THE UNIVERSITY OF TENNESSEE AT MARTIN

THE UNIVERSITY OF TENNESSEE AT MARTIN

The First One Hundred Years

Robert L. Carroll

HILLSBORO PRESS
Franklin, Tennessee

TENNESSEE HERITAGE LIBRARY

Printed in the United States of America

04   03   02   01   00   1   2   3   4   5

Library of Congress Catalog Card Number: 00-104992

ISBN: 1-57736-190-3

Cover design by Gary Bozeman
Cover and endsheet photos courtesy of the University of Tennessee at Martin.
Cover: Aerial view of UT Martin campus.
Front endsheet: Aerial view of UT Martin Campus, circa 1950.
Back endsheet: Paul Meek Library, 1998.

Published by
HILLSBORO PRESS
An imprint of
PROVIDENCE HOUSE PUBLISHERS
238 Seaboard Lane • Franklin, Tennessee 37067
800-321-5692
www.providencehouse.com

TO

Edward Clifton Pritchett
(August 22, 1909–September 20, 1998)
A tremendous father-in-law and a gentleman in the truest sense of
the word, his stories of UTJC encouraged me to undertake this
work. A 1928–30 alumnus, his love for the school and his fellow
students never diminished through the years.

My wife, Kay,
and our family
Steve, Pam, Heather, and Kristen Carroll; Cliff Carroll; and Kayla,
Tim, and Zane D'Arcy Goldrick

The many outstanding students
I was privileged to coach and teach
during my forty-one years at Martin

And my fellow faculty and staff members
during this period

Contents

Foreword

FROM MY BOYHOOD DAYS IN PALMERSVILLE TO THE governorship in Nashville, my life and the lives of many Tennesseans, especially West Tennesseans, have been touched by the institution we now know as The University of Tennessee at Martin. The excellent history written by Bob Carroll chronicles the establishment, the struggles, the growth, and the magnificent men and women who served this university and this region so unselfishly. Whether you knew the institution as Hall-Moody, UTJC, UTMB, or UT Martin, this book is a constant reminder of what we cherish and, in some cases, take for granted. Successful institutions, like successful people, usually reach their full potential through the help of others. The unsung heroes and the interesting characters are brought to life in this history that is sprinkled with insightful stories and touching memories.

When the Baptists founded Hall-Moody in 1900, few could have visualized that one hundred years later a primary campus of the University of Tennessee would have such an impressive physical plant and that so many young men and women would choose to continue their education at Martin.

As UT Martin celebrates one hundred years of higher education, we should all pause to reflect on what this institution has meant and continues to mean to our region. On many occasions I have publically stated that UT Martin is my university. It is a statement that I am still proud to make today.

Ned R. McWherter
Governor of Tennessee (1987–1995)

Preface

TIME IS UNKIND TO OUR MEMORIES, AND MY PRIMARY purpose in writing this history is to help preserve deeds of earlier years when a fledgling institution was seeking its place in the academic realm. Many people—including faculty and staff, students, and community leaders—helped to mold the school from its founding in 1900 to the present. The early struggles, the disappointments, the joys, and the growth are all a part of the history of UT Martin. My hope is that future generations will not forget those who worked and sacrificed to make the institution what it is today. They have left behind a lasting legacy. It is up to future generations to help the dream continue to flourish as a second century of service is launched.

Time and space limitations did not allow me to mention all the individuals and historical details associated with the school. There are many stories yet to be told, and, hopefully, others will accept the challenge. It is my hope that the names of earlier leaders, names synonymous with the college, will be remembered as we celebrate UT Martin's one hundredth birthday.

Acknowledgments

WHEN I DECIDED TO UNDERTAKE THE CHALLENGING task of writing a history covering the first one hundred years of The University of Tennessee at Martin, I knew plenty of assistance would be needed. Fortunately, I received it, and I wish to express my profound gratitude to everyone who assisted. If I overlook anyone who contributed, please accept my sincere apologies.

A gigantic thanks goes to the following:

Shelby Webb for her patience and skill in typing the manuscript;

Phillip Miller for correcting grammatical errors and offering suggestions;

George Horton Jr. who graciously sent copies of the Horton Papers, written by his father;

Mimi Coleman for her excellent research; and

Nick Dunagan for patiently reading the text and providing information.

Robert Muilenburg and "Bud" Grimes were invaluable in assisting with pictures, and Sarae Seratt also provided her typing skills.

A special thanks goes to Dieter Ullrich and Karen Elmore who went beyond the call of duty to locate historical materials. Dieter recently accepted a position at Millersville (Pennsylvania) State University, but his assistance continued even at a distance. Many others provided old newspapers and pictures, endured interviews, gathered information, and offered encouragement.

To each of the following I wish to convey my gratitude:

Larry Alexander

Mary L. Benson

Ernie Blythe

Harold Brundige

Tommy Bryant

John Bucy

Jim Byford

Connie Cantrell

Phil Conn

Harold Conner

Elmer Counce

Joe Croom

Phil Dane

Marvin Downing

Bill Duffy

Russell Duncan

Kay Durden

Aileen Edwards

John Eisterhold

Tom Farmer

Wayne Fisher

George Freeman

Mary E. Fuqua

John Gauldin

Bettye Giles

Dorothy Gillon

James Glasgow Sr.

Robert N. Glasgow

Houston Gordon

David Graham

Ralph Graves

Jacky Gullett

Jenny Hahn

Madge Harrison

Joe Black Hayes

Harry Henderson

Florence E. Hillis

Benny Hollis

Brad Hurley

Lucia Jones

Joe Johnson

Paul Kelley

Hollis Kinsey

Ron Lewellen

Pete Looney

Edith Edwards B. Masden

Doug Mayo

Nancy Lawson McDonald

Mack Moody

Ted Mosch

Grover Page

Ed Parham

Jim Payne

Margaret Perry

Randy Perry

E. C. Pritchett

James Riley

David N. Roberts

Steve Rogers

Martha Scott

Earl Shannon

Elizabeth Shannon

Linda Workman Shumate

Travis Shumate

Milton Simmons

Harold J. Smith

Gene Stanford

Verletta Stanford

Billy Stricklin

Frank Taylor

George Thomas

Jimmy Trentham

Steve Vantrease

Virginia Vaughan

Guy Wadley

Phil Watkins

Ed N. White

George White

N. B. "Buster" Williams

Lee Wilmot

Richard Wright

THE
UNIVERSITY
OF TENNESSEE
AT MARTIN

PART I

A History of Hall-Moody

NESTLED IN THE NORTHWESTERN CORNER OF Tennessee, Martin was a typical small rural town at the dawn of the twentieth century. Surrounded by thriving settlements in a predominantly agricultural region, the town had a population of 2,105.[1] The census of 1900 showed Weakley County to have a population of 32,546, a figure which surprisingly would exceed the census count in 1990.[2]

In many respects Martin was a typical mid-American rural community, but it was unique in that the town could boast of two colleges. Educational opportunities beyond the basics were lacking, and local citizens had taken steps to correct this deficit. In 1890, the Methodists founded McFerrin College, which survived until 1924. The Baptists, not to be outdone, established Hall-Moody Institute, the forerunner of The University of Tennessee at Martin, in 1900. This strong desire for education led the *Dresden Enterprise* in 1911 to declare Martin to be the "Athens of West Tennessee."[3]

Hall-Moody Institute was named for two prominent Baptist ministers, Elder J. N. Hall and Dr. J. B. Moody. Dr. I. N. Penick, pastor of the First Baptist Church in Martin for twenty-two years, was a key figure in convincing local Baptists and members of the Beulah Baptist Association (a group of about forty churches in Northwest Tennessee) to support the establishment of the institution. Numerous people generously donated time and money. The *Last Leaf*, the final yearbook to be published by Hall-Moody, praised the many individuals who supported the school until its demise in 1927. In addition to Penick, Moody, and J. N. Hall, persons cited for working to organize Hall-Moody included T. H. Farmer, T. M. Ryan, G. W. Hall, S. H. Hall, J. D. Hall, Dr. V. A. Biggs, P. A. Inlow, H. H. Lovelace, J. R. Lovelace, R. E. Nowlin, Elder G. L. Ellis, and Dr. J. C. Young. The Ladies Aid Society of the First Baptist Church in Martin was praised also for rendering valuable assistance.[4]

On October 2, 1900, while the Beulah Baptist Association was holding its annual session at the First Baptist Church in Martin, the cornerstone for the administration building, the first facility on the newly founded campus, was laid. Following dedicatory remarks, items, including a copy of the *Martin Mail*, were placed in the cornerstone. (These relics were uncovered when the building burned in 1970.) Diligent preparations for the opening of the school followed during the ensuing months, and regular classes commenced on September 2, 1901.[5]

The primary purpose for the founding of Hall-Moody, according to the *Last Leaf*, was to give religious and denominational training, plus general courses in education, to the young people in the area. The founders thought this specific training could be given only in a denominational school, and they embarked on their mission with ardent zeal. There was a public high school in Martin at the time, but the church fathers wanted a school which also would stress religious training. An early Hall-Moody publication warned, "This is not a reform school. We are too busy with energetic, ambitious ladies and gentlemen to waste time with worthless characters. We mean business, the students we have mean business, and we do not want any other kind to come."[6] Proper dress was required, and "sweethearting" was discouraged by the founding fathers.

The catalog also touted the town, stating "Martin is one of the prettiest, healthiest, busiest towns in West Tennessee, and it is known far and near as the most moral town in the State. There are no saloons or 'old sots' and no places of vice are tolerated one hour."[7] Saloons had been located in Martin until 1901 when the last one was closed. After this date, evidence suggests that alcoholic beverages manufactured at illegal stills in the backwoods of Weakley County could be purchased from bootleggers; however, the saloons in Martin were now out of business.

The school was located on the west side of Martin on the road to Union City. The Illinois Central Railroad ran north and south through the center of the town, and it was said that the Methodists lived east of the railroad and the Baptists resided to the west. Perhaps this influenced the location of the campus, which started with a modest beginning. The Methodists, as might be expected, had built McFerrin College on the east side of the Illinois Central Railroad.

Mrs. Ava Gardner Brooks, a member of the First Baptist Church of Martin, donated the land on which the aforementioned first facility on the Hall-Moody campus, the administration building, was built.[8] A two-story brick structure, this building housed administrative offices, classrooms, and eventually the library. It was, in fact, the primary classroom building throughout the Hall-Moody era. In 1912, a tower on the building was removed, two front wings were built, and four columns were added in the front.[9] The building remained the center of campus activity until 1959 when a new administration building was completed. By this date, the school had become the University of Tennessee Martin Branch, and the administration building later was named Hall-Moody as a tribute to the roots of the institution.

Other buildings were added as the campus gradually expanded. Temporary wooden buildings, including two-story dormitories for men and women and a dining hall, were built. The two dormitories, in order to maintain the proper decorum, were situated some distance apart. A small brick science building, erected before 1908, was located just north of the administration building.[10]

For several years, a building in downtown Martin, located in the Ryan Block on Lindell Street, housed the Hall-Moody Commercial College where students could study such subjects as bookkeeping, shorthand, typewriting, penmanship, commercial law, correspondence, and other business courses. The Commercial College, initially located in the administration building, was moved to the building on Lindell Street, and was returned to campus after the administration building was expanded. This department of Hall-Moody was discontinued in 1922 because of decreased demand. The last class consisted of ten students who received diplomas.[11]

The two frame dormitories were replaced in time by brick structures. Ellis Home for Girls, named in honor of Elder G. L. Ellis and later called Reed Hall, was built in 1919 for $35,000. Located immediately east of the administration building, the dormitory was connected to this building by a covered walkway.

In 1921, W. N. Lovelace gave the school three acres of land located northwest of the administration building. Lovelace Hall, a men's dormitory, was

Top to bottom:
J. N. Hall and
J. B. Moody

Present-day Lindell Street (looking north) in downtown Martin prior to 1908. Brick buildings would later replace the two wooden structures.

erected on this site for approximately $35,000. Similar in design to Ellis Hall, this residence hall was eventually renamed Freeman Hall. The latter names for both dormitories were derived from longtime hostesses.

Friends of the school helped to furnish the dormitory rooms. Pianos and Victrolas were placed in the reception areas and even bed clothing was given to the needy. Every effort was put forth to provide comfort for the students.[12]

A wooden gymnasium, located just south of the administration building and seating eight hundred, was built in 1924.[13] Heated by two coal-burning stoves, it was constructed so that it could be bricked at a later date, but this phase was never completed. An apartment building for married students was the remaining significant building on the Hall-Moody campus. It was located immediately south of the gymnasium.[14]

These seven buildings were situated on a campus which by 1927 had grown to over eleven acres, and the buildings and grounds had an estimated value of nearly $200,000.[15] At first, the main road to Union City, which was graveled, ran in front of the administration building and then directly west through the campus. University Street, then called Mechanic Street, extended west only to the present intersection with Lovelace Avenue. Later, the road through the campus would be closed and Mechanic Street would be extended until it connected with the road to Union City. During this time, the area west of the school consisted of woods, undergrowth, fields, and fences.

Mr. O. E. Baker and four female teachers constituted the first faculty when Hall-Moody began regular classes in 1901. During the period from 1901 to 1905, three others besides Mr. Baker held the presidency. These were Mr. M. M. Phillips, Mr. F. L. Norton, and Mr. J. A. Baber.[16]

One of the teachers to arrive on the Hall-Moody campus in 1901 was Frances Copass. In addition to many other duties, she headed the Expression

Department, according to the *Last Leaf*.[17] Fresh out of college with B.A. and M. A. degrees from Southwestern Baptist University (the name was changed to Union University in 1907) of Jackson, Tennessee, twenty-one years old, and lovely beyond description, she dazzled the town from the moment she stepped off the train. The Kentucky beauty was the talk of the town. The eligible bachelors pursued her, and some of her male students—as old as the teacher—tried to date her.[18]

Before long, the trustees regretted hiring such a pretty teacher. She was just too popular; her dates were too numerous. The trustees watched every move she made. She boarded in the home of one of the trustees, so observing her actions was easy. Her conduct was always ladylike and above reproach, but the school officials thought she had too many dates. They determined her social life was just too active, and it was interfering with her work. She had to go! Little did they know that their decision to fire her would result in a legal battle which would go all the way to the state supreme court.

On one occasion, she was instructed to take her zoology class, consisting of six boys and three girls, on a trip into nearby fields to catch insects, frogs, and other specimens for dissection in class. Armed with mosquito bar used as drag nets, the group ventured forth on the excursion, followed by a school official. He remained concealed until he caught the group sharing watermelons which had been "snared" by some of the boys from the field of T. H. Farmer, a trustee. "They gallantly shared them with the girls, and while the melons were being dissected on the ground, being too heavy to carry to the Institute, the principal appeared," according to trial testimony. The only criticism the principal offered at this time was that future classes should be divided. The jury undoubtedly viewed this as a harmless affair. This came out in the trial.[19]

Finally, because of her numerous dates and staying up late (past 10:30 P.M.), the trustees sent a committee of two to call on Copass concerning her behavior. She defended her actions and stated she had done nothing wrong. She remained firm but finally agreed to date only on weekends. The two delegates left without delivering the ultimatum that she would be fired if she didn't concede to the school's demands.[20]

On the following Saturday, Copass, having a free ticket and after getting permission from a trustee, accepted a date to a minstrel show. It was not over until after 11:00 P.M., and when her

The original Hall-Moody administration building. In 1912, the tower (some called it a witch's hat) was removed, two front wings were built, and columns were added in the front.

Above: The Hall-Moody Commercial College was located on Lindell Street in downtown Martin. It would be moved back to campus after the administration building was enlarged in 1912.

The first dormitories for men (right) and women (below) at Hall-Moody. They would later be replaced by Ellis Hall and Lovelace Hall.

Above: The science building on the Hall–Moody campus was erected by 1907.

Left: The Hall–Moody gymnasium when erected in 1924. It was built to be bricked, but this never occurred.

Below: The Hall–Moody dining hall, which was erected by 1907.

Ellis Hall (later named Reed Hall) shortly after construction in 1919.

date escorted her home, they sat and talked until nearly midnight. She also had another date Sunday night, again staying up late.[21]

This was too much for the trustees. Finally summoning enough courage, they asked for her resignation. She refused to resign because she thought she had done nothing wrong. The trustees then fired her. The termination notice to Copass stated, "We hereby dismiss Miss Frances Copass from Hall-Moody Institute on account of failing to comply with the demands of the Trustees." When she asked what demands she had refused, the reply was, "You understand." A request for another meeting with the trustees was granted, and Copass said she was sorry if she had done anything wrong and asked to be reinstated; however, the group remained firm in their decision to fire her. This was in December, and she had been on the faculty for four and one-half months. Following her dismissal, she sued the school for $275, the remainder of the year's pay, charging breach of contract.[22]

The case went to court in Weakley County with a large crowd pulling for Copass. Supporters of the school, many of whom wore Hall-Moody badges, also were present.[23] The trustees charged that her excessive dating—sixteen dates in four and one-half months—prevented her from devoting the proper attention to her job. It took the jury five minutes to reach a decision in favor of the beleaguered teacher.[24] The trustees would have to pay her $275. Her supporters were jubilant, but the trustees refused to drop the matter. They appealed the case to the Supreme Court of Tennessee, and it was heard in Jackson on May 10, 1902.

Judge John Summerfield Wilkes wrote the opinion for that court, and he displayed a delightful sense of humor. The problem boiled down to one fault, he stated in his opinion—the teacher was young and pretty. He reasoned that what was excessive dating for one person might not be so for another person.[25] He also acknowledged, with a subtle sense of humor, that the members of the state supreme court, while pondering legal questions, might stay up until midnight.[26]

In fairness to the Board of Trustees, Judge Wilkes stated:

> The school was a new one founded but a short time previously, and it was during its first term that this controversy arose. The Board was a new one and the teacher was new. There can be no doubt from this record that the Trustees were devoted to what they thought were the best interests of the school, and they were extremely solicitous as to the conduct and demeanor of its teachers. Their zeal and devotion and attention to the school and its interests cannot be too highly commended.[27]

Wilkes concluded:

> That they were sincerely and devotedly interested in the welfare of the school cannot for a moment be doubted; if they made any mistake in the management it arose not from a want of zeal, but from a want of experience and knowledge of the requirements of the situation.[28]

The only complaint against Copass relating to her job was that she did not maintain order in the study hall. She taught eight classes a day, each forty-five minutes long, and was required to monitor the study hall at the same time. It was asking too much, Wilkes reasoned, to expect her to teach a class and also keep a study hall full of sixty-five lively youngsters quiet at the same time. In

Named for W. N. Lovelace, this dorm for men was built in 1921.

addition, she was assigned to tap the bell for the different hours and classes. "She could not be held as an insurer of good order under such circumstances," Judge Wilkes observed.[29]

He added:

> It is requiring too much to hold the plaintiff as an insurer against any and all disturbances in a school-room. The trial Judge properly charged that she would be responsible for inattention and neglect only, and could not be held to keep order at all hazards. This would be requiring more diligence and a higher degree of control than is required of common carriers in the shipment of mules and other livestock, where the carrier is excused from such injury as results from the native unruly disposition of the stock, and we cannot require of this young lady, in the management of boys and girls in a school-room, a higher degree on control than is applied to shippers of livestock crowded into cars and subjected to many inconveniences.[30]

Wilkes further observed that even in the Supreme Court, with a marshal ready to check any disorder, a slight ripple of disturbance would occasionally arise. In the lower courts notwithstanding the efforts of the trial judge and sheriff, some disorder would also happen at times, he concluded.[31]

The state supreme court, after due deliberation, upheld the decision of the lower court. Wilkes observed that the study hall assignment and a limitation on dating were not specified in her contract, so she had fulfilled her obligations.[32]

T. H. Farmer

Also, a charge by the trustees that her friends had intimidated the jury with their behavior was dismissed. Copass received her $275, plus court costs.[33] The lovely teacher departed from Martin never to be heard from again.

In 1912, T. H. Farmer, a leader in the First Baptist Church for many years, wrote a short history of the church, and in it he alluded to the Copass trial as "a blessing in disguise." He stated that "she was backed and urged forward by some persons unfriendly to the school, and a considerable financial loss was thrust upon the trustees." But, in the final analysis, "this turned out to be the best investment they ever made," according to Farmer. The publicity generated by the suit made the public aware of "the most excellent moral tenets advocated by the trustees and taught by the faculty. . . ." Farmer concluded that "the impetus by this suit caused it [the school] to grow rapidly from year to year."[34]

When Hall-Moody was established, the academic "standards were high and the work thorough," according to the *Last Leaf*.[35] Needless to say, the first teachers at the school were required to be knowledgeable in many subject areas. The entire

English grammar class at Hall-Moody in 1904. (Courtesy of Patti Bucher)

program encompassed thirteen years, and the four instructors and the president taught a variety of courses. The school had primary, intermediate, and upper level classes, plus "extended" or "advance" work. Because of the "extended" classes, both Hall-Moody and McFerrin were sometimes classed as "colleges." The modern distinction between high school and college work had not been established at the time.

Using current terminology, the following analogy might best explain the academic organization at Hall-Moody during the early years.

Primary department—grades 1–6
Intermediate level—grades 7–9
Upper level—grades 10–11
"Extended" or college work—those classes beyond the 11th grade

While there was not a clear distinction between high school and college work at the time, this analogy offers a comparison with the modern academic structure.

The primary department included the first six grades, and it served as a demonstration school in teacher education throughout the twenty-seven years of Hall-Moody's existence. Following completion of the six primary grades, students could enter the three-year academic curriculum, or intermediate level. This was designed primarily for students preparing to take the college courses. Another option was the three-year teachers' curriculum. After completing this program, the equivalent of a ninth-grade education, students were certified to teach in an elementary school.[36]

In 1901, two different college courses of study were offered at Hall-Moody, a classical college course and a scientific college course. The classical college course included high school classes and two years of "extended" (college) work. The curriculum emphasized languages, mathematics, and science. Latin and Greek were required in each of the first three years, and French was a requirement in the last year. English was included for the final three years. The strong emphasis on languages was a trend which would be reversed within the near future, much to the dismay of many people.

The scientific college course consisted of high school classes and one year of college. Mathematics and science were required each year, and the language

The Primary Department at Hall-Moody. The photo was made about 1920.

requirement included a choice between Latin and German during the first two years.[37]

As time went on, Hall-Moody bestowed a variety of degrees including: A. B. (Bachelor of Arts), B. S. (Bachelor of Science), B. L. (Bachelor of Literature), L. I. (Licentiate Instructor), B. Ped. (Bachelor of Pedagogy), B. Accts. (Bachelor of Accounts), and B.O. (Bachelor of Oratory).[38] Most graduates received either the A. B. or B. S. degrees. The A. A. title (Associate of Arts) was conferred beginning with the 1918–19 academic year after the school was re-organized as Hall-Moody Junior College.[39]

The J. N. Hall Society of Religious Inquiry.

Training ministers for the Baptist faith became a primary aim for Hall-Moody from the very beginning. Dr. I. N. Penick, besides serving as pastor of the First Baptist Church, took the initiative in this endeavor. He taught ministerial students in his home without charge until the demand was sufficient to require a regular teacher. Dr. J. B. Moody, well-known as an author and teacher, accepted this assignment and headed the Theological Department from 1905–1915. This area enjoyed a rapid growth under Moody, sometimes referred to as "the greatest theologian in the ranks of the denomination."[40] He was followed by Dr. J. H. Anderson, who headed the department from 1915–21. Several others continued in this capacity until the school closed in 1927.[41] The lecture room at the First Baptist Church housed the Theological Department for the most part.

During the early years of Hall-Moody, the aspiring ministers at the college joined hands with community religious leaders to form the J. N. Hall Society of Religious Inquiry. Later, regular students, if they wished, could join the society. Activities of the group included lectures from outstanding ministers, debates on biblical topics, and research projects. Many young preachers were greatly encouraged by association with members of this society whose motto was: "Others."[42] Later, the Young Women's Auxiliary (YWA) was formed as an organization for the female students.

Classes at Hall-Moody were conducted from Tuesday through Saturday. This schedule allowed preachers to have Sunday services in their churches and then have a day for travel back to campus. The *Hall-Moody School Journal* made a strong argument for this schedule, plus other time savers. According to the publication, a ten-month schedule rather than nine months, excellent organization, and timely examinations resulted in a gain of two extra years of education over a six-year period. For those who used the usual Monday through Friday class schedule, quoting the *Journal*, "Monday is a blue day. Lessons are poor, teachers are cross, pupils are discouraged, and the lessons are usually re-assigned." The Hall-Moody method, the *Journal* continued, gained two days per week. Saturday was not lost since classes were held, and Monday, a non-class day, was spent preparing for the upcoming week. This was counted as another day gained. Schools which had classes on Monday just wasted a day, in the opinion of Hall-Moody officials. The logic of this argument failed to convince many schools, and they continued to use the Monday–Friday schedule.[43]

By 1905, the "heroic age," the early days of struggle had passed, and the school began to expand. "In this period of beginnings the wind blew and beat upon the little school, but it stood, for it was founded on a rock," according to the *Last Leaf*.[44] Dr. H. E. Watters, who came to Hall-Moody in 1904 as vice president and business manager, assumed the presidency in 1905. He was twenty-nine years old, capable, and energetic. A minister as well as a teacher, he attracted a capable faculty, and the school enjoyed solid growth during his eleven years as president.

Dr. Watters was charged with gaining additional support for the school, and he spent much of his time traveling widely doing fund raising, public relations, and educational work. He worked closely with state educational officials in summer institute work.[45] The purpose of the summer institutes was to help train and certify teachers.

The first major effort concerning summer institute work in the South was started in 1902 in Knoxville with the organization of the Summer School of the South. Philander P. Claxton—who later became United States Commissioner of Education and whose son, Porter Claxton, would be selected in 1927 as the first chief executive officer at the University of Tennessee Junior College—accepted the superintendency of the school. Sometimes referred to as "the largest summer school for teachers in America," it opened as a crusading effort to advance teacher education and improve schools. At first, the summer school was not associated with the University of Tennessee, but utilized university buildings and employed some faculty members. Later, facing competition from other summer institutes and with private funding sources diminishing, the university assumed responsibility for the school. Highly successful for several years with students from many states and featured speakers like John Dewey and William Jennings Bryan, the institute gradually

Dr. I. N. Penick, pastor of the First Baptist Church in Martin and a key figure in the founding of Hall-Moody.

A classroom scene at Hall-Moody around 1906. (Courtesy of Mrs. Alfred Samuel)

faded and closed in 1918. It had served a valuable purpose and was the fore-runner of the regular summer quarter at the University of Tennessee. Probably the greatest accomplishment of the school was to develop professional enthusiasm in teachers and a desire to improve educational standards.[46]

The efforts of the summer school had touched off a state effort to improve the teaching profession in Tennessee. Other summer institutes, supported by the state, were organized and operated. The Institute for West Tennessee was established at Hall-Moody Institute, and it was directed by Dr. Watters.[47] This afforded him the opportunity to have contact with many teachers in West Tennessee, and the prestige of the institution was enhanced.

From the beginning, the training of teachers was a priority for Hall-Moody, and the school became widely known for both teacher training instruction through the regular curriculum and the involvement of the faculty in the summer institutes. The 1909 *School Journal* claimed Hall-Moody to be "the greatest and best teachers' college outside of Nashville."[48]

When the school opened in 1901, county superintendents issued most teaching certificates based on an examination administered by the superintendent's office. This method of certification caused problems, and eventually, in 1913, the legislature placed teacher certification under the control of the state.[49]

Prior to this date, Hall-Moody, according to the 1909 *School Journal*, offered a primary or county certificate course. Those wishing to have additional

An early surveying class at Hall-Moody.

training could take the secondary or state certificate course. Upon completion of the primary and secondary courses, students could earn the L. I. (Licentiate Instructor) degree by finishing more advanced "college" courses.[50]

During the 1908–09 academic year, 226 students, 120 of whom were experienced teachers seeking additional training, were enrolled at Hall-Moody in teacher training.[51] Citing a record of splendid success, the *School Journal* boasted that 97 Hall-Moody students attended summer institutes in 1908 and only 4 percent failed the state examinations. The failure rate for students from other schools was 60 percent.[52] Similar results were recorded during other years. In 1912, Hall-Moody bragged that to date only 95 of 1,450 graduates had failed the state tests, contrasted with a state wide rate of 50 percent.[53]

During Watters' administration, Mr. M. W. Robinson served as vice president for six years, and he was the chief administrator during Watters' absence. In addition, Robinson also worked as assistant superintendent of public instruction for the state in 1911–12 and was later appointed supervisor for high school industrial work when this new position was created by the 1913 legislature.[54] Thus, Watters and Robinson were in key positions to promote Hall-Moody.

A major problem at Hall-Moody was the lack of an adequate library. Teachers helped to alleviate this situation by allowing the use of their personal books, but this was far from satisfactory. Watters solicited support for the library, and through his efforts Mr. Louis J. Parker contributed $1,000 for library books in 1912. An area was set aside in the administration building for the collection, and the library remained in this building throughout the Hall-Moody era.[55] It was not until 1951, long after the school became affiliated with the University of Tennessee, that the agriculture-biology-library building, later named Brehm Hall, was completed, and the library acquired more spacious quarters.

By 1913 there were four thousand volumes in the library. The 1915 catalog lauded the collection but advised that the library was "not a place for social enjoyment or idle pastime."[56]

The founders of Hall-Moody wanted the cost of attending the school to be within the means of all students, and the tuition charges were set accordingly. Scholarships of one hundred dollars were offered for sale to the general public, and these could be awarded to deserving individuals.[57] Funds from the sale of scholarships, tuition, and private contributions provided the financing of the school. From the beginning, the trustees personally financed a major portion of the budget. The Beulah Baptist Association gave a small appropriation, primarily for ministerial students. During the early years, the Tennessee Baptist Convention furnished no funds.[58] A lack of adequate financing plagued the school throughout its existence, and this problem eventually caused the school to close in 1927.

In 1901, all students paid a matriculation fee of one dollar for registering in any of the various courses at Hall-Moody. Listed below are the charges for the different courses for each ten-week term:

Primary Department, grades 1–3
$3.75
Primary Department, grades 4–6
$5.00
Academic Course, first and second year
$6.25
Academic Course, third year
$7.50
College Course, first year
$7.50
College Course, above first year's work
$8.75

Music, voice, shorthand, typewriting, and other specialized areas carried small additional charges. Students studying for the ministry and the children of ministers were charged one-half the regular tuition rate. Board was available for $2.25 per week. It was obvious charges were held to a minimum as a student could attend three sessions of ten weeks each for less than one hundred dollars.[59]

A bookkeeping class at Hall-Moody, circa 1921.

A former student who was reared near Trenton recalled how his father hitched his team of mules to a wagon and drove his son to Bradford so that he could ride a train to Martin. He arrived at the depot in Martin with a well-worn suitcase, an old iron trunk, and two dollars in his pocket. He worked his way through school, performing various jobs on campus. Apparently, the work ethic remained with the young student as he later became a highly successful businessman.[60]

Through the years, the charges at Hall-Moody increased, but every effort was made to keep the costs at a minimum. For the 1925–26 academic year, elementary school students paid $15 in fees, high school students paid $75 for tuition, and those enrolled in junior college paid $96 for tuition. Room and board for nine months cost $54 and $144, respectively. The financial problems of Hall-Moody were evidenced by the fact that the college went on an absolute cash basis beginning May 31, 1926. All tuition and room rents became payable in advance.[61]

During the early years of Hall-Moody, classes commenced in early September and continued until the first part of June. The school year was divided into four ten-week terms, and every effort was made to accommodate the students who enrolled with meager educational backgrounds. Special classes were arranged for students with academic deficits.[62]

The enrollment at Hall-Moody gradually moved upward. Records indicate the following attendance figures:

1903–04	193
1904–05	150
1905–06	322
1906–07	404
1907–08	484
1908–09	560

These figures included all students enrolled at the institution, and the 1908–09 enrollment included students from nine states.[63] Of the 560 enrolled in that year 35 were married, 76 were above twenty-five years of age, 29 above thirty, and 177 were above twenty-one years of age. The average age of the entire student body above the primary department was a little more than twenty-one years. Many of the older students were preachers and teachers who were seeking additional training.[64]

By 1908–09, the faculty had increased to seventeen, several of whom were well-known scholars. Dr. G. M. Savage, who served as chair of languages, had been at Southwestern Baptist University earlier. At the time, he had just returned from a year of study in Greece and the Holy Land. Touted by the *Hall-Moody School Journal* as one of the best Greek and Hebrew scholars in the country, Savage exemplified the well-trained faculty.[65]

A typing class at Hall-Moody in 1915.

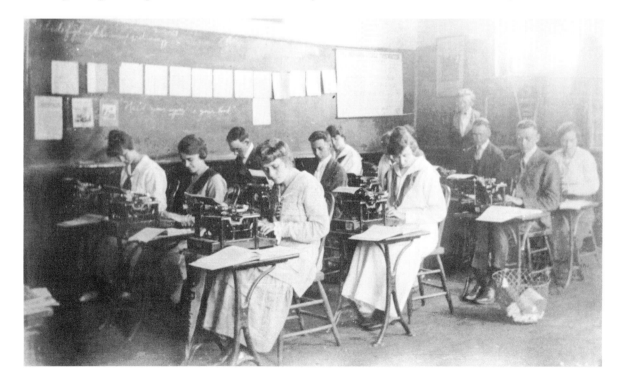

Pictured above are students enrolled in various musical and voice classes taught by Musa Hall, a popular faculty member who headed the music department at Hall-Moody throughout the existence of the school. Circa 1920.

One of the best known teachers was Musa L. Hall, who headed the Music Department throughout the entire existence of Hall-Moody. She started teaching music at a studio in Martin in 1896, and in 1901 she joined the Hall-Moody faculty, bringing her group of over thirty students with her.

The *Last Leaf* credits Hall and her assistants with teaching 733 pupils, 107 of whom were men and boys. Many of her protegees later taught music throughout West Tennessee. Her campus studio was in the administration building, and

> for twenty-seven years there emanated therefrom the 'drum-fire' of the piano artillery, the helpless cries of the beginning voice pupil, the piteous wail of the violin in the merciless hands of a would-be Kreisler or Kubelic, the groans of the despairing student of harmony and neglected musical history.[66]

Following the demise of Hall-Moody in 1927, Hall again established a studio on Mechanic Street (now University Street). The final yearbook referred to her as "the Alpha and Omega of the school." An alumnus fondly remembers her crossing the campus, "heels clicking, in a light dress with a green beret on her red hair which turned gray while teaching music to young and old in the little music room in the administration building."[67]

Travel to campus was not easy during the Hall-Moody era. There were no paved roads into Martin, and the local streets were gravel or cinder. It was not until the last years of the school that some main streets in Martin were paved. Few teachers and students owned automobiles, and many students came to school in wagons or buggies. Travel by train was a much-used method of transportation. The 1909 *Hall-Moody School Journal* bragged that seventeen passenger trains traveled through Martin each day on the Illinois Central and the Nashville, Chattanooga, and St. Louis railroads.[68] The latter railroad ran east and west, and the crossing of these two railroads in Martin afforded excellent transportation and gave the town an advantage in competition with surrounding towns. The Martin depot was a busy place on weekends, and nearby was the Railroad Park, the pride of Martin for many years. The 1921 valuation of the park and equipment was $250,000, and its amenities eventually included a restroom, something the ladies had sought for years.[69]

Various activities deemed proper for the social development of the students were scheduled. Picnics, receptions, excursions on the Mississippi River and to other sites, and musical programs were among the functions which enhanced the atmosphere at Hall-Moody. For several years, a student newspaper, the *Crimson and Gold*, was printed. Crimson and gold were the school's colors, depicting the rising and the setting of the sun.[70] Two annuals were published, the *Call* in 1921 and the *Last Leaf* in 1927.

Healthful exercise was encouraged, but organized athletic teams were discouraged during the school's early existence. As the *Hall-Moody School Journal* stated:

> We encourage athletics, but are unalterably opposed to certain games that exercise the body too violently and expose it to serious danger and at the same time weaken the moral fiber of the individual. We do not tolerate match games of football and baseball, or, in fact, match games of any kind. In the first place, we see no good in them, and in the second place, we see much harm. Those who really need exercise cannot get a place on a college team. Teams and match games beget reckless, boisterous dispositions, encourage gambling, and create too often an ambition for professional gaming.[71]

In time, this attitude would change, but limited funds and the large number of older adult students discouraged athletics during the early years.

In 1915, Dr. Watters resigned from the presidency of Hall-Moody Institute to devote more of his time to the ministry. The school had grown to over 500 students, and Watters had fulfilled the wishes of the trustees with his leadership.[72] However, even during this "period of expansion," financial woes lurked in the background.

Watters was succeeded by M. E. Wooldridge who would head the school for two years. He initiated a change in the policies and organization

A party of Hall-Moody students and friends picnicking at Johnsonville, Tennessee.

at Hall-Moody.[73] Teacher education, deemed necessary for the school's survival, had been put under state control in 1913. In order to meet the state requirements, the high school curriculum was revamped. The elementary programs also were altered to conform with state standards. Elementary work now consisted of grades 1–8, and the high school curriculum encompassed grades 9–12. A high school graduate was required to have credit for fifteen units, ten prescribed, and five elective.

The high school curriculum also became less classical and more scientific and vocational. During the fourth year the student was required to give two public orations as a requisite for graduation from high school. Throughout the history of Hall-Moody, priority was given to public speaking, and campus debates were scheduled in order to develop the speaking abilities of the students.[74]

Wooldridge, whose administration was termed for some reason as the "dark days" in the *Last Leaf*, was replaced by Mr. James T. Warren, a former vice president.[75] His familiarity with the school enhanced the further standardization of the elementary and high school programs to meet requirements established by the state Department of Education.[76]

The junior college curriculum also was standardized by 1917–18, and a clear distinction was made between high school and college work. Graduates of accredited high schools who had at least fifteen acceptable units could enroll. Students from unaccredited high schools were required to take examinations over their high school work before being admitted. Students entering from other colleges could transfer forty-eight hours, and a person had to be in residence for three quarters before the junior college degree could be received. Ninety-six quarter hours were required for graduation, of which forty-seven were required and forty-nine could be electives. Starting in 1918–19, the Associate of Arts degree was conferred on the junior college graduates.[77]

The Department of Ministerial Education continued to train ministers, missionaries, and other church workers during the entire history of the school. Though changes occurred through the years, religion continually occupied a position of importance at the institution, and school journals proudly stated that the pulpits of churches located in several states were filled by preachers who had received their training at Hall-Moody.[78]

During Warren's administration the two brick dormitories were constructed and a cooperative plan of dining room management was established. Students and teachers were furnished meals at actual cost. As the *Last Leaf* stated, "no better service was furnished anywhere at such reasonable rates." The yearbook also recorded the common comment, "Hall-Moody's meals are better than those offered in some of the best private homes."[79]

A loan fund for needy students also was established during Warren's presidency. Within a few years this fund contained $7,000–$8,000. A student could borrow from the fund and repay the loan with interest after graduation.[80]

The name of the school changed through the years. First called Hall-Moody Institute, the institution then became known as Hall-Moody Normal School, and finally Hall-Moody Junior College. As the school evolved, the name was changed to more properly reflect the role and identity of the institution.

During the early years when the school was called Hall-Moody Institute (HMI), Paul Meek, later to become head of the University of Tennessee Junior College, laughingly recalled that he and other McFerrin students referred to their counterparts at HMI as "half made idiots." Undoubtedly, the Hall-Moody students had equally derisive terms for the McFerrin enrollees as a keen competition existed between the two schools.[81]

1900
Hall-Moody Institute is founded. The cornerstone for the administration building is laid on October 2.

1901
Classes commence at Hall-Moody on September 2.

1902
The *Hall-Moody v. Copass* case occurs.

1905
H. E. Watters becomes president.

1912
The administration building is enlarged.

1913
Teacher certification is put under the control of the state.

1915
H. E. Watters resigns, and he is succeeded by M. E. Wooldridge.

1916
The Excelsior Literary Society and the Cliosophic Literary Society are formed.

1917
Hall-Moody is placed under the control of the Tennessee Baptist Convention.

Hall-Moody gets a new name—Hall-Moody Normal School.

Effective in 1917, Hall–Moody was placed under the control of the Tennessee Baptist Convention. From its founding in 1900 until 1917, the Beulah Baptist Association of Northwestern Tennessee controlled the school. In 1917, three other Baptist colleges—Carson–Newman in Jefferson City, Tennessee College in Murfreesboro, and Union University in Jackson—were placed under the auspices of the Tennessee Baptist Convention. The state organization felt higher education in the four colleges could best be served if they were all under a central authority.[82]

The entry of the United States into World War I had an evident effect on Hall–Moody. Some of the students marched off to war, and this great conflict ushered in a new awareness of world happenings. The cover of the *Call*, the 1921 yearbook, depicts a doughboy blowing a bugle, and the Excelsior Society in that same year noted that the Great War "threw its gloomy shadow over us and grasped within its clutches many of our best members."[83] At least one faculty member, H. C. Witherington, served in the military during World War I.

World–wide changes did not leave Hall–Moody untouched. As early as 1916, according to the *Last Leaf*, "there was a new type of student body arising."[84] The student body was younger and more assertive.

The Hall–Moody yell indicated the students were affected at least to a limited degree by the Jazz Age:

HALL-MOODY (1900–1927)

James T. Warren becomes president, replacing M. E. Wooldridge.

1921
The *Call* is published.

1922
Hall-Moody Normal becomes Hall-Moody Junior College.

1923
The Board of Trustees passes a resolution to permit intercollegiate athletics.

1925
Hall-Moody athletic teams start playing a strictly collegiate schedule.

1926
James T. Warren resigns as president, and is replaced by William Hall Preston.

A drive is launched to raise $75,000 to help alleviate the financial difficulties of Hall-Moody.

The Hall-Moody Boosters travel throughout the state seeking to gain students and support for Hall-Moody.

1927
The *Last Leaf* is published.

Hall-Moody Junior College is consolidated with Union University.

The last commencement is held at Hall-Moody on May 19.

Hall-Moody closes its doors on June 1.

The Excelsior Literary Society

Boom-a-rack-a, boom-a-rack-a,
Bow! wow! wow!
Chick-a-lack-a, chick-a-lack-a,
Chow! chow! chow!
Boom-a-rack-a, Chick-a-lack-a,
Ki! Y! Kin!
We are the Push from H. M. N.[85]

Literary societies were prominent on the campus from the earliest years. They met on Monday afternoons and provided debates, music, reading, and oratory. At first, the societies were organized by classes—freshman, sophomores, etc. But in 1916, these class groups gave way to two campus organizations, the Excelsior Literary Society and the Cliosophic Literary Society. Rivalry between the two groups was keen and each had its own colors, flower, and motto. Due to a lack of interschool athletics, these two societies competed in athletic contests against each other.[86] Among the female sports were basketball, volleyball, and tennis. The men, in addition to those three sports, fielded baseball teams.[87] These intramural games provided an outlet for youthful exuberance, but the students wanted to compete against other schools. Later, following the introduction of interscholastic sports, less emphasis was given to purely literary societies owing to the rise of many other student organizations.

Because of factors such as a lack of finances and an older student body during the earlier years of Hall-Moody, there was no demand for intercollegiate athletics. By 1922, however, competitive sports were gaining popularity, and a younger student group wanted to join the national trend. McFerrin College had fielded athletic teams for several years, and this probably was galling to the Hall-Moody students. Competition between McFerrin and Hall-Moody had existed through the years, but not on the athletic fields. Some referred to it as a "healthy denominational rivalry," but at times it was anything but healthy. Such was the case on Halloween night in 1916.

A group of Hall-Moody students encountered an outnumbered group from McFerrin; however, the McFerrin boys had acquired an ample supply of rocks as they crossed the Illinois Central Railroad. During the ensuing melee, the Hall-Moody forces were routed, some with broken teeth and assorted hematomas. They fled back to campus, regrouped into small gangs, and then committed the usual Halloween vandalism—on the western side of Martin.

One act of mischief was to persuade a teacher's cow to walk up some inclined planks into the barn loft. The next morning, the teacher had to call for help in rigging a block and tackle to lower the cow from the loft since cows are reluctant to walk down an incline.

The next day's chapel was devoted to the unreligious behavior of some of the students; however, all professed that they were not guilty since they were in their rooms studying. No one was ever exposed.[88]

The Cliosophic Literary Society

Perhaps to steer competitive spirits in a more wholesome direction, outside athletic competition finally arrived at Hall-Moody. Though "poorly equipped and trained" and with an informal coaching arrangement, Hall-Moody began football competition in 1922 with nearby high schools, compiling a record of three victories and three defeats. The baseball squad won nine of eleven games. The campus gym was not constructed until 1924, so basketball was given little attention.[89]

A new era in athletics dawned in 1923 when the Board of Trustees passed a resolution permitting, under specified regulations, intercollegiate athletics. This was contrary to earlier policies voiced by the administration and faculty that the evils of inter-school competition far surpassed the good. The *Last Leaf* lauded this change because it "brought to the school numbers of young people who otherwise would not have been reached by the school." The yearbook further stated that "the conduct of Hall-Moody athletic teams was a credit to the school, and they did their part in spreading school spirit wherever they went."[90]

The teams were known as the Sky Pilots.[91] This was a frontier term sometimes applied to preachers, but perhaps the students were thinking about both the glamorous flying aces of World War I and religion. Nevertheless, it was an appropriate nickname.

In 1923, two college teams were added to the football schedule. The Sky Pilots lost to Bethel College but defeated Murray State. The team won four games and lost three. The baseball squad had another successful season.

In 1924, the football team won seven games and lost two. A "lack of pitching" prevented the baseball team from having a stellar season. The new gym was now available, and basketball began to make forward strides.

Starting in 1925, Hall-Moody teams played a strictly collegiate schedule. Since there were only a few local junior colleges, mostly senior colleges were

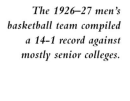

The 1926–27 men's basketball team compiled a 14–1 record against mostly senior colleges.

scheduled. The football team was 5–4–1 in 1925, and 3–5–1 in 1926 against this competition. The men's basketball team won 10 and lost 3 in 1925–26 and had a 14–1 record in 1926–27. The baseball went 10–8 in 1926. Much of the credit for the success of the football, baseball, and men's basketball teams was due to H. Kirk Grantham. A successful high school coach at Newbern, Tennessee, he came to Hall-Moody in 1925 as head coach and director of athletics.

The women had started playing basketball without a gym in 1923–24 against a mixed schedule of high schools and colleges. In 1925–26, they, like the men, faced an entirely collegiate schedule and finished 0–6. During the ensuing season, they fared somewhat better, compiling a 2–4 record.

In 1927, tennis teams for both men and women were organized for inter-collegiate play, and the matches were held on the local park courts.[92]

In 1926, James T. Warren resigned to become vice president of Tennessee College, and he was replaced by William Hall Preston.[93] The incoming president immediately encountered financial problems of a long-standing duration. Debts had been accumulating for almost the entire existence of the school. Members of the local board had helped with the debts through the years, but matters had now reached a crucial stage. A general campaign was organized to raise funds to meet the emergency.

In October 1926, a drive to raise $75,000 began, and $33,000 was pledged in about ten days. The workers were optimistic that the goal could be reached by April 30, 1927. Dr. J. E. Skinner, pastor of the First Baptist Church and president of the board of trustees, along with the field director, Mr. W. W. Jones, and others worked tirelessly, but their efforts were in vain. The goal was not attained.[94]

The Hall-Moody Boosters, composed of students and faculty members, joined others to work tirelessly for the school. The boosters traveled throughout the state in 1926, seeking to gain students and support for the institution.[95] The

The last (1926–27) Hall-Moody football team. The picture was taken near the area now occupied by the business administration building. Behind the team is the Union City Highway and the "Grove" where apartments are located today.

total enrollment for the 1926–27 year was 372, and a major effort was made to recruit future students.[96]

In the meantime, the Baptist State Convention met in Memphis, and it was decided that after June 1, 1927, Hall-Moody Junior College would be consolidated with Union University in Jackson, Tennessee. This would allow the church to concentrate its efforts on one school in West Tennessee.[97]

On May 19, 1927, the last commencement was held at Hall-Moody. For twenty-seven years the school had served well, but now its doors would close. During this period approximately 14,000 students had attended Hall-Moody, counting those enrolled in the elementary, secondary, and college divisions.[98] Elva Galloway, in her valedictory address to the graduates, quoted from the *Last Leaf*, a poem by Oliver Wendell Holmes. This final class was likened to "The last leaf upon the tree in the spring."[99] The final yearbook was appropriately called the *Last Leaf*, and it urged people, as Hall–Moody ceased to exist, "to recall its founding, its brave history, its students, its influence."[100]

In recalling the history of Hall–Moody, the *Last Leaf* notes:

> Hall–Moody's representatives shall not have occasion "to hang their harps upon the willows and weep when they remember her," but with calm assurance of her worth, shall proudly acknowledge their debt of gratitude, and so conduct themselves as to uphold her traditions, remembering that in honoring themselves, they honor their Alma Mater.[101]

H. E. Watters, formerly president of Hall–Moody and president of Union University in 1927, had a full page ad in the *Last Leaf* welcoming former Hall–Moody students to Union University.[102] Some went, including at least one faculty member, H.C. Witherington, but others, especially the athletes, remained behind to become students when the old Hall–Moody campus became the University of Tennessee Junior College. The Hall–Moody records were transferred to Union University, and on June 1, 1927, the school closed its doors. As the *Last Leaf* so aptly recorded, "Hall–Moody's brief life was overshadowed by clouds of financial worry and disappointments, but God, the master artist, turned all of the clouds into a glorious sunset!"[103] The school was now a part of history, but its loyal alumni would continue to reminisce about their beloved institution and the important role it had played in so many young lives.

TM PACER STADIUM
H. K. GRANTHAM FIELD

HOME   GUEST
DOWN   TO GO   BALL ON   QTR.

TENNESSEE

PART II

University of Tennessee Junior College
1927—1951

EVEN BEFORE HALL-MOODY INSTITUTE CLOSED ITS doors in May 1927, the citizens of Weakley and adjacent counties were very concerned that the loss of the college would deliver an economic as well as an educational blow to the region. Several of the area leaders wanted another agency to establish a college in Martin. For reasons not completely clear, the University of Tennessee was selected by the political leaders of northwestern Tennessee as the institution under whose administration the proposed junior college should be placed.[1]

Senator Sam R. Bratton of Union City, who represented Lake, Obion, and Weakley counties in the Senate, introduced Senate Bill 301, chapter 9 of the *Public Acts* of 1927. This bill provided for the establishment of a junior college in Martin, and it stated that the school would concentrate its academic offerings in agriculture, industrial arts, and home economics. The act passed both houses of the Tennessee legislature, and Governor Austin Peay signed the measure on March 29.[2]

The University of Tennessee now had a junior college to go with the main campus in Knoxville, the medical units in Memphis, and the agricultural experiment station in Jackson. The West Tennessee facilities strengthened UT's claim as Tennessee's state university and federal land grant institution; however, Harcourt A. Morgan, who had become president of the University of Tennessee in 1919 following the sudden death of Brown Ayres, was not overjoyed with the prospect of having a junior college in the UT family. Perhaps, Morgan complained, some "deep seeded politics may be involved."[3]

He was right. Politics did play a role, and so did economics. The citizens of northwest Tennessee thought their area deserved a college nearby, and they turned to their political leaders for help.

Numerous political figures were involved in the move to establish a junior college in Martin. Certainly Senator Bratton played a vital role, and another key individual was George W. Rowlett, a lawyer in Martin. Rowlett was a member of the board of trustees for Hall-Moody when the school closed, and in 1927 he became a member of board of trustees for the University of Tennessee, a position he held for over twenty years. Rowlett thus was a very influential player in the move to get UT to assume responsibility for establishing a junior college in Martin.

Squire John Hatler, a member of the county court at the time, was another person who worked diligently to get UTJC established. He traveled numerous miles throughout the county in a Model T Ford, urging people to support the college. He also was a key player when a $100,000 bond issue to purchase the Hall-Moody property came before the quarterly court.[4]

Foster Y. Fuqua, superintendent of the Weakley County schools and a leader in state-wide educational organizations, was presented with an engraved watch in 1927 by the Martin Chamber of Commerce for his work in helping to secure the junior college.[5] Numerous others also deserve plaudits for their efforts.

Morgan was still lukewarm. He did not openly fight the move for the junior college, but "he tried to offer one alibi and then another to get out from under accepting that institution."[6] Two factors which might have influenced his thinking were distance and money. Martin was 350 miles from Knoxville, and this new school could put a strain on the UT budget. Of course, the distance factor worked two ways. The long trip to Knoxville was a major reason why the people in northwest Tennessee wanted a college nearby.

Morgan devised a plan which he hoped would put an end to this foolishness. He proposed that the town of Martin and Weakley County each put up $100,000 to purchase the Hall-Moody property and make needed improvements. To his surprise and chagrin, they did it.[7]

It should be remembered that the community had just failed in an attempt to raise $75,000 to keep Hall-Moody from closing its doors. Undoubtedly, Morgan felt confident his proposal would also end in failure. It did not.

The General Assembly of the State of Tennessee gave Weakley County and the city of Martin permission to issue the bonds, subject to referendum, which would be used to purchase the Hall-Moody property. Senate Bill Number 385, chapter 172 of the 1927 *Private Acts of Tennessee* was proposed by Senator Bratton, and the act was passed on April 1, 1927.[8] Governor Peay signed it on the same day. House Bill Number 575, chapter 247 of the 1927 *Private Acts of Tennessee* was proposed by Speaker of the House Seldin L. Maiden and Representative R. E. Gallimore. This act was passed on April 5, 1927, and it also was approved by the governor on the same day.[9] Following passage of these two bills, the citizens of Martin and Weakley County approved the bond issues.

Thus, the University of Tennessee Junior College was born. During the legislative actions the school was officially called Tennessee Junior College, but it was later referred to as the University of Tennessee Junior College.[10] Ironically, Dr. James D. Hoskins, who followed Morgan as president of UT,

A 1930s picture of the administration building.

remarked in 1944 during the sesquicentennial celebration of the university that the establishment of UTJC was one of the most important accomplishments of Morgan's administration.[11] Additional accolades came in 1946 when *Look*, a prominent national magazine, listed the college as one of the top fifteen junior colleges in the nation.[12] However, starting in 1927, much had to be accomplished before the new school would reach national prominence.

During the summer of 1927, UT took charge of the former Hall-Moody campus which consisted of over eleven acres and six buildings. In addition, there was an apartment building for married couples at Lovelace and Hurt.

The campus buildings consisted of the administration building which was built in 1900 and remodeled in 1912, Ellis Home for Women (later Reed Hall), Lovelace Hall for Men (later Freeman Hall), a small brick science building, a wooden gymnasium constructed in 1924, and a frame dining hall. As mentioned earlier, the former Hall-Moody buildings and grounds had been valued at nearly $200,000.

The Hall-Moody buildings are gone now. The administration building, destroyed by a fire in 1970, was located in what is now the parking lot for the School of Business building. Reed Hall was directly east of the administration building and a covered walkway linked the two structures. The gymnasium was south of Reed Hall and occupied a portion of the present parking lot for the School of Business building. South of the gymnasium were the apartments for married students.

The small brick science building was in front of the administration building, near where the east wing of the School of Business building is today. The frame dining hall was located to the southeast of the old cafeteria, which

Above: The home economics building in the 1930s. Note that the campus road at the time ran in front of the building.

Right: Built in 1930, the industrial arts building is now known as Crisp Hall. (Courtesy of Billy Stricklin)

Below: The science building on the UTJC campus. It was built in 1929.

today houses the television studio. Freeman Hall was demolished in 1973, and Gooch Hall was built on that site.

The Hall-Moody buildings and land were purchased from the Tennessee Baptist Association for $65,000.[13] The remainder of the $100,000 bond issued by the city of Martin was used to purchase additional land adjacent to the western part of the campus.[14]

This acreage included a portion of the James E. Freeman farm, better known as Woodley Farm. Holland McCombs, for whom the home economics building would be named in 1987 during the sixtieth anniversary celebration of the founding of UTJC, liked to reminisce about his boyhood days on the farm of his grandparents. The vast expanse was called Woodley Farm because of the huge trees which dotted the landscape, according to McCombs. A nephew of Sam Bratton who led the fight in the senate to establish UTJC, McCombs would later enjoy an outstanding journalistic career as a correspondent, author, and executive for Time-Life publications.[15]

In 1927, the newly-purchased western part of the present campus was covered not only with trees, but also bushes and briers. This afforded UTJC students employment opportunities, since the area had to be cleaned up in order to beautify the campus. Dynamite was used at times to remove stumps, and in the fall of 1927 two students, reclining peacefully in a Model T Ford parked in front of the administration building, suddenly were jarred awake by a portion of a dynamited stump which went through the roof of the vehicle and landed on them.

The damage to the car amounted to $35.10, and the medical expenses for the more seriously injured student totaled $77.00. The other student apparently escaped with minor injuries. Since the university had no insurance to cover such incidents, the faculty divided the $77.00 equally and paid the medical expenses for the injured student. University of Tennessee President H. A. Morgan sent a personal check to cover the damage to the car.[16]

The University of Tennessee Junior College opened with ample funds for operation. The legislature provided $75,000 for an operating budget during each of the first two years. Also, the $100,000 bond issue by Weakley County helped to provide the means to build additional facilities.

In 1929, a science building and a home economics building were erected. In the following year, a gymnasium, a heating plant, and the industrial arts building were added. A cafeteria and a greenhouse followed in 1935. No other permanent facilities of any significance were built until the agriculture-biology-library building was completed in 1951.

The fields of study envisioned for UTJC were limited to agriculture, home economics, and industrial arts. Paul Meek, who became the chief administrator in 1934, commented, "We never really found out what it [industrial arts] was supposed to be."[17] Almost from the beginning, the industrial arts courses were slanted toward agricultural engineering, but it was not until 1944 that a full-fledged two-year engineering program was approved for the junior college.[18]

The first UTJC faculty/staff, 1927. Front row: Lavinia Roberts, S. R. Wood, Barsha Webb, Mary V. Burney, Florence E. Barnes. Second row: C. C. Cravens, Samuel Atkins, Eloise Berry, Samuel C. Collins, Madison Hall, Porter Claxton. Back row: J. Paul Phillips, Gladys L. Ogle, Richard G. Turner, H. Kirk Grantham.

Most of the engineering courses were being offered already, so this represented no great change.

Three education courses also were offered during the regular school year. Since these three courses were entitled "Teaching Rural Life" they were in harmony with the stated objectives of the new school at Martin.

The junior college almost from the beginning offered additional courses in education. These courses were designed for teachers who needed more training, and they were not listed in the regular catalog. The demand was there, but the authority to offer the courses was probably lacking. Nevertheless, separate mimeographed lists of these courses were sent to area teachers, and they could enroll either for a spring term encompassing April and May or a summer term, which ran from late May until early July. Finally, in 1934, these additional education courses, because of demands from local superintendents and others, became official and were listed in the catalog. The local school officials wanted to be sure these courses were sanctioned by Knoxville.[19]

Students wishing to enter the junior college had to be graduates of accredited high schools, and they were required to have a minimum of fifteen credits. These requirements were the same as those at Knoxville.[20]

The room and board charges at Martin for the fall quarter in 1927 were $72.00. Each student also paid a $7.00 per quarter maintenance fee, a laboratory fee ranging from $1.00 to $3.50, and a library fee of $1.00. Each also had to put up a damage deposit of $5.00.[21]

During the early years of the junior college, some health services were provided by doctors sent from Knoxville. George D. Wilhelm, a medical doctor on the UT staff, traveled to Martin in the fall of 1930 to give physical examinations to the students, and he reported an entering class which on the whole was "very healthy." The major problems encountered concerned tonsils, ringworm of the feet, flat feet, bad teeth, and bad posture. He found only two overweight girls and two overweight boys in the group.[22] In time, health services were handled by local doctors.

Amidst a community celebration, the University of Tennessee Junior College officially opened in September 1927. The school had an enrollment of 120 students and a faculty and staff of fourteen. The student body consisted of sixty males and sixty females, and the sophomore class was composed mostly of former Hall-Moody students.[23]

Calvin Porter Claxton was the first executive officer, and he served in this position until 1934. Born in 1898 and a 1919 graduate of UT Knoxville, Claxton was the son of Dr. P. P. Claxton, former United States commissioner of education. Following graduation, he farmed, served as principal of Bell Buckle High School, and then returned to Knoxville in 1926–27 to earn a master's degree in education.[24] Energetic, youthful, intelligent, and friendly, Porter Claxton faced a monumental task as the top administrative officer.

Administratively, Claxton reported to Dean C. A. Willson, head of agriculture and home economics at Knoxville. Emphasis at Martin was placed on those two areas, and Willson was assigned to direct the new addition to the UT family. Department heads in Knoxville hired the UTJC faculty and approved the courses to be taught. Needless to say, this arrangement severely limited Claxton's authority in selecting a faculty.[25]

He complained that department heads in Knoxville were sending to Martin "green teachers whom I have never seen and whom they do not know." An example of his lack of authority was illustrated by an incident in which two professors of English arrived in Martin one day to fill the same position. Claxton had not been notified that either had been hired, and he was somewhat bewildered. As it turned out, one professor was expected in Knoxville. Since only the position at Martin had been discussed with him, he naturally assumed this was where he was to be located.[26]

In a letter to A. W. Hobt, head of the Department of Physical Education at Knoxville, Claxton suggested that it would be best if the executive officer at Martin had the responsibility of hiring teachers so there could be a

Calvin Porter Claxton served as the chief executive officer at UTJC from 1927 until 1934.

Gene Stanford shortly after he joined the UTJC staff.

uniform policy. If the department heads in Knoxville continued to select the faculty, Claxton urged that only qualified and experienced teachers be employed. If untried instructors were hired, he felt the department heads had the responsibility to supervise and train them until they were up to par.[27]

What prompted the letter was that Hobt had sent to Martin an instructor in physical education with whom he became dissatisfied. Claxton defended her work and noted that Hobt had sent her to the junior college without training or graduate work. He urged that Hobt give her a chance or else send another teacher.[28]

For the most part, the staff at Martin was well trained. Many former students who later enrolled at UT Knoxville fondly remembered their instructors at the junior college as among the best. C. C. "Pop" Cravens, R. G. Turner, J. Paul Phillips, Edith Hunt, Stephen R. Wood, L. O. Colebank, C. E. Gatlin, and H. K. Grantham are a few of the early teachers cited as outstanding by their students.[29]

Charles A. Keffer, who served as director of the Agricultural Extension Service, took Claxton to task for the statement in a junior college publication that the school "gives instruction of the same high standard and credit as at Knoxville." Far from agreeing with Keffer, Claxton fired back, "I cannot agree with you that any exaggeration has been made in the statement that the local college gives instruction of the same high standard and credit as at Knoxville." He added that he would be very disappointed if Martin did not offer courses equal to those at Knoxville.[30]

Dean Willson, in a 1931 letter to Dr. Morgan, UT President, stated,

> We have been offering at the U.T. Junior College instruction for the first two years of collegiate work that shall be on a par with that offered at the University of Tennessee, or at least as nearly so as it is possible to do without the more expensive equipment and higher training of department heads that we have at Knoxville.[31]

However, in the same letter, Willson argued against adding a pre-medical curriculum at Martin, something the citizens of West Tennessee would demand and receive in the near future.

Claxton's salary in 1927–28 was $3,500 for twelve months. He was paid $2,500 for serving as the executive officer, and he received an additional $1,000 for teaching rural education.[32] To say he earned his salary is an understatement. His numerous duties included recruiting students, serving as dean of men, editing the catalog, handling college publicity, watching the budget, authorizing expenditures, writing petty cash checks, supervising chapel, greeting visitors, and filing reports with Knoxville. In addition to these and other responsibilities, he also taught two classes.[33]

Fortunately, Gene S. Stanford, twenty-one years old and a recent graduate of UT Knoxville, joined the staff as bursar in 1930 and relieved Claxton of many of the business headaches. Stanford remained on the staff as business manager until his retirement in 1972, and he was a key figure in the growth and development of the school. According to Stanford, Dean Willson asked him how he would like to be the bursar at Martin. He instantly replied, "Dean, I do not know what a bursar is nor do I know where Martin is, but I'll take the job!" The Great Depression was raging at this time, and jobs were very scarce.[34]

When the junior college opened, the faculty members who held the rank of associate professor or assistant professor earned $200–$250 per month. Teachers with a lesser rank generally were paid $150 monthly.[35] The majority of the faculty members had ten-month appointments. Later, during the depression, salaries would be slashed. A letter from Claxton to Willson, dated December 31, 1931, indicated how an approximate 10 percent salary reduction would be handled.[36] Cuts in the operating budget were also foreseen. This crisis would bottom out in 1933.

The only faculty member retained from the Hall-Moody staff was H. Kirk Grantham. He came to Hall-Moody in June 1925 from Newbern where he had been a very successful high school coach. He continued his winning ways at HMJC, coaching football, baseball, and men's basketball. Because of his winning record and the high esteem in which he was held, Grantham was hired as a member of the new UTJC faculty. He continued to coach football, baseball, and men's basketball. In addition, he headed the Department of Physical Education and served as director of athletics. Vertrees Vowell (1928 and 1929), Van Morgan (1930), and Frank Taylor (1931) were among the assistant coaches who helped Grantham.

Bob Wilkins, who served as the janitor for Hall-Moody, also remained in this capacity. Wilkins, who was well-known and beloved by the students, was a fixture on the campus for many years. The *Last Leaf* devoted an entire page to "Bob—the Most Loyal."[37] During an interview in 1947 with Dan Kroll, co-editor of the *Volette*, he mentioned that he had worked on the campus since December 1907. When he first arrived, related Wilkins, "The administration building had eighteen stoves, and I had to tote coal up the stairs in scuttles. Man, that was work—real man's work."[38]

H. Kirk Grantham was the only Hall-Moody faculty member to be retained at UTJC. A group of Martin business firms sent a petition dated April 18, 1927, to Dr. H. A. Morgan recommending that Grantham be retained by UT. This request indicated the high esteem which the community held for Grantham.

In that same year, 1947, Wilkins, who was then seventy-eight years old, contacted UT Trustee George Rowlett concerning any available retirement funds since declining health prevented him from continuing his janitorial duties. Rowlett wrote to Dr. C. E. Brehm, who was acting president of UT at the time, and he referred the matter to Paul Meek. As it turned out, there were no retirement funds, but Meek suggested that Wilkins be employed to work part-time as his health permitted in the library for eight to ten dollars a week. Wilkins, who was praised by Meek, Rowlett, and others for his devotion to the school, enthusiastically agreed to this arrangement.[39]

As part of his numerous duties, Claxton on occasions did have to deal with student disciplinary problems. One young man, who apparently had a disdain for class attendance, was dropped from the college. Immediately afterwards, he was the presumed leader in placing a bee hive in the front hall of the boys' dormitory and then arousing the bees with smoke. The result was angry bees, smeared honey, and jet-propelled students. Following the prank, he was barred from further attendance at the junior college, and Claxton notified the young man's father that his patience had been exhausted.[40]

Another incident which occurred on Halloween night in 1930 apparently resulted in no disciplinary action. About fifty college boys, with pranks in mind, marched downtown. The group was intercepted by the city police who fired three shots to disperse the crowd. As the *Weakley County Press* reported, "At each shot fired, several miles per hour was added to the speed of the dispersing crowd of boys." The students returned to campus, huddled briefly, and then called it a night.[41]

In November 1928, Coach Grantham notified some students, mostly athletes, that he had some extra tickets for the UT-Vanderbilt football game to be played in Nashville, if they could arrange transportation. Fourteen of them hopped a freight train, endured cold weather enroute to Nashville, but unluckily were apprehended in the freight yards by a railroad official. He asked for and received names, some fictitious, from the students. The official went to answer the telephone, and during this interval the young men fled. They attended the football game and then hitch-hiked back to Martin, except for two who again opted to "ride the rails."

As to be expected, a letter from a railroad official was sent to Porter Claxton, stressing the dangers and illegalities of riding a freight train. The official also requested payment for the ride to Nashville. The students were properly admonished by Claxton, but no fares were paid.[42]

Public relations also demanded attention from Claxton. The public reaction to campus dances and the "great milk

An entire page in the Last Leaf *was devoted to Bob Wilkins, a highly respected and well-liked campus figure. He was retained as a custodian at UTJC and again was very poplar among the students.*

war" of 1934 were examples of "town vs. gown" problems.

In 1927, Claxton, in correspondence with F. M. Massey, who served as dean of students for the university, stated he had made a decision against dancing. He was concerned that the public gossip and ensuing debates would harm the infant school. "This has been too long a church school and a church town. We had nothing to gain by instituting dancing, and lots to lose," he added. Facing the realities of youthful exuberance, he later softened his stance, and limited dancing did occur, much to the consternation of some local pious citizens.[43]

In April 1932, Rev. T. A. Duncan from Martin wrote President Morgan, apparently voicing concern about college dances. Dean Willson, at Morgan's request, drafted a reply in which he defended dancing as "the means of young people expressing joy." He also alluded to the Scriptures as having no admonition against dancing. He did stress that college dances should be limited and open only to college students. In addition, he stressed that the primary objective in attending college was to gain an education.[44]

In December 1933, remembering earlier local complaints, Willson advised Claxton that the homecoming dance should not have been advertised as such because of community reaction. Perhaps it would be better, he cautioned, to have a program in which there is singing, a one-act play, a moving picture, and other forms of entertainment. "The evening entertainment should be so varied that it could not possibly be called a dance," he concluded.[45]

Regardless of reaction, the young people would not be denied and college dances continued. Madge Harrison, who attended UTJC in the 1936–38 era and later was the first woman to be president of the University of Tennessee National Alumni Association, remembered with fondness the Friday night dances in the gym. "We used to really look forward to the Friday night dances. It was the highlight of the week," she recalled.[46]

Florence Elliott Hillis joined the UTJC faculty in 1933 in the Department of Physical Education. Noting that "the boys knew how to hold a girl but nothing else about dancing," she offered to teach ballroom dancing. To her surprise, nearly all the male students showed up for instruction at the first session. This further demonstrated strong student interest in dancing.[47]

The "milk war" occurred when an enterprising student began to buy and sell surplus college milk to local customers. Area dairymen complained about the competition. The reputation of the college herd, the known richness and cleanliness of the milk, and the emotional appeal to customers that they were helping a college student pay his way through college gave the young entrepreneur a decided advantage, according to one dairyman. It is interesting that

Florence Elliot Hillis, who is remembered by the students as "Miss Flossie." A UTJC alumna, she joined the physical education faculty in 1933. (Courtesy of Earl and Elizabeth Shannon)

two local dairymen also applied for the privilege of purchasing surplus college milk, so the dairymen were not completely united.

The situation was basically defused when Dean Willson advised Claxton and the dairymen that the students (the original student now had a partner) should not seek additional customers and their prices should be at the maximum local price. Needless to say, their customers wanted the students to continue. Willson did not ask the students to refrain from distributing milk but just to follow the aforementioned concessions.[48] Willson, in another letter to Claxton, was concerned that if milk could not be sold locally then others might complain about the selling of potatoes, hay, and other college farm products. His advice was to sell the farm products but not at lower prices.[49]

The junior college farm apparently was doing well. In October 1931, Willson wrote President Morgan that the farm was being maintained as "a laboratory for instruction of students—and also for the purpose of demonstrating better agriculture to the farmers of West Tennessee." Willson further stated that "two hundred and five acres are being farmed with one team of

---

1927
Hall-Moody closes and the University of Tennessee Junior College is established.

1928
Aloha Oe ceremony adopted from Knoxville.

"The Checkerboard" appears in the *Weakley County Press*.

First issue of the *Volette* is published.

1929
4–H Club begins summer camps at UTJC.

Science building and home economics building are erected.

1930
The *Volunteer Junior* is first published.

Gymnasium, industrial arts building, football field, and heating plant are constructed.

1931
Baseball is dropped as an intercollegiate sport.

1933
Enrollment plunges to all-time low.

Intercollegiate athletics are dropped.

1934
Paul Meek replaces Porter Claxton as the executive officer.

Citizens in West Tennessee issue a successful call for additional courses at UTJC.

Intercollegiate athletics are re-instated.

1935
Cafeteria and a greenhouse are built.

1936
UTJC gets its own post office.

mules, one general tractor, and a small garden tractor." He added that production costs, through the use of power, were at a minimum, and studies on production costs had been sent to the press, all county agents, and to Smith-Hughes teachers of agriculture. To possibly counter an argument that cheap student labor was responsible for low production costs, Willson indicated students were hired when possible, but they generally were not available in the summer when need was the greatest.[50]

The college opened with ample operating funds. The legislature in 1927 had allocated $75,000 a year for two years, and Claxton was optimistic that a substantial increase was possible in 1929.[51] The legislature did appropriate $90,000 a year, not quite what Claxton hoped for but still a good increase.[52] The proposed budget in 1931 was over $112,000, but then the Great Depression began to deepen. Reductions were made, and in 1933 UTJC had to operate on $36,000 a year. The total budget for the University of Tennessee was only $450,000 in that year.[53] The faculty at Martin was reduced to seven, the fall quarter enrollment plunged to ninety-two, intercollegiate athletics were

THE UNIVERSITY OF TENNESSEE JUNIOR COLLEGE (1927–1951)

1939
Baptist Student Union is formed.

1940
Civilian Pilot Training program is started.
Wesley Foundation is organized.

1941
Industrial arts building burns.
United States is plunged into World War II.

1942
A contract is signed to train naval aviation cadets.

1944
Two year program in engineering is implemented.
The naval aviation contract is concluded.

1945
World War II ends.

1946
The veterans return and the enrollment reaches a new level.
Temporary buildings are erected.
Academic departments are organized.
UTJC is ranked among the top fifteen junior colleges in the nation by *Look*.

1947
Two-year program in business administration is added.

1950
The Korean Conflict starts.
The battle is waged to elevate UTJC to senior college status.

1951
UTJC achieves four-year status, and the school becomes known as the University of Tennessee Martin Branch.

suspended, and a movement was started to abolish the school.[54] Others wanted to separate it from the University of Tennessee.[55]

Dr. James D. Hoskins, who became president of UT in 1933, opposed these movements against UTJC. He feared further loss of university funds, not to mention support in northwestern Tennessee. In 1933, the local chamber of commerce allocated $250 to send representatives to Nashville to talk with legislators about the college.[56] This assistance, plus support from other citizens, saved the day. The college barely managed to survive, and slowly the financial picture brightened.

During the 1933–34 period, the citizens of northwestern Tennessee, desiring expansion rather than closure of the school, petitioned for additional courses at the junior college. On February 21, 1934, the UT Board of Trustees Committee on the Junior College met in Martin. President Hoskins, Dean Willson, and Porter Claxton were in attendance, along with trustees George Rowlett, I. B. Tigrett, W. P. Ridley, and Thomas H. Allen. County superintendents from Weakley and the seven surrounding counties submitted a request for additional courses in liberal arts, education, and pre-medicine. In addition, they asked that all education courses be printed in the school catalog, athletics be re-instated, and every effort be made to increase the enrollment. As noted earlier, mimeographed lists of education courses for teachers had been sent to area teachers before the spring and summer sessions. The superintendents wanted these in the regular catalog to be sure they were sanctioned by the University of Tennessee.[57]

Later in the meeting, Milburn Gardner, representing the local chamber of commerce, read a paper from that organization requesting two years each in liberal arts, pre-medical and pre-dental training, and education courses. It was urged that foreign languages be included in the liberal arts courses. Again, restoration of intercollegiate athletics was urged, and it also was stressed that every effort should be made to gain additional students.

The chamber of commerce paper further urged that state appropriations for the junior college be placed in Weakley County banks instead of going to Knoxville. This did not happen. A plea for more local autonomy also was made.[58]

Paul Meek, around 1935, shortly after he became the chief executive officer at UTJC.

Hoskins agreed to re-instate intercollegiate athletics, to schedule enough courses in education for teacher certification, to provide the classes necessary for one year in pre-medicine, and to set up an adult education program for farmers and homemakers. In addition, a small fund was established for student recruitment.[59]

The final recommendation from the university officials, while not going as far as the West Tennessee delegations desired, did provide enough courses for two years in both education and liberal arts. The one-year course in pre-medicine was part of the liberal arts curriculum. The trustees, by accepting these proposed changes, went beyond the enabling act which had created the junior college in 1927. UTJC operated under this revised program approved by the trustees until World War II dictated changes.

The enrollment at the junior college had climbed to 180 during the 1929 fall enrollment but had declined to 92 for the 1933 fall quarter. Undoubtedly, the depression was the primary factor, but Americans tend to look for a scapegoat. Porter Claxton, for the most part, was delegated to that role.

Some, including George Rowlett, felt Claxton had not worked hard enough toward increasing the enrollment. Another complaint was that he was dating Evelyn Mabry, a campus teacher. They were both single, but some thought it not appropriate for the executive officer to date a faculty member. It is interesting to note that later, in March 1934, they were married.[60] The 1931 *Volunteer Junior* was dedicated to Claxton, evidence that he was admired by the students.

A needy student remembered that when he completed his work at UTJC and was preparing to transfer to Knoxville, Claxton gave him a personal check for fifty dollars. The student had compiled an admirable record at Martin while serving as an outstanding campus leader and athlete. Claxton's generosity was not forgotten, and following graduation from UT Knoxville the student presented Claxton with a signed blank check, urging him to fill in the amount he owed for the loan. Claxton never cashed the check.[61]

Others lauded the leadership, caring attitude, and diligent work by Claxton, but the final result was that he was transferred to Knoxville as assistant professor in rural education. He remained there for one year, did additional graduate work at George Peabody College from 1935–37, served as director of rural education at West Georgia College from 1937–43, and then worked for the federal government as an education specialist for the Institute of Inter-American Affairs and also for private agencies. He died in 1963 and is buried in Knoxville.[62]

Paul Meek became the chief executive officer at the junior college in September 1934. A native of Martin, Meek graduated from McFerrin College where he was an outstanding athlete. He originally planned to attend Vanderbilt University but later opted to enroll at the University of Tennessee. His college career was interrupted by a tour of duty in the U.S. Army during World War I, but he returned to graduate in 1919.[63]

Meek and Porter Claxton were classmates at the University of Tennessee. In fact, Meek was president of the senior class in 1919, Claxton was treasurer, and Martha Campbell, later Mrs. Paul Meek, was secretary.[64] Prior to his departure from Martin, Claxton wrote to Paul Meek wishing him well as the chief executive officer at UTJC. "It has been a great relief and pleasure to me to learn that it is you who have been chosen to succeed me here," Claxton wrote. "If I had the task of selecting the man in the care of whom I had most

The 1936 sophomore class was the largest graduating class in the history of UT Junior College at the time. Fifty-two members of the class enrolled at Knoxville during the next academic year. (Courtesy of Earl and Elizabeth Shannon)

rather leave the College, I would have chosen you. I am very sincere in this." The remainder of the letter offered any desired assistance and extended best wishes.[65]

Following graduation from the University of Tennessee, Meek had spent 1919–20 in Martin on a newly acquired farm. In the fall of 1920, he accepted a position as math teacher and football coach in Harlan, Kentucky, which was in the heart of the coal-mining hill country. Most of his meager squad had never seen a football game, and he started the team from scratch. This included building a football field.[66]

He liked to tell the story how in the first game, midway through the second quarter, a farmer, unaware of what was going on, led his mule across the field—pulling a dead hog behind.[67]

An outstanding athlete, Meek stood over six feet tall and weighed about 190 pounds. He was a handsome young man, and the hearts of many young mountain girls fluttered when they saw him. According to one of his students in Harlan, he was big, strong, and tough as rawhide. He could run faster, jump further, and throw harder than any of his players. What impressed the students the most though was that he didn't smoke, chew, drink, or use foul language,

nor did he allow his players to do these things in his presence. He taught the young men to play hard, but he wouldn't stand for any dirty football.[68]

Meek later became principal of the school and eventually superintendent. In the meantime, he and Martha Campbell were married in 1922. In 1934, he returned home to Martin as the executive officer at UTJC. Due to the depression, his beginning salary was only $2,700 per year.[69]

Meek, who would head the school until his retirement in 1967, now reported directly to Dr. Hoskins, who, as mentioned earlier, became president of the university in 1933. Willson and other deans maintained input concerning their respective areas, but the executive officer no longer reported administratively to the School of Agriculture and Home Economics.[70]

A major challenge facing Meek concerned the low enrollment. Hoskins urged Meek to make the college more regional in nature. In short, he was told the enrollment of out-of-county students needed to be increased.[71]

Meek and his staff swung into action. The 1934 fall enrollment, undoubtedly boosted both by the additional courses being offered and the reinstatement of athletics, surged to 229. The enrollment continued to climb, and 336 students were registered for the initial quarter in 1940. But then World War II broke out, and in 1943 only 115 students, including 24 males, enrolled for the fall quarter. Fortunately for the school, a contract to train aviation cadets had been secured. This helped the junior college survive until the veterans could come marching home.[72]

As the enrollment climbed, new faculty members were added. Earl M. Knepp, Harry Harrison Kroll, George Horton, and John E. McMahan were among those added in 1936 and 1937. McMahan, as head of the Department of Agriculture, was urged to increase the farm revenue. A better person could not have been chosen, though some of his student-workers complained about their low wages and "Mr. Mac's" exacting demands.

As old-timers recall, McMahan's chickens and peach orchards were his prizes. At least on one occasion, he complained about missing chickens. Feathers around one dormitory indicated some students had enjoyed fried

The gymnasium as it looked in the 1930s. (Courtesy of Earl and Elizabeth Shannon)

chicken. A missing hog also confirmed the source of an ample supply of barbecue in a dorm. Even faculty members were among the culprits who occasionally enjoyed a few free peaches. These dastardly deeds did not go unnoticed by the frugal McMahan, and he was constantly on the alert for such escapades.[73]

On one occasion, some students decided to display their abilities for covert operations by raiding another of Mr. Mac's joys—his strawberry patch. Operating under the cover of darkness with flashlights held low to the ground to avoid detection, "the raiders" crept into the field. Unknown to them, McMahan was hiding nearby. Taking a flashlight, he eased in among the strawberry snatchers as they moved quietly down the rows, savoring the luscious fruit. Suddenly, one student alertly noticed something was wrong. With a loud yell he announced, "Boys, there's one more flashlight than when we came in. Let's get the hell out of here!" A mild stampede followed. "Fellows, it's too late now because I know all of you!" McMahan bellowed. But the compassionate soul beneath the stern exterior emerged, and McMahan never sought punishment for the interlopers, some of whom reportedly didn't stop running until they approached the city limits of South Fulton.[74]

Another widely circulated story concerned a visit from one of McMahan's supervisors from Knoxville. As they toured the farm, the official opted to sample a couple of peaches from the orchard. McMahan extended his hand and supposedly stated, "That will be ten cents, please."[75]

The teachers, much like Claxton and Meek, had many and varied duties. Verletta Hearn, who joined the staff in December 1934, was hired as head of the Department of Home Economics with the rank of assistant professor. Her salary was $162 per month ($1,944 for the year—this was during the depression), and her duties included being department head, serving as dean of women, supervising the dormitories and dining halls, and teaching one-half load. The construction of the new dining hall, which was finished in 1935, also demanded her attention. In her "spare time" she was to supervise the school nursery. Other staff members had similar responsibilities.

After marrying Gene Stanford in December 1935, Hearn could work only part-time for the university due to a policy which stated that just one spouse could work for the school. Also, during the depression the prevailing attitude was that available jobs should be spread among as many families as possible.[76]

The football team during the 1927–29 seasons continued to play home games on the old Hall-Moody field located just east of present Gooch Hall and in front of the original administration building. The field was ninety yards long, and when a team moved the football down to the ten-yard line on one end it would be placed back on the twenty-yard line.[77] In order to entice fans to buy tickets, canvas was draped over the fence around the field on game days. The basketball team still used the wooden gym built in 1924, and the baseball team played at Harmon Field, a local facility.

A cafeteria was built on the UTJC campus in 1935.

In 1930, the new gym was completed, and a football field was built just north of that building. Constructed at a cost of $83,750 and featuring an inlaid maple floor, a swimming pool, excellent physical education facilities, and a large stage at one end of the gym, this was one of the most attractive structures in Tennessee.

The football field was one of the first lighted stadiums in West Tennessee. When it was first used in 1930, numerous people attended games, not only to see an outstanding team but also to view the marvel of night games. A cinder track, described as one of the best in the state, circled the field, and new tennis courts were located near the gym.

In 1974, at the urging of a host of Grantham's former players, the football field was officially named Grantham Field. He had been the major architect in planning the field. The stadium has been expanded through the years, but the field, with the exception of some

In 1974, at the urging of many of his former athletes, the football field was named in memory of H. Kirk Grantham. Mrs. Grantham and some of his former players observe the unveiling of the sign at Pacer Stadium.

turf improvements, is essentially as built in 1930. The original drainage system still functions very well.

The first UTJC football team had a total of nineteen players, most of whom had played on the 1926–27 Hall-Moody team. The basketball team, composed entirely of eight former Hall-Moody players, won the first Mississippi Valley Conference Basketball Tournament to climax the 1927–28 season. The Mississippi Valley Conference was organized in December 1927, and it consisted of schools, at various times, from Tennessee, Kentucky, Arkansas, Mississippi, and Missouri. UTJC was a member of the league from its founding until 1951.[78]

Athletic teams during the junior college era did surprisingly well, especially considering the caliber of opposition. Often times, the opponents were four-year institutions. During 1927–28, schools competed against included: Tennessee Polytechnic Institute, now Tennessee Tech (football); Southern Illinois University (football and basketball); Murray State (football, basketball, and baseball); the University of Memphis—known then as West Tennessee State Teachers College (basketball and baseball); Union; Lambuth; and Bethel (football, basketball, and baseball).[79]

Baseball, because of a lack of interest, was discontinued as an intercollegiate sport in 1931 and was not revived until 1957. Tennis and track appeared on the athletic scene, but both were in the infant stages. Gene Stanford, who had been a member of the tennis team during his undergraduate years at UT Knoxville, was an early coach of the netters.[80]

W. Everett Derryberry. (Courtesy of Earl and Elizabeth Shannon)

Due to the depression, all intercollegiate sports were discontinued in 1933. Emphasis was placed on intramurals, but students and the public were dismayed at the lack of intercollegiate competition.[81] It is interesting to note that the enrollment plunged to an all-time low in that year.

In 1934, at the urging of local groups, athletics were resurrected. Major Bob Neyland, legendary football coach at UT Knoxville, visited Martin in July 1934 and hailed the revival of football at UTJC. Speaking before a large and enthusiastic crowd, he also praised the selection of W. Everett Derryberry, one of his former players, as the new football coach.[82] Derryberry, a Rhodes Scholar following graduation from UT Knoxville, had joined the faculty at Martin in 1933 as head of the English department. Under Derryberry's direction, the football team enjoyed three successful years, including an undefeated season and the Mississippi Valley Conference championship in 1936. Following the premier season, Derryberry retired from coaching to concentrate on his academic duties. In 1938, he joined the faculty at Murray State as head of the English department, and he later served as president of Tennessee Tech for many years.[83]

The 1930 football team which finished 8–2 and lost the Mississippi Valley Conference championship in the final game to West Tennessee Teachers (now the University of Memphis) by a score of 14–13.

Derryberry's assistant in 1934 was Gordon Smith who received $300 for coaching during the football season. His assistant in 1935 was Ralph Hatley, later to become the head football coach at Memphis State (which became the University of Memphis in 1994). Cecil "Sonny" Humphreys was Derryberry's assistant in 1936. In 1937, he became an assistant coach at Memphis State, and he took twelve players from the undefeated 1936 UTJC team with him. Nine of them became starters, and Memphis State had two outstanding years. Humphreys, who served for two years as an assistant coach at Memphis under Allyn McKeen, was elevated to the head position when McKeen accepted the top job at Mississippi State. He later became president (1960–72), and then served as the first chancellor of the State Board of Regents (1972–75).[84]

Grantham continued to serve as men's basketball coach, director of athletics, and head of the physical education department until 1937 when he went into the Pepsi-Cola business in Tupelo, Mississippi. Hollis Kinsey, a former student-athlete at Hall-Moody and UTJC, was a partner in the enterprise. Grantham resided there until his death in 1963.

Tragedy struck the UTJC football team in 1935. James Edward "Jimmy" Long, a sophomore tailback from Union City, suffered a severe head injury during a game at Northwest Mississippi Junior College, and died early the next morning at a hospital in Memphis. During the fourth quarter in a hard-fought game, Long broke loose for a forty-yard run. When tackled his head hit the ground with a terrific impact. He stood up, remarked he was a little dizzy, and then slumped unconscious as he sat on the bench. Dr. O. M. Derryberry, the brother of coach Derryberry, gave Long immediate attention and called for an ambulance to rush him to Memphis. Unfortunately, he had suffered the rupture of a blood vessel within the brain, and nothing could be done.

According to newspaper accounts, the biggest crowd ever to attend a funeral in the area was present for his services.[85] The 1937 annual, the *Volunteer Junior*, was dedicated to the memory of Jimmy Long, and in 1993 a plaque was erected at UT Martin in remembrance of this outstanding young man.[86]

Nick Denes, who later had some excellent teams at Western Kentucky, took over the coaching duties in 1937. He was assisted that year by Phil Dickens who had earned the nickname, "Phantom Phil," while playing as a tailback at UT Knoxville. Dickens later was the head coach at Wofford College, the University of Wyoming, and Indiana University. "Bo" Rice, another UT grad, served as Denes's assistant during his second year.[87]

Rifle teams for the men and women also appeared on the UTJC campus in 1937. The members of both teams belonged to the National Rifle Association, and C. E. Gatlin was the sponsor. The women's team competed against the University of Mississippi, San Francisco Junior College, Wheaton College of Illinois, Hofstra College of New York, and Pennsylvania State Teachers College. The men competed against the same teams except the Muscle Shoals Rifle and Pistol Club was substituted for the University of Mississippi. The women also fired against, not at, a team of UTJC faculty members, but the results were not available.[88]

James Edward "Jimmy" Long from Union City who died in 1935 from a head injury he received in a football game.

In the 1939–41 era, Paul Hug, assisted by Joe Black Hayes, handled the coaching responsibilities. Except for the brief stint (1934–37) when Kirk Grantham coached basketball and Everett Derryberry coached football, the head football coach also headed the basketball program.

During the war years (1942–45), regular athletics were suspended; however, in 1946, with the return of the veterans, athletics were revived. Paul Hug was the head coach, and he was assisted by James C. Henson. In 1947, Henson was elevated to the top position, and Vincent Vaughan was employed as his assistant. Both would continue in their respective positions for the remainder of the junior college era.

Henson, a former standout football player and track performer at Mississippi State, served in numerous capacities during his early years at UTJC. He coached football and basketball, headed the Department of Physical Education, served as director of athletics, and taught a chemistry class. Colleagues and students both remember his philosophy of life, good humor, and amicable manner.[89]

Students at UTJC emulated students on the Knoxville campus with some traditions and customs,

The basketball team in the mid-1930s. The tall player in the center is Floyd Burdette, who later was the head basketball coach at Martin for nineteen years.

but others were their own. In 1928, the Aloha Oe ceremony was adopted from Knoxville.[90] In the ceremony the sophomores at Martin would light their torches (candles) from the parent torch to go forth and spread the light of leadership and learning. This was a very touching exercise which normally occurred on the football field at night. The lights would be turned off, and the students would form a procession with their lighted candles.

A student newspaper, the *Volette,* was started in 1928, and it continues today, though it is now called the *Pacer.*[91] An earlier campus publication, the *Checkerboard*, was the forerunner of the *Volette*. Space in the *Weakley County Press* was provided each week, and campus news was printed in the column entitled "The Checkerboard."[92] This feature lasted from January to May, 1928. During the depression and World War II, issues of the *Volette* were limited, but the newspaper has enjoyed a continual publication from January 1929 to the present. An annual, the *Volunteer Junior*, now the *Spirit*, was first published in 1930.[93] The "Checkerboard" articles were compiled in book form in 1928, and some deem this as the first annual. Due to the depression, the yearbook was not published from 1933 through 1936.

The students participated in such activities as a public speaking club, a dramatics club, an agricultural club, a home economics club, an orchestra, a lettermen's club, and a glee club. Clubs and other organizations were encouraged during the junior college years, but fraternities and sororities were prohibited. One of the most active clubs on campus during this era was the

Student Christian Association which included members from all church groups. In 1939, the Baptist Student Union was organized, primarily through the efforts of Joe Black Hayes.[94] He later recalled that their first meetings were held on the stage in the gym. The Methodists organized the Wesley Foundation in 1940, and the Church of Christ and others soon had their individual clubs.[95] This led to the demise of the Student Christian Association.

Many students who were members of the Wesley Foundation fondly recalled the efforts of Betty Henson who directed the Wesley Foundation for many years. They particularly remembered the fun times and excellent food provided by Betty and James Henson on Sunday nights.[96]

When the veterans returned after World War II, they formed the Bluejackets Club (Navy, Coast Guard, and Merchant Marine veterans) and the Army Club. Later, they would join hands as the Veterans Club.[97]

The Barnwarming Dance and Carnicus were important campus events. On one occasion, a newspaper article announcing the engagement of a former queen of the Barnwarming Dance stated she had been queen of the "*Bar*warming Dance." Needless to say, this did not endear the paper to her and her family.[98] Carnicus, derived from "carnival" and "circus", was an annual show sponsored by the Department of Physical Education. Started at UTJC in 1934, it featured tumbling exhibitions, dance routines, a queen (Carni) and a king (Cus), skits, and clowns. The gym normally was packed for this event.[99]

When the junior college first opened in September 1927, rules and regulations were few and mostly enacted by the students themselves. Claxton thought the students were adults and should be given the opportunity to govern themselves. F. M. Massey, dean of students at Knoxville, received a letter from Claxton, dated October 11, 1927, in which Claxton praised the behavior of the students and outlined what rules had been established.

Chapel was held routinely, and the men in the residence hall had voted that drinking, gambling, and rowdy behavior would not be tolerated, Claxton reported. If a person spit on the floor or came in after 10:30 P.M. and made unnecessary noise, he would be fined fifty cents. Those who drank and/or gambled faced harsher penalties, including expulsion from school. Claxton added that the women at this time had not formulated a code of conduct, but they were required to check out and give their destination when leaving the dorm. They could date when they wished, but they had to be in the dorm by 11:00 P.M.[100]

Needless to say, more stringent rules followed. After all, UTJC had just taken over the campus of a church school, and community expectations had to be met. Some of the new regulations were advocated by the students and some by the administration. The women, as to be expected, faced more restrictive hours. The general curfew for a long time during the week was 9:00 P.M. for the women, but the weekend hours were more liberal. They still were required to check in and out of the residence halls at night and were prohibited from dating on Tuesday and Thursday nights since Wednesday and Friday class schedules were heavy.[101]

An observation was made that the library was a heavily used facility if all who checked out to go there did so. Slick windowsills indicated a few of the young ladies enjoyed sneaking out of the dorm after hours. Proper dress for all students was expected, and modesty was the order of the day. For example, when walking across campus to a physical education class the women were asked to wear a coat over their shorts.[102]

Most of the students worked either on campus or in Martin. Campus wages, during the early years, were 10¢ to 12¢ an hour, and students eagerly sought these jobs. One student, who washed dishes in the old dining hall which was replaced in 1935, recalled that the sink was a washtub. The floor sagged in the middle and formed a collection pocket for grease. Walking was hazardous, and sanitary conditions, at best, were questionable.[103] Other jobs had equal drawbacks, but most students had to work. As many testified later, "We were all in the same boat. None of us had any money, and any job looked good."

In 1936, the fall quarter enrollment had climbed to 299, and the junior college acquired its own post office. It was located in a room on the west side of the administration building.[104]

In 1937, the campus had a sudden but temporary increase in campus inhabitants. During the great flood in that year, many of the residents in areas along the Mississippi River had to flee from their homes, and a large number of the displaced people from Lake County found refuge in Martin in churches, homes, and on the UTJC campus. The shop in the engineering building, the gym, and other quarters were quickly arranged for the flood victims. A witness to the event recalled, "It was a sad sight to see these folks, many of whom had lost everything, and the people in Martin and other communities gladly responded to meet their needs."[105] Another person remembered, "The campus went all out to help these unfortunate people. They were a very appreciative and cooperative group, though some of the men had to be reminded that they couldn't shoot the squirrels on campus. At home, they were accustomed to hunting squirrels, and some, at first, thought they were in a hunter's heaven."[106]

By 1939, the war clouds in Europe had gathered, but the ominous signs at first did not hamper the growth of the junior college. Then, abruptly in December 1941, the United States was plunged into World War II, and most of the men marched off to war. As noted earlier, the existence of the junior college was threatened again by a scarcity of students. Fortunately, the program to train naval aviation cadets was procured, and this enabled the school to survive.

A factor which helped the junior college acquire the contract with the Naval War Training Service was that the school had started the Civilian Pilot Training Program in October 1940. Participants in the Civilian Pilot Training Program who passed the ground school and flight examinations received a private pilot's license. It is interesting to note that many of the graduates from this program became military pilots during World War II. Most of the aviation courses were later taught to United States Army Air Force cadets who trained at Martin from late December 1941 until June 1942 when the Army terminated its program at UTJC. Shortly afterwards, when the naval aviation cadets arrived the school was well prepared.[107]

In the background of this 1935 photo is the administration building and the old science building. Note that the campus road ran in front of the buildings on the quadrangle.

Gill-Dove Airways where aviation cadets trained during World War II.

In August 1942, a contract was signed with the Civil Aeronautics Administration to provide elementary courses in pilot training for the Naval War Training Service. This program continued until August 1944, and over five hundred cadets went through classroom training, flight instruction, and the physical fitness program at Martin during this interval.[108]

Paul Meek and his staff, well aware of the consequences of the war for the junior college, worked diligently to get the flight program. This training course would keep the faculty together, and, even more importantly, provide a wartime service.

Meek displayed bulldog tenacity in his efforts. When he received a call one Saturday from naval headquarters in Atlanta informing him that the junior college did not have adequate transportation for the cadets, he immediately stated that a bus had been ordered and would arrive the following Tuesday. Of course, a bus was not expected, and Meek was in a precarious position. On Sunday, to solve the dilemma, he dispatched Earl Knepp and Gene Stanford to Cairo, Illinois, with instructions to purchase a bus, by whatever means necessary. They found one on the black market worth about $2,500, paid $5,000 for it, and drove it home. Pictures of the bus with cadets boarding it were fired to Atlanta.

Meek, as anticipated, had to answer questions from Knoxville concerning this hasty purchase. Suffering through the expected chastisements, he agreed that in the future he would first contact the proper officials at Knoxville before making any other such requisitions. It was good that Meek had gambled on the purchase because within a few days no buses were available at any price. If he had first sought permission from Knoxville, it could have delayed the purchase by weeks.

Later, Gene Stanford, when informed that this was a rather daring deed, remarked, "Maybe so, but it also could have gotten us fired!" Stanford, who was the business manager at the time, smiled when he recalled that it required nine regular students to equal the income received for one naval cadet.[109]

During 1943–44, the second year of the Naval War Training Service, the faculty at Martin taught fourteen Navy classes with a total of 387 students. At the same time, 115 students were enrolled for the 1943 fall term in the regular college program. The total of 502 students taxed the faculty and facilities to the fullest. During the two-year period 1942–44, a total of 538 cadets received aviation training at Martin.[110]

The instructors from the junior college, though not in service, wore uniforms and taught such courses as "Plane and Ship Recognition, Civil Air Regulations, Theory of Flight, Aerology, Navigation, Communications (Code and Semaphore) and Aircraft Engines."[111] The faculty members, for the most part, divided their time between teaching the cadets and the regular students. It is interesting to note that Paul Meek, an aviation enthusiast, had taken training and could fly an airplane.

The physical training program was under the guidance of Joe Black Hayes and H. O. Finley. Hayes, an outstanding guard and captain of the 1937 UT Knoxville football team, also served as director of athletics for the school during the war years. Following the culmination of the naval aviation program in August 1944, Hayes joined the United States Navy. He later was a member of the Middle Tennessee State University staff from 1950 until his retirement in 1981.[112]

The flight training was at Gill-Dove Airways, owned by Gill Staulcup. His wife's name was Dove, and thus they called their business Gill-Dove Airways.[113] This site was about two miles from the college, and the cadets flew from there in Piper Cubs. After eight hours in the air with an instructor, the cadets next made a solo flight. Following this, the successful cadets received an initiation by their colleagues with a toss into a mud hole or the swimming pool.[114]

The first two flight instructors at Gill-Dove Field were James Holly and James Bandy, who taught students in the Civilian Pilot Training Program. When World War II started, both immediately joined the Army Air Force and were sent back to Martin to train the Army cadets. When the Army program was terminated, Holly and Bandy were ordered to report to Memphis. They were then transferred to the United States Navy, and once more they were sent

Left to right: 1st Lt. Charles Lafayette Nickell, AAF, Bold Spring; 1st Lt. John Calvin Kelley, AAF, Burlison; A/C Ben Julian Brock, V-5, USNR, Greenfield; T/Sgt. Fred Thomas Maddox, AAF, Martin; Sgt. Robert Lee McKinney, Jr., Inf., Fulton, Ky.

Left to Right: 1st Lt. Dwight Lon Paschall, Engineers, Puryear; Lt. John Thomas Edwards, AAF, Gleason; Pfc. Warren Athol Clendenin, Mountain Inf., Springville; Capt. Horace Franklin Butler, Engineers, Martin; Pvt. Lee Tyree Neill, Inf., Milan; Capt. Wm. Ralph Pauley, AAF, Russellville, Ky.

Left to right; Ensign Wayne Roland Bryant, USNR, Kenton; 2nd Lt. William Jennings Brann, AAF, Dresden; 2nd Lt. Joe Harris Mann, Brownsville; 2nd Lt. Edward Reid Osborne, AAF, Arlington; Sgt. Tillman Ezelle Thompson, Inf., Camden.

Left to right: S/Sgt. James Harold Smith, Inf., Martin; Pvt. John Kay Nunnally, QMC, Grand Junction; Lt. Larimore Colvett, Inf., Alamo; 2nd Lt. James A. Hooper, AAF, Toone; Lt. George Anderson Pinner, AAF, Covington.

Left to right; Major Walter Sidney Butler, Jr., AAF, Huntingdon; Capt. John William Dickinson, Jr., AAF, Brownsville; Lt. Ned Calvin Pentecost, AAF, Martin; 2nd Lt. Ottis Oneal Outlaw, AAF, Stewart; Lt. Cecil Raymond Robertson, AAF, Westmoreland.

Left to right: Ensign Woodrow Wilson Williams, USNR, Nashville; 2nd Lt. Luther Albebrt Donoho, Jr., Marine Air Corps, Martin; ARM 3/c Richard Owen Maiden, Naval Air Corps, Dresden; AMM 3/c Brown H. Smith, Naval Air Corps, Pikeville; S/Sgt. Edward C. Morrow, AAF, Waynesboro.

Left to right: S/Sgt. Herschel Dotson Lynn, Inf., Waynesboro; S/Sgt. Robert Houston Bratton, Jr., AAF, Williamsport; 2nd Lt. Edward Lewis Harris, AAF, Knoxville; Sgt. David Nolen Gentry, Signal Corps, Franklin; 2nd Lt. Warner Wright Harrison, Cavalry, Savannah; S/Sgt. James Durward Counce, AAF, Corinth, Miss.

Left to right: Lt. Ancil Ross Williams, Jr., AAF, Savannah; Pfc. William Joe Scott, Inf., Martin; 2nd Lt. Harry Ellsworth Haney, AAF, Dresden; Sgt. Wilbert Bernard Vincent, Inf., Bolivar; Sgt. William Locke Vaughn, AAF, Linden.

Previous page: A composite of UTJC alumni who lost their lives in World War II. (Courtesy of Joe Nickell)

to Gill-Dove Field, this time to train naval cadets. Assisted by other instructors, they remained in Martin until August 1944 when the naval aviation program at UTJC ended. Holly later recalled that "the cadets were sent to us from all over the country. Some of them had never even driven a car. There were some real tough customers in that group."[115]

When the contract to train the naval cadets expired in August 1944, a contract to provide elementary flight training was signed with the Tennessee Bureau of Aeronautics. This agreement established forty scholarships to be used to instruct Tennessee public teachers and prospective teachers in aviation. Gill-Dove Airways again provided the flight instruction for the junior college under the terms of this contract.[116]

Gill-Dove Airways no longer exists. After World War II, one hangar eventually was converted into a nightclub known as the Strata Club, and it was a favorite place for the college students to dance the night away. Today the buildings are gone, and a new high school and a city park have been erected on the grounds.

The cadets were housed in the college dormitories and in the gym. Temporary, more military-like names were attached to their quarters. Meals were provided in the cafeteria, and they joined the regular students for socials. After all, there was a scarcity of male students.

One spinoff from the naval aviation program was the addition of a regular two-year engineering program. When the junior college opened in 1927, industrial arts was to be offered along with agriculture and home economics; however, it did not appear as an official course of study until 1931–32. During the cutbacks in 1933, the curriculum was dropped and was not reinstated until the 1936–37 school year. In the following year, it was changed to the "Curriculum in Agricultural Engineering."[117]

During World War II, while planning for the growth of the college after the war, the junior college staff and local citizens recommended a two-year course in engineering. President Hoskins and the board of trustees confirmed the need, and a basic two-year curriculum in engineering was officially instituted at Martin in 1944.[118] As noted earlier, this represented no great change since most of the courses were already being offered.

The campus almost did not have a facility in which engineering could be taught because the industrial arts building was virtually destroyed by a fire on June 21, 1941. Starting in 1929 and lasting until 1964 when the camp was moved to Milan, the facilities at UTJC were used each summer by 4–H Club members. The camp, which eventually ran for four weeks, became so large that not enough space was available in the two college dormitories. Tents were used for the overflow. In the late spring, workers waterproofed the tents with oil and stored them in the attic of the industrial arts building. Spontaneous combustion probably caused the tents to ignite and flames engulfed the building. Gene Stanford, on his way to play tennis, discovered the fire at 5:40 P.M. He later reminisced that somehow his tennis racket, along with much school property, was lost during the turmoil of the fire.[119]

Firemen from Union City and Fulton rushed to Martin to help the local fire department battle the blaze, but hampered by inadequate water pressure, they could not save the building. The walls, foundation, warped beams, and debris were all that remained of the one-story building.

Several students and staff members managed to salvage some of the building's equipment. While doing this, a number of the students and firemen barely escaped injury when the roof caved in. Stephen R. Wood, head of the industrial arts department, dived headfirst out of a window to escape the falling debris.[120]

Paul Meek was preparing to attend the University of Chicago for summer work on his doctorate when the building burned. He later remarked that "My doctoral program probably went up in smoke along with the industrial arts building."[121] The United States was plunged into World War II shortly afterwards, and Meek was never able to pursue his doctorate. Later, in recognition of his many contributions to the community and higher education, Meek was awarded an honorary doctorate by Lambuth College.[122]

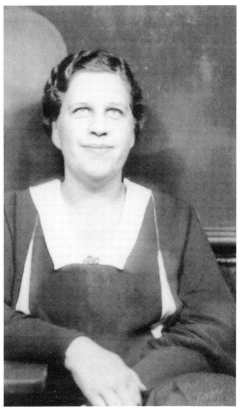

Myrtle Phillips joined the UTJC staff as registrar in 1929, a position she occupied until 1964.

The loss of the industrial arts building posed a serious threat to the campus. University authorities appealed to Governor Prentice Cooper for help since regular university funds were inadequate to meet this emergency. Cooper promptly responded with an authorization for $75,000 from his emergency fund to rebuild the facility, and a construction contract was approved in August 1941. It has been noted that this was the fastest known acquisition of money and approval of a large construction project in the history of the university.[123] Fortune smiled on the junior college because building materials would soon go primarily to the war effort, and the facility was desperately needed, especially since UTJC would be deeply involved in defense activities.

The industrial arts building later became known as Cooper Hall, and it retained this name until 1996 when it was renamed Crisp Hall. Harry L. Crisp II and his wife, Rosemary, contributed funds to enhance campus technology, and the building was renamed in memory of Harry L. Crisp Sr. To maintain the policy of naming campus dormitories for former governors of Tennessee, Atrium Hall then became known as Cooper Hall. Thus, the name of a governor who assisted the university in time of need is still memorialized at UT Martin.

During World War II, Myrtle Phillips, who had joined the staff in 1929 as registrar, wrote and mailed a campus publication entitled *Campus Chatter,*

The "Wooden Box" was a pre-fab dormitory for men. This picture was taken in 1947. (Courtesy of Billy Stricklin)

chiefly to alumni in military service. The campus had not employed an alumni director up to this time, and Phillips had carried out the alumni work that was done through the years. Assisted by Earl Knepp and Florence Blackman, Phillips kept in touch with the servicemen throughout the conflict, keeping them abreast of each other and campus happenings. *Campus Chatter* was first published August 15, 1943 and continued until July 15, 1946.[124]

Russell Duncan, a UTJC alumnus and later director of the UT Martin student center, remembered how Phillips would call him concerning servicemen who were in the Kennedy Veteran's Hospital in Memphis. Duncan was employed by the UT medical units in Memphis during the war, and he would visit the young men who were hospitalized.[125]

Unfortunately, forty-two former UTJC students lost their lives during World War II. Records indicate about nine hundred junior college alumni served during the conflict. On June 8, 1946, a campus memorial service was held for these young people who had made the ultimate sacrifice. During the ceremony, Paul Meek paid tribute to the fallen servicemen, and Tom Prewitt from Bolivar, representing UTJC alumni and his military comrades, gave a very moving speech in remembrance of the forty-two who had not returned from the war.[126]

During his talk, Prewitt remembered the joy of receiving the *Campus Chatter*. He remarked:

> The publication that the school has sent all over the world has done a great deal toward keeping us as close together as possible. I can recall from my own experiences that great feeling of joy and anticipation which I got each month about the arrival of the *Campus Chatter*. For a few minutes I was able to forget

the rigors of a wartime experience and picture myself back at home with all my old friends. It served in no small way to bolster the ever-ebbing morale of a lot of boys on all the fields of battle.[127]

Homecoming activities followed the memorial service, but it was a homecoming unlike most. Sadness mingled with joy. Those in attendance were thankful the conflict was over and normalcy had returned. They greeted fellow alums warmly, but the vacant places left by those who had fallen dimmed the joy.

The 1947 *Volunteer Junior* was dedicated to the memory of those lost in battle, and their names appropriately were inscribed in the front of the annual.

After World War II, the veterans aided by the G.I. Bill of Rights, flocked to colleges across the nation. The 1946 fall quarter enrollment at UTJC spiraled to 649, of which 532 were males. Fortunately, the naval aviation program had held the faculty together, but temporary housing and classrooms had to be quickly arranged. Also, additional faculty members were needed.

After the war, the school purchased some surplus property including eleven structures at Camp Tyson near Paris, Tennessee, and twenty-five dwellings at Camp Breckinridge near Morganfield, Kentucky. Neville B. Williams, a local general contractor, won the bids for dismantling, moving, and re-erecting the buildings at Martin. He earlier had been the contractor for the home economics building, the science building, the football bleachers, barns, sidewalks, and other campus projects. That he was a strong supporter of the junior college was evidenced by the fact that he often times would do the requested work and then wait for payment until funds were available.[128]

Gene Stanford, in a 1994 letter to N.B. "Buster" Williams Jr., son of Neville B. Williams Sr., fondly recalled the many contributions to the campus by the senior Williams. He gave special praise to Williams for re-assembling the tornado-wrecked cottages from Camp Breckinridge, the moving of a much needed boiler to campus, and for re-erecting the buildings from Camp Tyson. Stanford concluded, "I always felt that the college received more than a dollar's worth for every dollar we paid him."[129]

These temporary buildings were used for classrooms, offices, and housing. Among these structures were the Mt. Pelia Apartments (in the vicinity of the Paul Meek Library), what came to be known as the R.O.T.C. building (just south of the humanities building and eventually housing classrooms, the post office, the bookstore, and R.O.T.C.), apartments for married students and faculty members (situated south of the old administration building and in the "Grove"), and a two-story dormitory for men (located near the present location of Clement Hall). The residents in the latter structure referred to themselves as the "Knights of the Wooden Box." The buildings from Camp Breckinridge, actually small cottages, were located in the area now occupied by the Ned McWherter Agricultural Complex. This housing complex was sometimes referred to as "Incubator Hill."[130]

The women students were housed in Freeman Hall and Reed Hall, and the single men found additional housing in Martin. The Dodd, Fuqua, Thornton, Hunt, Howell, Ryan, Patterson, Phillips, Wilson, and Hurt houses were among those where male students resided. The "Grove," besides being the site of some barracks-style apartments, was filled with house trailers. "Trailer Village" contained twenty-two trailer homes obtained through the Federal Public Housing Authority in 1946 as well as a number of privately owned trailers. Everything was crowded, including classrooms, housing, and the cafeteria. George Horton later remarked, "Going from one end of the science building hall to the other between classes was like trying to gain two yards against an Alabama Rose Bowl team!"[131] Mary Lynn Travis Benson, a UTJC alumna and a recent graduate from UT Knoxville, joined the faculty in 1946, and she recalled that the science building was so crowded she had to teach physics in the home economics building.[132]

The dining hall for many years served meals family style, but the influx of students resulted in a change to cafeteria-style service. Also, an addition to the dining facility was necessary in order to accommodate the long lines of hungry students. Eating establishments which catered to the students sprang up near the campus. Mr. and Mrs. Riley G. Wilson, better known as Ma and Pa Wilson, fed a large number of students in their home for several years. The Dinner Bell and later the T Room were two restaurants which appeared after World War II. The American Café and others were located in downtown Martin.

With the enrollment expansion came occasional incidents, some caused by non-students. An episode which could have had fatal consequences occurred in December 1945. Four service men, who were not UTJC students and while under the influence of "demon rum," arrived in a boisterous mood at the women's residence hall one evening seeking some young ladies who would go dancing. The dorm matron rebuffed the young men and advised them to leave. They did so, but then decided to "smoke out the girls." Locating a big pile of leaves which had blown against the dorm, they started a fire. The flames swept through a vent and set fire to the floor and some foundation timbers. Fortunately, the fire was quickly extinguished, and a disaster was averted.[133]

An effort was made by college officials to get a grand jury indictment against the four young men, but the grand jury was not in an indicting mood, especially since the accused had served in the military during World War II. The four did agree to pay $125 for the fire damage and demonstrated sincere remorse over the incident.[134]

Earl Knepp later laughed about an incident which occurred in the boys' dorm, the "Wooden Box." The dorm mother asked Knepp to investigate the report that a student had drawn the picture of a naked woman on a wall in his room. Knepp checked, and the young man had drawn a beautiful woman with the appropriate anatomy. Since it was an excellent work of art, Knepp thought it was a shame to destroy the drawing, so he asked the student to just put some clothes on the young woman. A couple of days later, Knepp decided to check to see if the student had complied with his request. He had—the young lady was now wearing shoes.[135]

To meet increasing enrollment projections, the administrative staff was reorganized in 1946. Five faculty members were elevated to heads of departments. John E. McMahan (Agriculture), J. Paul Phillips (Education), Helen L. Hawkins (Home Economics), Newton Hall Barnette (Engineering), and George Horton (Liberal Arts) assumed these new responsibilities. In 1947, a two-year program in business administration was added, and Jasper F. Grover was named to head that department.[136]

As the University of Tennessee Junior College forged a stronger presence in West Tennessee, recommendations were voiced by area people that it should be elevated to four-year status. In 1934, when additional courses had been added at the junior college, West Tennessee citizens had led the battle. Once again, they stepped forward on behalf of the school. The Organization for Expansion of the University of Tennessee Junior College was formed, and the group, composed of prominent citizens from throughout the area, presented strong arguments in favor of elevating the school to senior college status. Their basic argument was that opportunities for college training in West Tennessee lagged behind East Tennessee and Middle Tennessee. In July 1950, the group met in Trenton and planned their strategy.[137]

In the meantime, the UT Board of Trustees, at a meeting of the Executive Committee on December 12, 1949, appointed Trustees Charles R. Volz from Ripley, Frank Ahlgren from Memphis, and Sam J. McAllester from Chattanooga "to study the advisability and legality of making the University of Tennessee Junior College at Martin a four year college in Agriculture, Home Economics, Engineering, and Business Administration."[138]

On September 15, 1950, Volz, who served as chairman of the UTJC expansion committee, submitted a report which recommended that the curricula be expanded to four years in agriculture and home economics with the addition of the necessary related courses in liberal arts. This would be effective in the fall quarter, 1951. The full board of trustees voted not to accept the committee recommendations at that time but asked for further study. The charge to the committee still included engineering and business administration. At this time, the expansion committee was enlarged from three to five members. Clyde B. Austin from Greeneville and E. W. Eggleston from Franklin were the two additions.[139]

The West Tennessee citizens' organization was represented at the September meeting, and Charles G. Tomerlin, acting secretary for the Union City Chamber of Commerce, presented strong arguments on behalf of the group favoring expansion of the junior college. As the spokesman for the West Tennessee delegation, he emphasized that West Tennessee needed and deserved the expansion of UTJC to senior college status. A pamphlet entitled "Make the Junior College A Four-Year School" was widely circulated and contained rather convincing arguments for the elevation of the school.[140]

Officials at the University of Tennessee initially displayed misgivings about the expansion of the junior college. Fred C. Smith, vice president of UT, in reply to a request from President C. E. Brehm, sent a memo to him on May 6, 1950, in which Smith and four deans concluded that the costs for four-year programs in engineering, agriculture, business administration, and home economics would be prohibitive. Smith suggested efforts should be directed to making UTJC the best two-year school possible.[141] Since the school in 1946 had been listed by *Look* as one of the top fifteen junior colleges in the nation, this position apparently had been attained already.

President Brehm gradually began to favor the move for expansion. Charles Volz, as a board of trustees member, was a very vocal advocate for expansion. In a letter to Brehm dated July 19, 1950, he stated point-blank that the people in West Tennessee "are aroused" and "insistent" that the junior college be expanded.[142] Undoubtedly, these persuasive statements influenced Brehm to acknowledge the validity and strength of the West Tennessee movement. He later issued a twelve-page statement in which he listed the reasons why UTJC should offer four years in agriculture and home economics. He mentioned that an analysis of the student body at Knoxville showed 58.8 percent from East Tennessee compared with 13.9 percent from West Tennessee. To Brehm, this indicated UT was not adequately serving the youth of the western region.[143]

Harold Brundige introduced the bill in the Tennessee House of Representatives to elevate UTJC to senior college status. Interestingly, he is a member of the First Baptist Church in Martin which was a leader in establishing Hall-Moody Institute.

In October 1950, the Board of Trustees met again, and once more a delegation from West Tennessee was present to request that the program be expanded to provide for four years in agriculture and home economics. Engineering and business administration were not mentioned, probably because of demand. Also, it would be easier to gain expansion in two areas rather than four. The Volz committee reported that the junior and senior years in agriculture and home economics could be added for $80,000 in additional funds, and the committee recommended again that this be done.[144] Once more, a call was made for further study.

President Brehm, following the procedure established by President Hoskins in 1934, appointed a faculty committee to study the proposal for the expansion of the junior college. This group reported back that the total expansion cost would be $108,500. In addition, the faculty group listed a need for additional classroom, office, laboratory, and library space at a cost of $1,181,700. It was also noted that a women's dormitory should be built, and the cost of this was listed at $396,000.[145]

In early December 1950, the committee appointed by the Board of Trustees submitted two reports. The majority report, read by Volz, recommended the addition of the additional two years in agriculture and home economics. Sam J. McAllester and Clyde B. Austin filed a minority report opposing the expansion. The board of trustees adopted the majority report favoring the expansion, and in December 1950 approved four-year status for the junior college. Now it was up to the legislature to act.[146]

In the meantime, a movement was underway to move Memphis State College into the UT family. For several years, some Memphians had pursued this idea. The University of Tennessee itself had recommended the strengthening of bonds between Knoxville and other elements of public education all the way down to the elementary school level. Dr. Andrew D. Holt was hired as assistant to the president at UT in August 1950, and he was given the responsibility of seeking solidarity with the various educational segments. Both Holt and Brehm reasoned that this proposal to put Memphis State under the administration of the University of Tennessee might help to achieve this aim.[147]

The Memphis Chamber of Commerce, Memphis political boss Ed Crump, Governor Gordon Browning, President Brehm, Frank Ahlgren (a trustee and also editor of the *Memphis Commercial Appeal*), and others favored the move. A faculty committee appointed by Brehm was favorable, and the board of trustees by a ten to seven count on December 4, 1950, voted for the proposal to admit Memphis State to the UT family. Sam J. McAllester, a trustee from Chattanooga, gave the minority report opposing the move. It was now up to the 1951 legislature.[148]

Following the meeting of the board of trustees, one of the most heated debates in Tennessee history ensued, and it spilled over into the legislative session. Newspapers, alumni, governmental agencies, and others joined the debate and took sides. Brehm spoke in favor of the proposal, but ex-President Hoskins, then eighty-one years old, urged more study.[149] For the most part, East Tennessee opposed the move, West Tennessee favored it, and Middle Tennessee was a battleground. The opposition was too great to overcome, and the end result was that the Memphis State proposal died in the senate mill.

In the meantime, the bill to elevate UTJC to senior college status managed to survive. Harold Brundige, a young attorney from Martin who served in the House of Representatives from 1951 to 1955, introduced House Bill 264 Chapter 27, which permitted the school to offer four years in agriculture and home economics. Also, the bill proposed that the name of the college be changed to The University of Tennessee Martin Branch.[150]

When questioned about how the Martin movement survived when the Memphis State proposal died, Brundige replied, "We were successful because we were well organized." He and others cited the work of Hardy Graham, Harry Lee Vincent, Jack Burdick, and Charles Tomerlin from Union City, Doug Murphy, Wilbur Vaughan, Wayne Tansil, James Riley, and others from Martin, George Thomas and James Glasgow Sr. from Dresden, State Senator Dallas Hall from Tiptonville, and Cooper Alexander from Jackson, plus Paul Meek and others from the junior college. Also remembered were Noel H. "Bud" Riley from Ridgely, a member of the House of Representatives; State Senator Broeck

During a visit to UTJC on November 15, 1950, Governor Gordon Browning receives flowers from Janice Miles as Charlie Tomerlin looks on. During the visit, Browning stated, "I will stand up and fight for a four-year course in agri-culture and home economics in Martin." He kept his promise.

Cummings from Rutherford; and Robert A. "Fats" Everett, aide to Governor Browning.[151] A special tribute was given to Governor Browning. Brundige observed, "Gordon Browning was the one primarily responsible for the success of the move to make Martin a four-year institution. He talked to the legislators individually to gain their support, and we had the necessary votes before the bill ever went to the floor."[152] Brundige and others also worked tirelessly to acquire the necessary support, especially in Middle Tennessee. Also remembered were the efforts of Charles R. Volz, who chaired the board of trustees committee which served as the catalyst necessary to launch the campaign. On February 13, 1951, the legislature passed the bill, and Governor Gordon Browning approved it on February 15, 1951.[153]

Shortly afterwards, the legislature authorized an appropriation of $108,000, the amount recommended by the faculty committee, to expand the programs in agriculture and home economics. All other courses continued to be limited to two years. These included business administration, education, engineering, liberal arts, predentistry, premedicine, prenursing, and prepharmacy.[154]

Paul Meek undoubtedly was in a quandary during the initial stages of the move to elevate the junior college to four-year status. He probably hoped it would happen, but he remained loyal to his superiors. While addressing the UTJC faculty on September 17, 1948, Meek stated that he agreed with the university administration that Martin should remain a junior college, and he asked the faculty to help quiet talk concerning expansion.[155] A year later, on September 16, 1949, he gave the same report to the faculty. He briefly alluded to the ambitions of Memphis State to become a part of UT, and he closed with the caution that "there is no immediate call for comment." He further advised that Dr. Brehm had told him to "listen and say nothing." He considered that wise counsel for the faculty, and he closed by saying, "When the university administration instructs us concerning this matter, it will then be time enough for us to speak."[156]

It was a year later that Volz's committee recommended the expansion of the curricula at Martin. Comments prior to this time could have hurt the school's elevation, but now Meek and others apparently were able to openly solicit support.

The University of Tennessee Junior College, which had served the area well from 1927 to 1951, thus became the University of Tennessee Martin Branch, and a new era was launched. There were numerous individuals deserving of plaudits for their efforts, and time has not diminished the debt owed to these dedicated workers.

PART III

The University of Tennessee Martin Branch
1951—1967

THE ARRIVAL OF THE DECADE OF THE 1950s, SOMETIMES referred to as the "nifty fifties," brought both optimism and apprehension to most Americans. Johnny and Jane had marched home from World War II, and normalcy, of sorts, had returned. The Atomic Age, for better or worse, had arrived; 3-D movies with accompanying glasses fascinated moviegoers; the hula hoop was the rage; the television set was becoming an essential household item; *Playboy* and *Sports Illustrated* were first published; the Barbie doll debuted in 1959; and young girls—and some not so young—were raving about the new hip-swinging singing idol, Elvis Presley. Most of the older generation and some youngsters preferred to go around humming the song, "Davy Crockett." Some of the more daring—including Estes Kefauver, the United States senator from Tennessee—even wore coonskin caps. Along with these came the cold war, the Korean Conflict, McCarthyism, and a Senate investigation of organized crime in the United States.[1] As the youth of America pondered the future, a greater number saw the need for a college education, and increasing numbers trekked to institutions of higher learning. Fortunately for aspiring college students in the West Tennessee area, the offerings at Martin were expanding to meet their needs.

A new era dawned at Martin in 1951 as the college donned the cloak of senior college status and acquired its new name—The University of Tennessee Martin Branch. The school was empowered to offer bachelor of science degrees in general agriculture and general home economics. All other courses remained limited to two years, but within a few years requests for additional four-year degrees would emerge. The two-year courses were business administration, education, engineering, and liberal arts, which included predentistry, premedicine, prenursing, prelaw, and prepharmacy.

West Tennessee was an outstanding agricultural region, and as farming became both more mechanized and diversified there was a demand for additional training in that field and also in home economics. The new degrees at UTMB were designed to satisfy those needs. When UTJC was founded in 1927, agriculture and home economics were the major courses, and the new degrees continued the emphasis in those areas. Within a decade, however, more small industries began to emerge in West Tennessee, and with this growth came a demand for additional degrees. Again, as in the past, local citizens saw the need and led the movement for increased offerings at Martin.

In 1951, the junior and senior years in agriculture and home economics at Martin were based on courses earning five quarter-hours of credit. The freshman and sophomore years were basically the same as at Knoxville, but the last two years were not developed for transfer credit to UT Knoxville. Students were advised to transfer at the end of the sophomore year if they intended to do so.[2]

The faculty of the College of Agriculture and School of Home Economics at Knoxville, working with their counterparts at Martin, developed the curricula for the new degrees at UTMB. One of the faculty members from Knoxville who came to Martin to assist with the curricula changes was Harold J. Smith, later to become head of the School of Agriculture at Martin. The elevation of these two programs resulted in the addition of twenty-nine new courses of study at Martin. Department heads in Knoxville directed and supervised the work at Martin. In fact, the College of Agriculture and School of Home Economics supplied several teachers, including the department head for home economics, during the first year.[3] After the initial year, the faculty at Martin was in place, and temporary assignments from Knoxville were no longer necessary. J. E. McMahan continued to head the Department of Agriculture and Mary Rachel Armstrong became head of the Department of Home Economics in 1952.

Senator Estes Kefauver, escorted by All Students Club President Pete Gossett, is shown as he visited the campus during the 1953–54 academic year. The students are standing on the sidewalk in front of the gym. The "Grove" is in the background.

Interestingly enough, several former students and faculty members recall that UT Knoxville did not make any strong overtures to the early UTMB graduates to entice them to pursue graduate work at Knoxville. Other institutions, the University of Illinois in particular, expressed greater interest, and several students earned Ph.D. degrees from Illinois. Among these were Joe Key, Phil Watkins, Pete Gossett, and Jere Freeman. Faculty member Norman

Campbell also elected to attend the University of Illinois, where he received his Ph.D. in chemistry in 1962. Joe Key became a highly recognized plant physiologist and a faculty member at the University of Georgia; Phil Watkins returned to Martin as a faculty member and is currently vice chancellor for student affairs; Pete Gossett later became vice president of the Institute of Agriculture at UT Knoxville; and Jere Freeman has enjoyed a prominent career in industrial research. Much of the credit for urging the UTMB graduates to seek advanced degrees belongs to Mr. McMahan. Watkins recalls "that 'Mr. Mac' didn't ask if we were going to graduate school; he just wanted to know where we wanted to go."[4]

Other graduates in the 1950s were equally successful in their careers. Cavit Cheshier, a campus leader while attending UTMB, later earned a doctorate and was executive director of the Tennessee Education Association for several years; Ted Welch, a prominent Nashville real estate developer, served as commissioner of finance and administration under Governor Winfield Dunn; and Bob

An aerial shot of the campus made in the 1950–51 period. Note that work has started on the men's dorm and Moody Avenue is being closed (right foreground). (Courtesy of Val Umback)

It became necessary to establish an election commission on campus to prevent multiple voting by some students. Overseeing an election, standing left to right, are George Horton and Grady Taylor. Horton directed the election commission for several years, and Taylor was a very popular biology professor.

Parkins has enjoyed a successful career as a farmer and owner/editor/publisher of the *Mirror Exchange*, a newspaper in Milan. Numerous others have made notable achievements in their chosen professions.

The two new degree programs did not immediately bring a great increase in the enrollment at Martin. The first graduating class on June 1, 1953, consisted of ten graduates in agriculture and four in home economics. The next year, eight degrees were granted in agriculture and three in home economics, but growth was underway.[5] In 1951, 416 students were enrolled for the fall quarter, and by 1960 this figure had climbed to 1,123.

A major factor in curtailing a more rapid initial increase in the enrollment was the outbreak of the Korean Conflict. When North Korean forces swarmed across the 38th parallel in June, 1950, the United Nations, with the United States in the forefront, went to the aid of South Korea. Once more, as in the past, the youth of America heeded the call to arms, and college plans were put on hold. Fortunately, the bitter and bloody struggle ended in a prolonged truce talkathon when the warring forces abandoned the battlefields for the peace table in Panmunjom. As the fighting decreased and the talking increased, a truce was forged, which allowed the military to release many of its personnel. Aided by educational benefits in the so-called G.I. Bill of Rights, veterans once more entered halls of higher learning, as they did following World War II. The

University of Tennessee Martin Branch, as it had done earlier, welcomed these additional students, many of whom were returnees.

A sign of the growing importance of the Martin campus was signaled when the board of trustees as a whole, for the first time since the school became affiliated with the University of Tennessee, met at Martin in April, 1952. President Brehm, in his introductory speech, remarked that the board of trustees was meeting to dedicate the men's dormitory at Martin and also to celebrate the twenty-fifth anniversary of the campus. He further added that it was good for the board and the students to meet each other. He concluded with the statement, "The board recognizes that the Martin Branch is a great asset to the University as a whole."[6] Cavit Cheshier, president of the All-Students Club, gave an appreciative response on behalf of the student body. Interestingly enough, the board at the time also agreed to admit black applicants to the law college and the graduate school at Knoxville without further court action. Earlier, four black students had successfully petitioned the courts for the right to enter the law college and the graduate school, and the board's decision was to admit other black applicants "similarly situated" without requiring them to seek relief through the courts. This decision did not apply to undergraduates, and thus it did not affect Martin, which offered only undergraduate programs at the time.[7]

In September, 1952, the Reserve Officer Training Corps (ROTC) made its appearance at UTMB. It was under the direction of the University of Tennessee Military Science Department at Knoxville, and only the first two years (Military Science I and Military Science II) were offered at Martin. To

The Aloha Oe ceremony in the football stadium, circa 1950.

ROTC cadets undergoing inspection.

complete the last two years, the advanced course, students had to transfer to Knoxville. Agriculture students who elected to earn the bachelor of science degree at Martin could complete only the first two years of ROTC.[8] It was not until the fall of 1964 that the four-year ROTC program was started at Martin.

Another change which occurred after the school moved from junior college to senior college status was the appointment of a member of the board of trustees from Weakley County. The General Assembly of Tennessee created this new position, and Wayne Fisher from Dresden was appointed by Governor Frank Clement to fill this spot in 1953. A businessman and former superintendent of Weakley County schools, he served very ably on the board of trustees until 1981, and during his tenure he was a staunch advocate for the Martin campus.[9]

In order that the needs of the Martin campus could be properly addressed, the board of trustees appointed a Martin Branch committee from their membership in 1951. Trustee Charles R. Volz was the chair of this committee until his death in 1956, and Wayne Fisher followed as the next chair. James T. Granberry, Ben Douglass, Harry W. Laughlin, and Tom Elam were among the trustees who served very ably on the committee. Elam was appointed to the board of trustees by Governor Frank Clement to fill the vacancy when Volz died.[10]

Paul Meek, the guiding and stabilizing force at Martin since 1934, received a title change from executive officer to dean when the school was elevated to senior college status.[11] His leadership was a crucial factor as the junior college struggled to stay afloat during the depression and World War II. The school emerged from the war years with expansion in both enrollment and curriculum, and the tenacity of Paul Meek was a key element.

Other long-term faculty and staff members played vital roles during these trying times. Gene Stanford, George Horton, Earl Knepp, J. E. McMahan, Myrtle Phillips, J. Paul Phillips, Harry Harrison Kroll, and David C. Allen were among the "old-timers" who had worked diligently to steer the school through the troubled waters of the 1930s and the 1940s. Once again, as the 1950s brought new challenges, these educators, who had been joined by some faculty newcomers during the post–World War II era, rose to the occasion.[12]

Many of the newcomers who had joined the faculty and staff ranks during and following World War II became familiar campus figures. Among those were Horace B. Smith (history), Norman A. Campbell (chemistry), Lloyd A. King (chemistry), Harriet E. Fulton (music), Ed M. Chenette (English), James Odell Jones (engineering), John Shannon Murphey (English), and William H. Baker (business). Staff members who were equally well-known by the students were Mrs. H. A. Patterson and Cora Campbell (managers of the dining hall), Alice M. Smith (school nurse), Russell Duncan (student welfare and manager of the bookstore), and William Wade "Red" Freeman (superintendent of the physical plant).[13]

Trustee Wayne Fisher is presented with a plaque of appreciation by Elmer Counce on behalf of UT Martin. After Fisher's retirement in 1981, Jimmy Harrison, Nancy Overton, and currently, Barbara Castleman have served as the Weakley County representatives on the Board of Trustees.

In April 1952, the board of trustees met as a group on the Martin campus for the first time. Governor Gordon Browning is seated at the end of the table and C. E. Brehm is at Browning's right.

The campus was deeply saddened by the deaths of two of the faculty members in 1955—David C. Allen and John Shannon Murphey. Many of the students were taught the rudiments of public speaking by Allen, and their affection for him was sometimes demonstrated in campus skits. Murphey served as adviser to the veterans, and he was a highly respected and beloved English instructor. The 1956 annual was dedicated to the memory of these two outstanding individuals.[14]

J. Paul Phillips, the head of the Education Department and the husband of Myrtle Phillips, died in 1953, and he was replaced by Glenn Gallien, who had recently served as superintendent of Wayne County Schools. Mr. Phillips, who possessed a quiet and friendly personality, is well remembered as a psychology teacher. The students, in remembrance, dedicated the 1954 yearbook to him.[15] Puffing on his ever present pipe, Mr. Phillips sometimes entertained his classes with demonstrations in hypnosis.

A former student, John Gauldin from Dyersburg, recalled that he was preparing to take the entrance exam for the United States Naval Academy in the spring of 1951, and he was very apprehensive. While a student at Martin he roomed with Mr. and Mrs. Phillips, and the night before the exam Mr. Phillips asked John if he was worried about the test. John confirmed that he was nervous and apprehensive. Mr. Phillips asked him to sit in a chair by him, be very relaxed, lower his head, and close his eyes. Mr. Phillips told him he would do well on the exam the following day, and that at 9 P.M. he was going to go up to his room, go to sleep, and be refreshed and relaxed the next morning. John said he didn't feel that he had been hypnotized, but shortly afterwards he told Mr. Phillips that he was going to go to bed and be ready for the next day. John said he sat on the bed and turned on his radio. He remembered the radio program because the news concerned the recalling of General Douglas McArthur from Korea by President Harry Truman. The next thing John remembered was waking up at 8 A.M. He had just fallen over on his bed, and when he awoke he still had his clothes on. He was initially concerned that he had not slept very well since he had not taken his clothes off, but once he showered and dressed he felt refreshed, relaxed, and ready to go. He went to Union City, never felt the first pang of nervousness, and did exceedingly well on the entrance exam. After this, he was a firm believer in hypnotism and was very appreciative of the efforts of Mr. Phillips to assist him.

J. Paul Phillips taught psychology and other subjects from 1927 until 1953.

John graduated from the naval academy and was a military pilot for ten years. Following his stint in the military he returned to Dyersburg and has been a banker for over thirty years.

A Barnwarming scene from the 1950s.

John also recalled that some of the Newbern residents purchased an old school bus, and it was used to transport ten to fifteen students to Martin each day for classes. At times, John would ride the bus to Newbern, go on home to Dyersburg, and then catch the bus for the return trip to Martin the following morning.[16]

Regular student activities, such as dances, were very popular during the 1950s. Donning the appropriate attire, the students danced the hours away at the Winter Wonderland, the Engineers Ball, Barnwarming, the Christmas Dance, and other socials. Contrary to the old complaint, "There ain't anything to do on campus on weekends," most students delighted in the weekend events.[17]

The faculty members also joined in the fun with competitive outings like a milking contest. Cows would be brought to the football stadium and male and female teachers would demonstrate their milking abilities to the cheers of faculty and students. The first to fill his or her pail was the champion in the men's and the women's divisions. The cows endured these amateurish efforts with their customary stoicism.[18]

Green "beanies" and odd dress were much in evidence in the fall as freshmen endured the expected initiation. The cry "air raid" echoed across the campus, and on this command freshmen were required to "hit the dirt." Shaved heads, much to the chagrin of Paul Meek, were also prominent. Some students, at their own option, sported Mohawk hair cuts. Again, the administration frowned on this fad, and many a young man was advised to "get a decent hair cut."[19]

In the mid-1950s, "panty raids" made an appearance as another student diversion. Some male students would raid the girl's dormitories seeking "panties." Often times, young ladies would still be in the desired apparel, and administration officials and parents were equally upset with this antic. On some occasions the "raiders" suffered surprising opposition from the besieged parties. One young man barged into a room intent on getting his intended prize only to be met with a solid blow to the chin and a swift kick in the groin. Needless to say, he decided discretion was the better part of valor, and he painfully departed from the premises.[20]

To counterattack the "raids" the faculty and staff were organized into the so-called "dawn patrol." During most of this era the campus had only one night watchman, so help was needed. At the first hint of trouble, faculty and staff members hustled to assigned positions, normally around the coed dormitories. Some of the more daring females would encourage the "raiders," but, if identified, they too faced disciplinary action.[21] Several young men had their college careers interrupted as they were sent home to explain to their parents that they were guilty of misconduct.

On one occasion, a staff member, stationed in the peach orchard to apprehend "raiders" fleeing back to Mt. Pelia Lodge—which housed regular male students at this time—heard the excited young men returning from the night's adventure. Prior to entering their dorm the students decided it would be best to hide in the orchard to see if pursuers were hot on their heels. As luck would have it, one of the more alert young men sensed the presence of someone nearby. As he crawled over to the prone figure, he whispered, "Friend or foe?" The staff member softly replied, "Friend." When the student had crawled to about three feet away the staff member shined his flashlight in the young man's face. Several peach trees were de-barked by a mass exodus of students from the orchard.

Entering the dorm, the staff member found a sweaty student doing pushups. He reached down, picked some peach tree leaves from the young man's head, smiled, and departed, leaving behind a red-faced individual with uncertainty etched on his face.[22]

An ongoing quest by some students through the years involved the unauthorized acquisitions of exams. When the campus had only a lone watchman at night, some students would watch him while others would enter, or try to enter, offices in search of upcoming tests. Ingenious methods were used by the interlopers, but some faculty members were equally ingenious in protecting their exams.[23]

C. E. Gatlin, a UTJC faculty member who later taught at Texas A & M, discovered that his exam had somehow been acquired by some students. To remedy the inappropriate acquisition, he quickly made out another test. As the students were demonstrating their knowledge, or a lack of the same, on the examination, a bewildered student approached Gatlin and asked, "Prof, are you sure this is the right exam?"[24]

On another occasion a professor, who often bragged that his exams could not be stolen because he slept with them, was visited in his office by some enterprising students. One distracted the teacher while another student "borrowed" an upcoming test from the desk of the unsuspecting professor.[25] In time, as campus security increased, this student activity became less profitable.

A fun event sanctioned by the administration was Sadie Hawkins Day. Based on Al Capp's comic strip *Li'l Abner,* the female students were the pursuers for the day, and they would invite their "captured" young men to a finale dance presided over by Li'l Abner and Daisy Mae, two students selected for this honor based on their likeness to Capp's characters. Dressed in Dogpatch style, the men sported corsages of assorted vegetables furnished to them by their "captors." The women

Li'l Abner (Lonnie Yager) and Daisy Mae (Kaye Taylor) at "Sadie Hawkins Day" around 1953.

paid the admission charge based on the size of their waist lines—some undoubtedly took a deep breath before the measurement. "Marrying Sam," the lovable Dogpatch parson, was also present for a "hitching" ceremony.[26]

Campus beauties to appear in the yearbook, the *UTMB Volunteer,* were selected by a campuswide vote until 1959. During this time, the Agricultural Club sponsored a regular beauty revue, and the winner represented the campus in beauty pageants; however, the court was not pictured in the annual. In 1959, the All-Student Club sponsored the first beauty revue where the queen and her court were the beauties to be featured in the yearbook. The contestants vied in formal, swimsuit, and talent competitions. In 1960, a question and answer session was added. Mary Lou Harding was crowned as the 1959 queen under this new format. Nancy Lawson, the 1958 winner who placed third in the

"Miss Tennessee" competition, was named queen in 1960, the only contestant to win the beauty revue two times.[27]

The beauty revue project was undertaken by the All-Students Club at the request of members of the student body. Two nights were devoted to the competition, and clubs and organizations sponsored entrants. During the first night's competition, nine finalists were chosen, and they competed for the title during the second session. The person chosen as queen was entitled to represent UTMB in various contests throughout the year.[28]

The chorus, directed by Harriet Fulton, was a popular student activity throughout the '50s. Handel's *Messiah* and other performances captivated campus and area audiences.[29]

Aspiring thespians had the opportunity to display their talents when Vanguard Theater was organized in 1955. At first, all public performances of both music and drama were given in the gymnasium, and classes were taught in various places. Eventually the music department was housed in the old administration building after the new administration building was completed.

Nancy Lawson is the only contestant to win the campus beauty revue two times, 1958 and 1960.

These quarters were not very satisfactory because the entire building was shaky when Vanguard Theater had musical productions with dancing.[30] As some cynics remarked, "It was a good old building; several hundred pigeons which roosted in the attic could not have been wrong!"

On one memorable occasion, a stagehand, lowering some swings from the attic in a Vanguard production, slipped and put his foot through the ceiling. A pile of accumulated dirt, undoubtedly enriched by pigeon droppings, descended directly upon the piano and the head of the accompanist. Thirty minutes later, after the accompanist and the piano were cleaned, the production continued.[31]

For safety reasons, the old administration building was eventually abandoned, and Vanguard Theater was housed in the old science building. Music and drama classes were taught in Reed Hall and the new administration building. Finally, in 1970, the fine and performing arts building was completed, and the music, art, and drama departments had their own building, a new and modern facility.[32]

In the fall of 1950, partial athletic scholarships were offered in football and men's

Harriet Fulton is directing the chorus in the early 1950s scene.

basketball. The scholarships consisted of room (in Mt. Pelia Lodge), books, and a job whereby the recipient could earn about $20 per month. Earlier athletes had been assisted in finding campus employment and housing was sometimes arranged, but regular athletic scholarships were nonexistent. The results of the new emphasis were evident as the 1950 football team posted a 5-3 record following a winless 1949 season.[33]

Guy L. Wadley, as captain of the 1949 football team, had the customary responsibility for team captains of reviewing the season highlights at the annual football banquet. He pondered about the bright spots in a winless season, and he finally decided to talk about why the team did not record any victories. His primary point was that their opponents, unlike UTJC, offered athletic scholarships. If future teams were to be successful, some type of scholarship assistance was needed, Wadley concluded.

The next day, as he walked in front of the administration building, he heard someone call his name. He turned around and saw Paul Meek beckoning to him. As Wadley recalls, "We sat on the steps, and Mr. Meek stated that he felt I had offered a valid argument for assistance for athletes. He further stated that he would discuss the matter with the athletic committee."[34] Paul Meek, true to his word, did as promised, and in 1950 partial scholarships were offered.

Many former athletes knew that Paul Meek, though primarily an academician, was aware of the vital role of athletics on a college campus. They also thought he did everything possible within a limited budget to support the athletic teams. The overwhelming majority of faculty and staff members followed Meek's example, and most could be seen at athletic contests, oftentimes selling tickets and helping in other ways.

In 1952, Floyd "Red" Burdette returned home to head the UTMB basketball program. A native of Martin, Burdette had served for seven years as the head basketball coach at the University of Alabama just prior to his appointment at Martin. Vincent Vaughan, assistant coach under James C. Henson, remained in this capacity.[35]

Henson, with Vaughan's assistance, continued to lead the football program. In addition, he was head of the Department of Physical Education and served as director of athletics.

In 1957, Bob Carroll, who played his first two years at Martin and was a 1956 graduate from the University of Wyoming where he garnered academic All-America honors, became the head football coach. Guy D. Penney was his assistant for two years prior to being named head coach at Morehead State. Grover L. Page and Ross Elder joined Carroll's staff in 1959. During this era, all coaches had teaching responsibilities along with their coaching duties. This would continue until 1975 when the first full-time coaches were employed.[36]

Baseball had been dropped in 1931, but it emerged again as an intercollegiate sport at Martin in 1957. Ed Chenette, a member of the English staff, was approached by several students interested in playing baseball. They asked that

Faculty members Bettye Giles, Harriet Fulton, Catherine Bettis, and Mary Rachel Armstrong are pictured in the early 1950s.

he help to organize a team and serve as the coach. He agreed, administrative permission was granted, and baseball once again was an intercollegiate sport at Martin.[37]

Men's track made its debut in 1959 as an intercollegiate sport. Earlier efforts had been on the intramural level. Athletes from other sports and regular students comprised the initial team which was coached by Ross Elder.[38]

Women's intercollegiate athletics were on the horizon, but they had not yet arrived at Martin in the early 1950's. In 1952, Bettye Giles, the recent recipient of a master's degree from UT Knoxville, joined the physical education staff and became a guiding force for women's athletics at Martin. Even though the women's tennis team competed against other colleges, and with a high degree of success, it was not until 1956 that the team acquired varsity status after a formal petition to the UTMB Athletics Board. The women had no scholarships at this time but "the prestige of having a varsity letter was priceless to our women athletes," Giles recalled.[39] Other women's sports and eventually scholarships would follow.

In 1958, the board of trustees, acting on a motion by Trustee Tom Elam, approved the waiving of tuition and fees for athletes at Martin. No more than thirty awards could be in effect at any one time.[40] A 7–0–1 football season against tougher competition followed this action. Later, the number of awards would be increased.

The 1950s also produced the first football players from the school to be recognized as All-Americans. End Hugh Lashlee was selected to play in the Junior College All-American All-Star game in 1956. In 1958, against a schedule

Homecoming parade in 1960. The Carter Hotel, in the background, would later be used to house approximately forty male students as the campus enrollment mushroomed. The City State Bank is located on the site today.

which now included only senior colleges, Marvin "Buddy" Long, also an end, earned All-America honors. In the following year, fullback Bobby Fowler, who still holds many of the school's rushing records, received All-America accolades. Fowler, who signed with the Chicago Bears, was the first football player from Martin to ink a professional contract, and he is the only player to have his jersey retired.[41] In 1956, for the first time in the school's history, a Martin team appeared on television. The UTMB-Memphis Navy football game was televised locally.[42]

Not all of the attention at athletic events was directed to the players. Shirley "Gussie" Galey, a cheerleader, will long be remembered for her original "Tennessee Spirit" cheer. Excitement rippled through the crowds as she chanted, along with appropriate moves, "It's over here, it's over there, it's in the air, it's everywhere—what? The Tennessee Spirit!!"[43] Her performance was so impressive that other schools came up with their own rendition of the cheer.

Bobby Fowler was the first UT Martin football player to be drafted by a professional team (the Chicago Bears), and he is the only football player to have his jersey retired by the school.

Mt. Pelia Lodge was not the epitome of a plush athletic dormitory. Former athletes laughingly recall that the dorm, one of the war surplus buildings purchased after World War II, had heating problems. The coal-burning furnace was located in the basement, which generally flooded during a heavy rain, but the furnace did belch an ample supply of soot to the rooms. Each morning, the athletes looked like characters in a minstrel show. The rooms over the furnace, when it was operable, received some heat, but those farther away got only a meager amount. On one occasion, some residents pointed out that their room was cold—a thin crust of ice covered the water in the commode.

Shortly afterwards, as the furnace continued to deteriorate, the athletes were temporarily

moved to newly constructed rooms in the basement of Browning Hall until steam heat could be installed and renovations made. After returning to Mt. Pelia Lodge, the athletes, proud of their improved quarters, planted shrubs—which they had "borrowed" from Mr. McMahan's nursery—around the building, improved the gravel parking lot and painted the areas needing it. Later, as more men's dorms were built in the 1960s, the football players moved to Reed Hall, and eventually all athletes were housed in Browning Hall. Mt. Pelia Lodge continued to be used for men's housing when the regular dorms were fully occupied.[44]

A photo of the A–B–L Building facing University Street. Completed in 1951, many said this building gave the campus a sense of permanence.

After the arrival of Coach Burdette, the basketball players, prior to the move to Browning Hall, were housed in another war surplus building located at the corner of Lovelace and Hurt Streets. The players referred to their residence as "Tall Vol Lodge."[45] After all athletes were moved to Browning Hall, this building served as temporary quarters for some music classes.[46]

As the enrollment increased, it was imperative that additional facilities be built. In 1951, the A-B-L (Agriculture, Biology, Library) Building was completed. Governor Gordon Browning and other dignitaries were present on September 6, 1951, for the dedication of this facility, later to be named Brehm Hall in memory of former UT President C. E. Brehm.[47] Until this date, the library had occupied cramped quarters in the administration building. Mary Vick Burney, who had served as the librarian throughout the junior college era, undoubtedly was elated to finally have a spacious and modern library. Her services on behalf of the students were acknowledged when the 1955 yearbook was dedicated to her. George Horton later recalled that he, Earl Knepp, and others spent countless hours planning the A-B-L Building, a very welcome addition to the campus.[48]

In 1952, a men's dorm housing 150 was completed. This was the first dormitory to be built at Martin, other than temporary war surplus buildings, since the school had become a part of the University of Tennessee system.[49] In 1949, a group of UTJC students, led by Joe Fuller, had sent a petition to Governor Browning urging him to support the building of men's and women's dorms at Martin. Browning had earlier vetoed a bill providing for dorm construction at Martin because, as he stated in his reply to the petition, it placed "a half million dollar bond issue on the general fund of the State of Tennessee." He added that the trustees had the authority to sell revenue bonds based on the rent income from dormitories, and he suggested this was the logical course to follow. Browning assured the petitioners that he would address this issue at the next meeting of the board of trustees.[50] Aware of the dire need for housing, Browning did as promised and later came up with funds to help complete three of the planned five units of the men's dormitory.

Another problem encountered in building the men's dorm concerned the closing of Moody Avenue which ran north and south through the campus just west of the original administration building. The site selected for the men's dorm was most feasible if the portion of Moody Avenue which extended through the campus were closed. At least one of the city aldermen opposed the closing of the street; some favored it, and an intense debate, with some name calling, ensued. A hotly contested city election occurred in June 1950, and the result was a more favorable city administration which eventually agreed to the closing of Moody Avenue through the campus. Paul Meek, through diligent and diplomatic efforts, worked tirelessly to remove this obstacle to the erection of the men's dorm.[51]

A dorm designed to house 236 women followed in 1957. A national steel strike delayed the construction of this facility. It had been authorized for construction by the board of trustees in 1955, but was not ready for occupancy until September 1957. When finally completed, it was discovered that additional funds totaling $14,000 were needed to properly

A photo taken during the dedication of Clement Hall in 1966. At the table (L-R) are Congressman Robert A. "Fats" Everett, Governor Frank Clement, President Andy Holt, Paul Meek, and Mrs. Meek.

equip the building. Governor Frank Clement endeared himself to the campus when he promised to get the funds to finish the project, which he did. This dorm would later be named Clement Hall in his honor.[52]

Earl Knepp, who by this time had been assigned the duties of resident engineer, recalled that open house for Clement Hall was a near catastrophe. On Saturday, the building was cleaned and ready for the occasion, but early Sunday morning, the day of the open house, Knepp received a frantic call. Water was two inches deep in the entrance, the lounge, and some of the rooms. The mechanical contractor was summoned. A hot water line in the ceiling that had not been soldered was quickly fixed, soggy ceiling tiles were replaced, and water was vacuumed from the floors. Open house was held as scheduled.[53]

As early as 1952, Trustee Charles Volz had reported to the board of trustees that there was a definite need for a new administration building at Martin. Most administrative offices were located in the administration building, which was the first structure to be completed on the old Hall-Moody campus. Time had taken its toll on the building, and more space was needed. After 1952, each

Picture taken about 1960 after the administration building is completed. "Incubator Hill" is at the far end of the football field. Faculty members lived in the pre-fab houses facing Moody Avenue. The Ned R. McWherter Agricultural Complex now occupies that area. (Courtesy of Val Umback)

report by the Martin Branch committee included the request for an administration building.[54]

Finally, in 1957, the board of trustees allocated funds from the legislative appropriation to construct an administration-classroom building at Martin. It was later decided, on the recommendation of Trustee Wayne Fisher, that the building be air conditioned since summer classes would be taught there. The State Building Commission, which had been established by legislative action in 1955 to approve state building projects, authorized the construction of the facility, the first air-conditioned building on the Martin campus.[55]

Completed in 1959 at a cost of $589,371, this three-story structure was named Hall-Moody in a ceremony in February 1968, as a tribute to the roots of the institution. Governor Buford Ellington led the dedication and the board of trustees at that time officially recognized the date 1900 (when Hall-Moody Institute was established), as the official founding date of UT Martin.[56] Blount College, another church-related school, was the acknowledged predecessor of UT Knoxville, and this precedent was followed at Martin.

When originally occupied, offices of the dean (now chancellor), bursar, registrar, student personnel, and public relations shared the building with education, business administration, English, French, and home economics. As the school grew, the classrooms were moved to new quarters.[57]

1950
The war in Korea starts.

1951
The school acquires four-year status, granting degrees in general agriculture and general home economics.
A-B-L building is completed.

1952
ROTC is started at UTMB.
Men's dorm is built.

1953
First degrees granted to agriculture and home economics graduates.
The appointment of a member of the board of trustees from Weakley County is approved.

Mid 1950s
"Panty raids" appear on the Martin campus.

1955
Vanguard Theater is organized.

1956
First Hall-Moody reunion on the Martin campus is held.

1957
Education is elevated to four-year status.
The initiation of degree programs at Martin is placed under the board of trustees rather than the state legislature.

1959
President C. E. Brehm retires, and Dr. Andrew D. "Andy" Holt is named as his successor.

New construction on the Martin campus in the 1950s came to a close with the building of a home management house for the Department of Home Economics. Since 1951, when a degree in home economics was authorized, the program had been handicapped by the lack of a campus house where students could be taught using the most modern appliances and technology. This building was equipped and ready for occupancy in the spring quarter of 1959.[58]

Shortly after the school achieved four-year status, a movement to offer degrees in additional fields was started. Once again, as in the past, area citizens aware of the educational needs of West Tennessee, sprang into action. A meeting of the Organization for Expansion of the University of Tennessee Martin Branch was held on May 17, 1956, at the Gateway Restaurant in Martin. Many of the same citizens who had worked to move the school to senior college status were present, including Charles G. Tomerlin from Union City, who served as secretary. George C. Thomas from Dresden, Harold Brundige and Ed Eller from Martin, and State Senator Broeck Cummings from Rutherford were among the invitees who had been involved in the earlier campaign.[59]

President Brehm had already informed the board of trustees that additional courses would be needed at Martin in the future, and citizens of West Tennessee verified his statement. With the exception of the development of the two-year

THE UNIVERSITY OF TENNESSEE MARTIN BRANCH (1951–1967)

The administration building, the first air-conditioned building on campus, is erected.

The first graduation exercises at the end of the summer quarter are held.

1960

The board of trustees adopts a resolution favorable to the establishment of social fraternities and sororities at UTMB.

1961

Business administration and liberal arts gain four-year status.

First black student enrolls at UTMB.

1962

Marching band is formed at UTMB.

1963

President Kennedy is assassinated in Dallas.

Library is opened on Sundays.

1964

Faculty members are to be paid for summer teaching.

Four-year ROTC program is implemented.

1966

The University of Tennessee National Alumni Association grants the first outstanding teacher awards.

1967

The school gets a new name—The University of Tennessee at Martin.

A gathering of the Hall–Moody alumni at UT Martin in 1977. George Horton, a key figure in organizing the group, is standing at the right on the second row.

engineering program, university officials, in the past, waited until area citizens had asked for additional courses before acting. As early as 1954, citizens had petitioned Trustee Charles Volz to request additional degrees at Martin, and he reported this request to the board of trustees. Between 1954 and 1957 committees appointed by the trustees and President Brehm studied the need for curricular expansion. The faculty committee appointed by President Brehm suggested the need for expansion in three areas—business, education, and liberal arts. Department heads William H. Baker (business administration), Glenn S. Gallien Sr. (education), and George Horton (liberal arts) stated very ably and with the proper documentation the reasons why their departments should be elevated to degree status; however, in November 1956, the board of trustees, after carefully considering costs and other aspects, decided that only education should be elevated "at this time." The liberal arts and business courses necessary to implement the degree program in education would be added, but four-year degrees in these areas would have to wait.[60]

Unlike the degree programs established in agriculture and home economics in 1951, the degree program in education followed the program at Knoxville. Students at Martin could select a degree in elementary, secondary, or business education. Education quickly forged a strong campus presence, and

in 1959, for the first time in the school's history, graduation exercises were held at the end of the summer quarter.[61]

In 1958, Jimmy Trentham became the first graduate to receive a degree in education. He had attended Lambuth College earlier before transferring to Martin to complete his degree requirements. Trentham, who earned a Ph.D. degree at Vanderbilt in 1965, later became a highly respected biology professor at Martin and also served a stint as provost and vice chancellor for academic affairs.[62]

One dark cloud still looming on the horizon was the requirement that additional courses at Martin had to be approved by the legislature. In 1957, this requirement was removed when the legislature placed complete control, including the initiation of new degree programs, under the board of trustees. This act gave the board the same authority as they had at the other University of Tennessee campuses.[63]

When UTMB achieved senior college status it was obvious alumni activities needed accelerated attention. Myrtle Phillips, along with her duties as registrar, had informally served as alumni officer through the years. Elmer Counce, who joined the Department of Agriculture staff in 1951, became the first director of alumni affairs and placement on a part-time basis in 1952. In 1957, at the request of Counce, two UTMB alumni representatives were added to the alumni executive council of the UT Alumni Association. This forged stronger ties between the UTMB association and the General Alumni Association.[64]

In the summer of 1956, alumni of Hall-Moody Institute, headed by E. I. Brundige, held the first of many reunions on the Martin campus. At this initial reunion, the Hall-Moody Alumni Association was born, with Brundige as president. The group met annually for a picnic until 1972. In that year Hollis Kinsey, a Mississippi businessman who had attended both Hall-Moody and UTJC, hosted the alumni function at his home in Tupelo. For the next five years, Kinsey, president of the association in 1973–74, hosted an annual luncheon on the Martin campus.[65] As the number of Hall-Moody alumni dwindled through the years, the group began to meet with the UTJC alumni. Most of the Hall-Moody alumni are gone now, but their love for their cherished institution

As the enrollment increased at UT Martin, so did the length of the registration lines.

remained bright through the years. It was especially meaningful to this group when the board of trustees in 1968 officially accepted Hall-Moody Institute as the forerunner of UTJC and all former students at that institution were declared to be UT alumni.

In 1959, Dr. C. E. Brehm retired as president of the University of Tennessee. A well-known figure throughout the state with his old battered "legislative hat," Brehm was a staunch supporter of the Martin campus. From 1917 to 1943, he served as director of the Agricultural Extension Service of the University of Tennessee. He was dean of the College of Agriculture and director of the experiment station at Knoxville from 1943 to 1946. When Dr. James Hoskins retired in 1946 at the age of seventy-six, Brehm became acting president, and he served in this position until 1948, when he became president. Always neatly dressed with his ever present bowtie, Brehm, still wearing his old battered hat, became a familiar figure in Nashville, urging legislative support for the UT campuses. In recognition and appreciation for his staunch support of UTMB, the 1959 annual was dedicated to him.[66]

Dr. Andrew D. "Andy" Holt became the sixteenth president of the University of Tennessee in 1959, and once more UTMB had a strong ally in that position. A native of Milan, Dr. Holt had joined the UT staff as an administrative assistant to the president in 1950 and later became vice president.[67] His abilities, energy, and reputation as a popular folksy speaker led to his appointment as president. Gregarious and charismatic, this nationally known educator proved to be an outstanding leader, and he delighted audiences with his entertaining talks when he visited the Martin campus. As the 1960s approached, new challenges emerged, and Holt proved to be equal to the demands as a new decade was embraced.

The 1960s was a period of phenomenal growth for UTMB. The fall quarter enrollment in 1960 was 1,123, and it surged to 4,197 in 1969. Additional buildings sprang up, the campus expanded, new degrees were offered, and the school became known as the fastest growing college in the state. But during this time of unprecedented growth, worldwide changes were taking place which would mar the idyllic scene.

Nationwide, the 1960s opened with a wave of idealism when John F. Kennedy was elected as president. One of his early acts was to establish the Peace Corps, but the 1960s turned out to be everything but peaceable. The Bay of Pigs fiasco, a continuation of the cold war, and a deeper involvement in Vietnam made students more aware of world happenings. Traditionally identified with "panty raids" and other frivolous goals, by the late 1960s students throughout the nation became more serious and began to question policies of "the establishment." The military draft was a primary target, and popular student chants were, "Hell No, We Won't Go," "Draft Beer, Not Students," and "Make Love, Not War." This student unrest eventually trickled down to the Martin campus, but the conservative background of the majority of students left only a token number who sought to emulate the anti-establishment trend on many campuses. An eventual by-product of the national student unrest were more relaxed rules and policies at Martin, especially in relation to dorm hours, but the violent unrest on some campuses was never evident at Martin.[68]

As in past wartime conflicts, many students left the friendly confines of the Martin campus and marched off to battle, this time in the rice paddies and jungles of Vietnam. Most of the students who stayed behind thought support for those called to duty was a top priority. These were their former classmates,

Dr. Andrew D. "Andy" Holt delighted crowds with his humorous talks when he visited the Martin campus.

and the vast majority advocated support for their friends who had been called to serve their country in an unpopular war.

The war was also brought closer to the campus when J. Houston Gordon, a 1968 UT Martin graduate, was chosen to represent Lt. William Calley in the appeal of his conviction for his part in the infamous My Lai massacre. A third generation alumnus of UTM, Gordon had received his law degree from the UT Knoxville College of Law. He was on the staff of the United States Army legal

This 1964 photograph shows the stadium shortly after completion. The half-back with the football is Mack Moody (21).

department in Washington when he was selected to represent Calley, who was court martialed in 1971 for his involvement in the 1968 attack that killed one hundred Vietnamese civilians. Calley's sentence was not overturned, but he was freed from custody on the basis of legal rulings. Gordon received national attention during the appeal, a far cry from his quiet days as a student at UT Martin. Gordon is presently a highly successful attorney in Covington, Tennessee, and he has served on the UT board of trustees, the University of Tennessee National Alumni Association Board of Governors, the UTM Development Committee, and as president of the Tipton County alumni chapter.[69]

Another UT Martin alumnus, Charles O. Davis, wrote a book in 1996 entitled *Across the Mekong*. Davis, a 1961 graduate and a member of the football team, recounts his experiences in Laos from January 1965 until June 1967 as a helicopter pilot for Air America, an independent airline that was under contract to the United States government to support various cold war activities in Southeast Asia. The pilots, among other duties, were frequently assigned rescue missions of downed United States military and Air America pilots, oftentimes under enemy fire. Davis later was a member of the Air National Guard and retired with the rank of Lieutenant Colonel. He presently is a pilot with US Air and lives in Alexandria, Virginia.[70]

The assassinations of President Kennedy (after only a little over a thousand days in office), Martin Luther King Jr., and Robert Kennedy cast a further cloud over the era. These tragic events, coupled with nuclear uncertainty and the expanding war in Vietnam, dampened the spirits of most Americans, but fortunately there were bright spots. The space race was on, and most Americans marveled at the accomplishments of their country. A crowning moment came on July 20, 1969, when Neil Armstrong walked on the surface of the moon.

A local bright spot was expanded offerings on the Martin campus. Business administration and liberal arts were elevated to four-year status in 1961. When education was expanded to a four-year program in 1957, ninety-one new courses were added. Forty-two of these were in liberal arts and twenty in business, and these additions greatly enhanced the elevation of these two departments to degree-granting status.[71]

Additional buildings were necessary as the enrollment mushroomed. The engineering/physical science building was completed in late 1961, and an addition to Clement Hall was made in 1962. A new steam plant and a fieldhouse, featuring a sunken arena and a seating capacity of 3,500, were built in 1963.[72]

Faculty and staff members, area citizens, local governments, and businesses joined hands to raise $150,000 to build a new modern football stadium which seated a total of 6,500. It was dedicated at the first home game in 1964 when UTMB battled Middle Tennessee State in a 0–0 tie. It was necessary to acquire private funds to build the stadium since the University of Tennessee liked to brag that no state funds had been used to build the stadium at Knoxville, and Martin was expected to follow suit.[73]

New residence halls were erected rapidly. McCord (1964), Austin Peay (1966), Ellington (1967), and Atrium (1969) residence halls were built to meet the needs of a burgeoning enrollment. The Grove Apartments, built in the area once occupied by house trailers and barracks-type apartments following World War II, were completed in 1965. A modern university center, again replacing a war surplus building, was erected in 1966. In 1968, the Paul Meek Library was built. For the first time in the history of the school, the library had a building which did not have to be shared with others. Another much-needed classroom building, the humanities building, was constructed in 1969.[74]

A major factor in the enrollment increase at Martin was a recruiting network involving faculty members. Initially organized to a limited degree in the 1930s, recruiting efforts by 1954 were conducted in four regions. Three regions covered West Tennessee and the other region included Middle Tennessee and nearby out-of-state areas. Each region was assigned a coordinator and about ten faculty members. Working tirelessly and often times at their own expense, these faculty members visited high schools, prospective students in their homes, agricultural extension agents, and others who could help entice students to enroll at Martin. This network continued until 1967 when recruiters were hired by the office of admissions.[75]

George Horton, who was the coordinator for region three, was uncanny in his enrollment predictions. In 1946, he predicted the fall quarter enrollment would be 650. It was 649. For the 1964 fall quarter enrollment Horton predicted 982 freshmen would register and the total enrollment would be over 1,800. The actual enrollment figures were 983 freshmen and a total enrollment of 1,847 students. Other predictions by Horton were equally accurate.[76]

Unlike the scene on some campuses, integration occurred rather quietly on the Martin campus and helped to bolster the enrollment. The first black students enrolled in 1961, the same year in which black undergraduates entered UT Knoxville. Jessie L. Arnold, one of the first black students to enroll at Martin, entered in the summer quarter of 1961.[77] Leonard Hamilton was prominent among the black students who became campus leaders. A standout basketball player, Hamilton was chosen as Mr. Volunteer in 1970. He is the current head basketball coach at the University of Miami (Florida). In 1972, Wendell Wainwright, a popular campus leader, was chosen as Mr. Pacer in a campuswide election. Emmett Edwards, a biology major from Covington, Tennessee, served as a student trustee on the board of trustees in 1975–76, the first black to sit on the board. Reginald Williams, a very popular campus figure, served two terms, 1983–84 and 1984–85, as president of the Student Government Association. Other black students earned prominent niches through the years as campus leaders.[78]

The board of trustees, at a meeting on the UTMB campus on January 25, 1960, adopted a resolution favorable to the establishment of national social fraternities and sororities at Martin. In the past, these organizations had been forbidden at Martin.[79] Phi Sigma Kappa (1960) was the first national fraternity established. Other fraternities organized in the 1960s included Pi Kappa Alpha (1961), Alpha Gamma Rho (1963), and Alpha Tau Omega (1964). Other fraternities would follow in later years.[80]

Among the sororities established in the 1960s on the Martin campus were Chi Omega (1961), Alpha Delta Pi (1961), Zeta Tau Alpha (1961), and Alpha Omicron Pi (1966). Additional sororities would also be founded in the future.[81] These organizations quickly became an integral part of campus life, and wholesome competition—with the exception of a few incidents where the competition became too "spirited" and fisticuffs and other incidents ensued— was fostered. The Panhellenic Council and the Interfraternity Council were established to help govern the activities of the Greeks. Competition during rush was keen, as it was for All-Sing—which was started in 1962—homecoming events, and other activities. Through the years, a few incidents occurred to blemish the records of the Greeks, but the total picture gives a very favorable nod to the fraternities and sororities for their untiring efforts with campus and community activities.

The Pikes practice for their run with the football to Murray State.

An event filled with intrigue occurred in October 1962, when the Phi Sigs journeyed to Murray State and "borrowed" the coveted cannon of the ATO fraternity. The cannon was traditionally fired at football games when the Racers scored. The Phi Sigs wanted to reverse the trend and fire it when UTMB scored. They planned to return the cannon at halftime, but somehow the ATO's discovered where their cannon was. Following many phone calls, it was returned to the rightful owners, and in a spirit of cooperation, the cannon was fired during the game when either team scored, to the delight of fans from both schools. As a climax, both fraternities marched onto the field at halftime and held an impromptu cannon-firing together.[82]

The Pikes from Martin and Murray also adopted the tradition of running a football from the visiting campus to the host school before a game. This fifty-mile trek added to the competitive spirit of the game as the Pikes, with banner flying, dashed onto the field just before the kickoff to deliver the game football to the officials.[83]

A mishap marred one of the Pike runs to Murray in the early 1970s. When approaching an underpass in Fulton, Kentucky, the clearance for the rental truck was not checked. The result was a smashed top and a stuck truck. The riders and beverages for a pregame party with the Murray State Pikes were unloaded, the back tires deflated, thus allowing the vehicle to be freed. A check for $78 per month was sent to the rental company for ten months to pay for the damages.[84]

On another occasion, a runner was advised that brief running attire was permissible, but trotting down the highway in just a jock strap was going a little too far.[85]

Another welcome addition to the UTMB campus was the arrival of a marching band. The initial group, consisting of forty-five members, made its debut in 1962 at the UTMB-Austin Peay football game. The members also formed small pep bands to add to the excitement at basketball games. Glenn Wiesner, director of the band, properly predicted that the band would be much larger in the near future.[86]

In 1961, for the first time in the school's history, golf became an intercollegiate sport at UTMB. The initial team, coached by Grover Page, who would head the golf program through four decades, was composed mostly of football and basketball players.[87]

After a long absence, rifle teams appeared once again on the athletic scene. Earlier men's and women's teams, organized in the 1930s, had been dropped during World War II, but in 1963, both men's and women's teams were re-established. Sergeant Milton Jackson, a member of the ROTC staff, coached the initial teams which enjoyed surprising success against major opposition.[88]

In September 1962, Paul Meek, who had guided the school since 1934, was elevated by the board of trustees upon the recommendation of President Andy Holt from dean to vice president of the University of Tennessee in charge of the Martin Branch.[89] In 1965, he was promoted to vice president of the University of Tennessee and chancellor of the Martin Branch.[90] These promotions recognized both the growing importance of the UTMB campus and the administrative achievements of Dr. Meek.

In 1962, Gene Stanford was promoted from bursar to business manager, Horace B. Smith was elevated from student personnel director to assistant dean of student affairs, and Norman Campbell was named assistant dean of instruction. In addition, Campbell remained head of the Department of Liberal Arts.[91] These changes were further evidence of the escalating growth of the school.

The assassination of President John F. Kennedy in Dallas on November 22, 1963, cast a cloud of profound shock and dismay over the UTMB campus. When the rumor reached the campus that President Kennedy had been shot, classes were interrupted or dismissed and the campus community gathered around radios and televisions awaiting further news. Shortly after 1 P.M., a bulletin was released confirming the death of the President. As the *Volette* reported, "Coeds with tears in their eyes and college men with sincere and solemn expressions were stunned at the news."[92] The school was closed on Monday, November 25, as the nation observed a day of mourning for the fallen President, and a campus memorial service was held in the newly constructed gym at 10 A.M. on November 26. As another tribute to President Kennedy, the flag on campus was flown at half mast from sunrise to sunset for thirty days.[93] Few events would shake the campus and the nation as deeply as the assassination of the young and energetic President.

Halloween, generally a time of mischief, was no exception in 1963. Some students confiscated several crates of eggs from Mr. Mac without his consent or knowledge. Stashing the eggs in strategic spots around the campus, the egg chunkers pelted unsuspecting victims. Shortly afterwards, three city police cars arrived at one of the men's dorms. The students outside the dorm made a hasty retreat to their rooms. The police challenged them "to come out and face us like men!" But, unfortunately for the police, several students were concealed behind shrubs, and when the officers got out of their squad cars they were met with a barrage of eggs. Deciding that discretion was the better part of the valor, the police hastily departed the scene. The culprits, however, had been identified, and the following day they had to pay for 120 dozen eggs, and they were assigned to campus cleanup duty.[94]

On other occasions, students, thinking perhaps that they were being treated unfairly, matched wits with the city police. One time, two officers entered Browning Hall searching for some students presumed to be guilty of traffic violations. Unsuccessful in their search, the police returned to their vehicle only to find that it had been jacked up and placed on blocks. Naturally, none of the students knew how this happened.[95]

Another mischievous incident occurred when the police went to a dorm to investigate a minor disturbance. While they were in the dorm, their squad car disappeared. It was found the next day in a nearby field concealed in tall weeds. The students surmised that the car must have been left in neutral and rolled into the field, carefully concealing itself without any student assistance. The police disagreed, but no one stepped forward to acknowledge responsibility.[96]

A change welcomed by the students occurred in 1963. A request by the students that the library be opened on Sundays was addressed and the facility was made available from 2 to 5 P.M. on Sundays, effective during the fall quarter of 1963.[97] As the enrollment increased, more students were on campus during weekends and use of the library increased accordingly.

Another change, which faculty members cheered, occurred in 1964. Prior to this date, they were not paid for teaching summer classes. As a general rule, the faculty members taught once every three years unless their department was small. In that case, they taught more often. Starting in 1964, faculty members who taught in the summer received extra pay.[98]

On September 1, 1964, Myrtle Phillips, who had become registrar in 1928, retired.[99] A meticulous record keeper, Phillips had served the campus well during her tenure; however her exacting demands at times irritated a few faculty members, and a couple of long running feuds became legendary. Harry Harrison Kroll and Phillips were friendly but staunch antagonists. Kroll had a

Harry Harrison Kroll, a noted author and an English professor at Martin from 1936 until his retirement in 1958. One of his novels, **Cabin in the Cotton,** *was made into a movie.*

tendency not always to follow instructions from Phillips, and some suspected that he delighted in this amicable feud.

Henry C. Allison, who joined the faculty as a physics instructor, replaced Phillips as registrar. A World War II veteran who had served in the Pacific aboard a PT boat, Allison was a popular campus figure for years. An outstanding physics teacher, his cordial personality and helpful attitude made him an excellent choice to succeed Phillips. His title would later become dean of admissions and records.[100]

In 1964, J. E. McMahan also announced that he was stepping down as head of the Department of Agriculture after twenty-seven years in that position. Deserving plaudits poured in from students, colleagues, alumni, and others who had fond memories of their association with "Mr. Mac." He would remain on the faculty teaching horticulture until his retirement in 1971. Dr. O. Glenn Hall, a charismatic and very capable replacement, assumed the duties as the new department head on January 1, 1965.[101]

At this time, the UTMB farm became the eleventh experiment station in the UT system. At first, Dr. Hall also served as the superintendent of the farm. Harry Henderson, who had attended school at Martin and later received his bachelor's and master's degrees at UT Knoxville, served as farm supervisor, farm manager, and eventually farm superintendent. After the farm became an experiment station, research at Martin received additional attention.[102] During earlier years, some excellent research had been done by faculty members whose primary responsibility was teaching.

The University of Tennessee National Alumni Association began to recognize outstanding teachers on the University of Tennessee campuses in 1966. Two awards were presented at Knoxville, one at the medical units in Memphis, and one at Martin in the first year. Wayne Chester, an assistant professor of geography, was the first recipient of the award at Martin.[103] Through the years, numerous other outstanding teachers have been recognized by the UTNAA for superior teaching.

As 1966 faded into history, UTMB was a beehive of activity. Campus growth and changes would be lauded; however, additional changes in 1967 lurked around the corner. Once more, the school name would be changed. Since 1951, the school had been called the University of Tennessee Martin Branch. Now, to recognize the growing importance of the campus, a new name—The University of Tennessee at Martin—would be bestowed upon the school.

CAMPAIGN FOR QUALITY
U T MARTIN
MARTIN, TENNESSEE
38238

May 3 1985

PAY TO THE
ORDER OF   UT MARTIN   2,021,000.00

Two Million Twenty-one Thousand & 00/100 DOLLARS

FOR Campaign for Quality   UT Alumni and Friends

PART IV

The University of Tennessee at Martin
1967–2000

CHANGE AND EXCITEMENT WERE VERY EVIDENT ON THE
Martin campus in 1967. Change reigned as the school name was changed, Paul
Meek—the guiding force for the institution since 1934—retired, and Archie
Dykes became the new chancellor. Excitement gripped the campus and
community when the football team posted a 10–1 record including a
Tangerine Bowl victory; Linda Sue Workman, Miss UT Martin, won the
coveted title of Miss Tennessee; and Martha Harrison Sublette was chosen as
the number one baton twirler in the nation.

The changes began on May 2, 1967, when Governor Buford Ellington
signed Senate Bill No. 488 which officially changed the name of the school
from The University of Tennessee Martin Branch to The University of
Tennessee at Martin. This marked the beginning of a new era for the institution.[1]

The retirement of Paul Meek on September 1, 1967, marked the end of an
illustrious career in higher education. Meek had led the school through the
dark days of the depression, the turbulence and uncertainty of World War II,
and the growth and expansion of the campus in the 1950s and 1960s. Aided by
his wife, Martha, Meek had served the school in an extraordinary manner for
thirty-three years, and well-deserved praise flowed in as he retired.

Proof of the high esteem in which Meek was held was evidenced by the
naming of the library for him in 1968. With tears in his eyes, Dr. Meek thanked
the crowd which gathered when the honor was bestowed on him. President
Andy Holt in his remarks stated, "The heart of any campus is the library, and
that's why it is named after Paul Meek."[2]

Archie Dykes, fresh from a postdoctoral fellowship in academic administration at the University of Illinois, assumed his new duties on September 1, 1967.
At this time, he became the youngest administrator of a higher educational
institution in the state. Prior to his postdoctoral work, Dykes was on the UT

Chancellor Archie Dykes is shown serving as the chef during a student cookout.

staff as director of the University of Tennessee-Memphis State University Center for Advanced Graduate Study in Education.

During earlier years, he was a high school teacher and principal at Church Hill High School. Just prior to going to Memphis, Dykes was superintendent of the Greeneville City Schools.[3] An experienced administrator, he continued the growth and expansion of the campus as the school embarked on a new era with a new name—The University of Tennessee at Martin.

An event which brought excitement to the campus was the appearance of the 1967 football team in the Tangerine Bowl. A brief summary of the season by Bob Carroll, head football coach at the time, is provided as follows:

> As we approached the 1967 football season, the UT Martin coaching staff and players were cautiously optimistic that a banner year could be on the horizon. The team had finished strong during the previous season, and graduation losses had been minimal; however, the squad was not large numerically, and the possibility of injuries to key personnel was an ongoing concern.
>
> The team gave a solid performance in our season opener against archival Murray State, winning 16-9. Victories over Millikin University (70-0), Southeast Missouri (39-0), and Jacksonville State (38-0) followed. On a hot,

muggy afternoon at Delta State, we lost a hard-fought 19-18 game. Could we rebound from this discouraging loss? A 44-36 win over Middle Tennessee the following week demonstrated the tenacity of the team. The next game was at nationally ranked Troy State. In perhaps the most outstanding game of the season, the players dominated the Red Wave, pounding out a 20-12 victory. This win earned the team national attention. A 22-0 shelling of Florence State, now the University of North Alabama, the following Saturday was darkened when stellar fullback Bobby Hayes suffered a broken leg.

By this time, our jubilant fans were mentioning the Tangerine Bowl, and during a 48-14 romp over Arkansas State Teachers, tangerines were thrown into the stands by the cheerleaders. Optimism was running high, but we were in the Mid-East Division. This championship was held in Murfreesboro, and to go to the Tangerine Bowl and challenge for the Atlantic Coast Championship we would have to cross over divisional boundaries. The country was divided into four divisions, and in the future the winners would meet to determine a national champion. But in 1967, only divisional playoffs had been implemented, and a team was expected to play within its geographical area.

A group of determined local people, led by Doug Murphy and "Cotton" Pitts, swung into action. They thought our team deserved to go to Florida. Phone calls and telegrams flowed to the NCAA and Orlando. Due to the efforts of many supporters, we were allowed to cross divisional boundaries and play West Chester State (Pennsylvania) in the Tangerine Bowl.

We still had the season finale at Austin Peay on Thanksgiving Day, and an NCAA official urged me to have the team ready for this game so as not to embarrass the selection committee. We awoke that morning to a cold and dreary day with snow on the ground, but the team was red hot. We pounded the Governors, 47-6.

We flew into Florida, accompanied by the cheerleaders, the band, school dignitaries, a large number of students, and other fans. For the first time in the history of the school, we were on national television, and our fans who couldn't go to Orlando poured in messages that they would be watching the ABC channel.

West Chester, who had played in the Tangerine Bowl the year before, was ranked fifth in the nation in the college division and had received the Lambert Trophy as the most outstanding team in the East. We were the underdog, but our players were relaxed and confident.

The coach from West Chester was in a dilemma. He had brought sixty-six players to the game, but NCCA rules permitted only thirty-eight to dress. He asked if I had a similar problem, and I explained we did not since we had only thirty-nine players and I had told one he was the first alternate.

Even our coaching staff was outnumbered. The West Chester staff was composed of eight coaches, while my staff consisted of Grover Page, Jack

The 1967 Tangerine Bowl Champions.

Beeler, and Ross Elder. We did have one advantage—our ardent fans. Their spirit was contagious, and the UT Martin colors were everywhere.

Light showers which fell throughout the game could not dampen the enthusiasm of our fans, and our players responded, dominating the Golden Rams in a 25-8 victory. The director of athletics at West Chester bluntly stated after the game, "UT Martin just whipped our butts."

In retrospect, what I most fondly remember is a close-knit and fun-loving group of dedicated athletes who were a pleasure to coach. There were some truly outstanding players on the squad, but egos were not a problem. What they accomplished brought national attention to UT Martin, and they can forever be proud of their achievements. Their successes since graduation indicate they are still winners. Gary Doble, one of the captains of the Tangerine Bowl team and later president of the University of Tennessee National Alumni Association, typifies this group of outstanding young men.

As I recall this memorable event, I especially remember Tommy Baker, Julian Nunamaker, Larry Ramsey, Jim Wiggins, Coach Jack Beeler, and Coach Ross Elder, who are no longer with us.

Later, the Tangerine Bowl would become the Citrus Bowl, and as I watch the games today my thoughts return to 1967 when a virtually unknown team from rural northwest Tennessee carved a niche in gridiron history.[4]

Linda Sue Workman, a student from Portageville, Missouri, who had been selected as Miss UT Martin, won further acclaim for the school when she was named Miss Tennessee in 1967. Proving that beauty runs in the family, Ali Shumate, the daughter of Travis and Linda Workman Shumate, entered the state competition as Miss Knoxville in 1995, and also won the title of Miss Tennessee.[5]

Martha Harrison Sublette, chosen from thousands of competitors, was selected as the number one baton twirler in the nation in 1967.[6] Her parents, David and Madge Harrison, were UTJC alums and her mother, as mentioned in the UTJC section, would later become the first woman to serve as president of the UT National Alumni Association.

In 1968, the University of Tennessee was converted to a statewide administrative system. A university self-study had revealed the need for such a system which would provide greater independence for the UT campuses and, at the same time, provide for better coordination of the activities of the campuses within the system. As a result of the study, the statewide system was formed. California, Texas, North Carolina, and other states had similar setups. Each campus chancellor, although still responsible to the president, had his/her own staff and was afforded more autonomy. At this time, campuses were located in Knoxville, Martin, and Memphis. In June 1969, the University of Chattanooga joined the UT family as the University of Tennessee at Chattanooga, and shortly

Football players Bobby Hayes (30) and Larry Shanks (41) are pictured in 1967 with Linda Sue Workman shortly after she was crowned Miss Tennessee.

afterwards, in 1971, UT's Nashville Extension Center became the University of Tennessee at Nashville. These campuses, plus the agricultural extension service and other divisions, afforded a formidable challenge for the new statewide system.[7]

In 1968, a new sport, rodeo, emerged on the Martin campus. Dr. Niels Robinson, a faculty member in the School of Agriculture and affectionately known as "Doc," was approached by six students—Glen Bruce, John Pettit, Tommy Sanders, Clint Callicott, Marvin Youngerman, and Danny Glover—about starting a rodeo team. Doc agreed to be the sponsor, thinking that the project, like many student endeavors, would die by the next day; however, the students were persistent. They procured a horse and saddle, sold raffle tickets on them, and raised about five hundred dollars. From this meager beginning the rodeo team was off and running, and UT Martin's first rodeo was held on Memorial Day weekend in 1969. Within five years, the team membership increased from four to about twenty-five, and in 1973 UTM joined the National Intercollegiate Rodeo Association, the first team in Tennessee to do so. Also at the same time, UT Martin became a member of the tough Ozark Region, which included thirteen colleges from eight southern states. The first year the team finished last in the Ozark Region, but this was just the beginning. Within a brief period, the rodeo team from Martin would become a dominant force within the group.[8]

Pictured left to right: Chancellor Archie Dykes, Dr. N. W. "Doc" Robinson, alumnus Bob Parkins, and Dr. Harold J. Smith. Robinson was the rodeo coach at Martin for many years and Smith headed the School of Agriculture from 1967 until 1987. A dive bomber pilot in World War II, Smith is credited with dropping a bomb down the smokestack of a Japanese battleship.

In 1974, U.T. Martin's rodeo team finished second in the Ozark Region and made its initial appearance in the NIRA national finals, the first team east of the Mississippi River to achieve this honor. In 1976, the rodeo team won its first Ozark Region title, and nineteen others would follow through 1999. During the 1974–1999 period the team made twenty-five trips to the national finals. The best finish was in 1985 when the team was third in the nation. Three UT Martin cowboys achieved the pinnacle of rodeo success by winning the National All Around Cowboy award. They were Skip Emmett (1975), Tony Coleman (1977), and George Mesimer (1981).

The women's rodeo team also made impressive strides, winning the Ozark Region in 1996 after several second place finishes. They have earned eight trips to the national finals through the years and finished third in the nation in 1992 for their best finish.

Dr. N. W. Robinson, in addition to his teaching duties, served as the coach until his retirement. In 1978, Tony Coleman was employed as a part-time coach, and he also was named the first full-time coach in 1991 after Doc Robinson retired. Coleman led the team until 1996 when George Mesimer, Coleman's assistant, took over while the search for a replacement was underway. Mesimer coached the team in 1996, and once more they were in the College Rodeo National Finals. Coach John Luthi, who had headed the rodeo program at Fort Scott (Kansas) Junior College, was hired as head coach in 1997.

The team lost its most ardent supporter when Doc Robinson died in 1994. The arena in the Ned R. McWherter Agricultural Complex is named in his honor, and he was the first person to be inducted into UT Martin's Rodeo Hall of Fame.[9]

A rodeo scene in the Ned R. McWherter Agricultural Complex.

Tragedy struck the rodeo team in the fall of 1994 when Valerie Devillers, a twenty-year-old team member from Verac, France, was killed in a riding accident at the practice area.[10] A stunned campus gathered en masse for a memorial service to this outstanding young coed who loved rodeo. As Chancellor Perry sadly observed, "Although Valerie had only been part of our campus a short time, she had so quickly become a part of our university family."[11]

The first rodeo at UT Martin was held at J. E. Cantwell's Golden Sunset Horse Ranch in Greenfield. The next year, in 1970, the rodeo was moved to the Obion County Fairgrounds, and in 1977 it was located at Bo Dodd's farm near Martin. The next move was in 1979 to an outdoor arena on campus. During these early years, the only certainty was rain. As several rodeo fans observed, "If a drought threatens, just hold the rodeo and a flood will follow." This problem was solved when the Tennessee General Assembly appropriated $1.6 million for construction of an agricultural pavilion at UT Martin in 1982. It was a multipurpose facility which became the site of numerous agricultural related activities and home for the rodeo team. Completed in 1984, the West Tennessee Agricultural Pavilion, which provided an indoor arena with ample seating, was complemented by the construction in 1989 of a two hundred-horse stalling facility. The complex was named in honor of Governor Ned Ray McWherter. A native of Dresden, Tennessee, McWherter was a proven friend of UT Martin, and it was appropriate that the complex be named in his honor.[12]

Two large paintings designated for the McWherter Complex were donated to UT Martin. Unfortunately, while previously stored, bird droppings had accumulated on the paintings, and they required cleaning. During the cleaning process some of the paint faded and Aaltje VanDenburg, a long time UTM faculty member and an art teacher, was asked if she could touch up the paintings. She stated she could, and while she was on a ladder working on a pastoral scene a maintenance worker ambled by. He studied one of the paintings and then asked VanDenburg, "Do you know what's wrong with one of the paintings?" "No," she replied. The maintenance worker wryly commented, "Both of the horses are studs, and they wouldn't be in the same pasture." VanDenburg smiled and said, "I can handle that problem," and with a couple of swift strokes with her brush one of the studs became a filly.[13]

In 1980, the rodeo team received further support when the Rodeo Booster Club was formed. Also, in that same year, Martin Rodeo and Roundup Days was started. Featuring a prayer breakfast, a Miss Rodeo Roundup contest, musical entertainment, a golf tournament, a parade, a barbecue dinner, and dances, the week-long event has proven to be very popular. A steadfast crew of volunteer workers exemplified by Mimi Coleman, Dale Bolding, Gloria Howell, David Vowell, Mac Barber, Marvin Alexander, Harry Lee Caudle, Barbara Davis, Linville and Martha Freeman, George Mesimer, Dennis Simpson, Bob Smith, Bill and Lucile Sharrock, Ron and Barbara Cooper, Gary

Roach, and others have provided invaluable support through the years to the rodeo team. Faculty members LeeRoy Kiesling, now retired, and Rodney Thomsen have served as advisors to the team.[14]

In later years, Doc Robinson recalled an earlier incident involving a Brahman bull which got loose and ran wild through the streets of Martin. The bull stormed through a campus housing unit where some student wives were sunbathing. The last thing they expected to join the leisure activity was a Brahman bull. Needless to say, the activity was cut short by the arrival of the unexpected interloper, who slightly injured one of the sunbathers. Continuing his escapade into downtown Martin, the bull encountered the Martin police, who tried to corral him with blue lights flashing and sirens wailing. They discovered this was not the proper procedure to capture a rampaging bull. Fortunately, a veterinarian managed to give the animal a tranquilizer, the bull was loaded into a truck, and shortly afterwards, he was sold. Doc confessed that when he found out where the bull had been that day, it was the nearest he came to nervous collapse.[15]

As former students reminisce about their college days, they generally recall their excellent and more colorful or eccentric professors. Sometimes the professors embodied all these characteristics. An English professor from the 1960s, J. Wallingford Boothe, is a perfect example of such a teacher. He joined the faculty in 1960, and oftentimes he could be found between classes practicing yoga by standing on his head in the hallway. He also was a highly recognizable figure as he hurled his tall frame across campus with gargantuan strides, white socks flashing. One day, as some students were driving downtown, they offered Boothe a ride. "No thanks," he replied. "I'm in a hurry."[16]

Lois Lord was another well-remembered faculty member from the same era. A member of the Biology Department and an excellent, though unconventional, teacher, she had a searing tongue for malingerers. She ruled in her classroom. With a cigarette dangling from her lips, she would hoist her generous frame upon her desk and impose the rudiments of biology on her students in no uncertain terms. Most were very appreciative, and many remember that she made every effort to assist students who were having difficulty in biology. She later taught at Lambuth for many years.[17]

Another often recalled campus figure, though not a faculty member, was William Wade "Red" Freeman. A UTJC alumnus, he joined the junior college staff in 1948 as head of the physical plant, a position he held until 1964. From that date until 1974 when he retired, he was in charge of the motor pool. Tall, slender, and red-headed with a warm smile and an engaging personality, Freeman was very popular among both students and faculty and staff members. He died less than a month after retirement, and a memorial garden near Gooch Hall was erected in his memory in 1976.

In March 1969, the *Tennessee Spirit*, an alumni publication, was started. Prior to this date, the only alumni publication had been *Campus Chatter,* which was published during World War II. David Small, head of alumni affairs at Martin at the time, worked with the campus public relations staff to produce this new publication. In 1970, while Buddy Mitchell was director of alumni affairs at UT Martin, the publication was renamed the *UTM Spirit*. In 1973, when Carol Strawbridge was head of alumni affairs, the title was changed to the *Campus Scene*, its present title. Mary Beth Davidson of the public relations staff assisted Strawbridge, and after Strawbridge resigned in 1974, Davidson assumed primary responsibility for the publication. Public relations, now called the Office of University Relations and headed by Robert D. "Bud" Grimes, currently produces the *Campus Scene*. Dale Dombrowski followed Davidson as editor. After he accepted a new position at Kentucky Wesleyan, Jennifer Glass assumed her present responsibility as editor.[18]

Nationwide, the 1970s could be described as the era of turbulence. Soaring energy prices, inflation, Watergate and other scandals, student unrest, and the continuing Vietnam War caused many Americans to be pessimistic. Some bright spots emerged when a cease-fire in Vietnam in 1973 allowed American forces to come home, and the country celebrated its two hundredth birthday in 1976. But cynicism remained evident as the country endured the tentacles of change.

A scene from a Madrigal Dinner. R. L. Brittain, Walter Haden, and Bob Todd were among those who served as Lord of Misrule for the festive occasion.

The 1970s could also be labeled the decade of change for UT Martin. A new president assumed the leadership reins for the University of Tennessee; UT Martin selected a new chancellor; student demonstrations occurred; the athletic teams entered a different conference and received a new nickname;

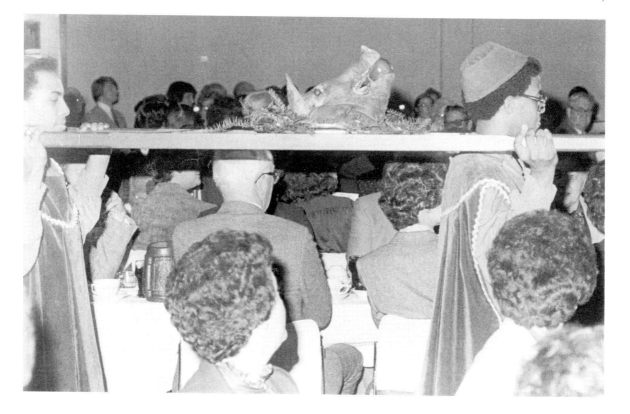

some sports were dropped; several coaching changes occurred; women's athletics became more prominent; the "Push for St. Jude" was started; new fraternities and sororities were organized; additional buildings were erected; "streaking" appeared on campus; dorm restrictions were eased; several "old-timers" retired; new programs of study were started; and the enrollment continued to increase, though not as rapidly as in the 1960s.

The economic woes of the nation were felt at UT Martin. Salary increases for faculty and staff fell sharply below the rate of inflation, and the enrollment, which had surged in the 1960s, rose by only 570 students during the 1970–79 period.[19] Progress continued, but the pace had been slowed.

Students at Martin did enjoy a more liberal atmosphere. Dorm mothers and sign-out procedures in the dorms were replaced by head residents and student assistants. Curfews virtually disappeared, and students could now formally rate their professors. Some pressed for the right to have alcohol on campus, but the pendulum had not swung that far.[20]

Venezuelan students, along with their beloved sport of soccer, joined the student body in the 1970s. International Week, which introduced UT Martin students to different cultures, also appeared. Dean Rusk, Julian Bond, Ralph Abernathy, and Irving Levine were among the keynote speakers, some controversial, who addressed campus audiences in the 1970s.[21]

Another noted speaker to appear on campus in the 1970s was George Bush. On November 17, 1978, Bush, former director of the Central Intelligence Agency (CIA), became the first speaker to address a crowd in the new physical education-convocation center. The building had been occupied since 1976, but there were no seats in the arena until 1978. During his talk, Bush announced that he would seek the presidency in 1980, but he was slated to serve two terms as vice president under Ronald Reagan before being elected in 1988.[22]

Additional fraternities and sororities, including the first ones organized by black students, were founded in the 1970s.[23] The United Collegians, forerunners of the Black Student Association, sponsored the first Black History Week in 1970. Among the more noted speakers sponsored by the BSA was Stokely Carmichael, who addressed a campus audience in 1977.[24]

Student entertainment was not neglected as Ray Charles, Stevie Wonder, Marshall Tucker, Barry Manilow, and other performers appeared on campus. In 1975, over 5,500 fans crowded into Pacer Stadium to hear Charlie Daniels, Barefoot Jerry, Wet Willie, and the Outlaws.[25] Some concerts—for example, Cheech and Chong and Wet Willie at Homecoming in 1976—were not financial successes, but the Student Government Association worked diligently to provide top entertainment for the students.[26]

In 1969, Dr. Andy Holt announced he would retire in 1970 as president of the University of Tennessee, and the board of trustees immediately began the arduous task of selecting his successor. A selection committee appointed by the board, after receiving input from several constituencies, narrowed the list of candidates to Edward J. Boling, UT's vice president for development; Archie Dykes, the chancellor at UT Martin; Webster Pendergrass, vice president for agriculture; Cecil C. Humphreys, president of Memphis State University and formerly a football coach at UTJC; John Chalmers of Kansas State University; and Noah Langdale Jr., president of Georgia State College.

As had been done successfully in the past, the board of trustees selected an in-house candidate, Dr. Ed Boling, as the seventeenth president of UT. A number of students and professors opposed his selection, and the result was a demonstration on the Knoxville campus in January 1970. The selection process was the primary focus of criticism by the demonstrators, not Boling. The demonstration ended after a four-hour confrontation between the demonstrators and the administration, students supportive of the administration, and campus and city policemen. Boling, in Nashville at the time, pledged that his administration would involve students in decision-making in the future—but not under pressure. True to his word, Boling later implemented changes whereby students were placed on some key committees, affording them opportunities to express student views.[27]

Boling followed a very popular president, Andy Holt, but he did not try to emulate him. Boling had served under Governor Buford Ellington as commissioner of finance and administration, and he understood state government. A World War II veteran, he also had worked in the private sector. Energetic, knowledgeable, and a meticulous planner, Boling had served UT well as vice president for development. Lacking the folksy and charismatic style of Holt, Boling used his own quiet but firm manner, coupled with his experience in state government and higher education, to be a very successful leader of the rapidly expanding UT system.[28]

As noted earlier, student discontent with the protracted war in Vietnam surfaced at Martin, but the violence evidenced on some campuses was averted at UTM. Some students and a few faculty members did sponsor a peace march from downtown Martin to the campus. This was on May 13, 1970, nine days after the slaying of four Kent State University students by National Guardsmen. The march route down University Street passed the AGR and ATO fraternity houses, and city administrators were fearful of an encounter there with students opposed to the march. Permission for the march was granted by the city, but the marchers were requested to walk as far away from the fraternity houses as possible. Several faculty members, at the request of Chancellor Dykes, served as observers. The major concern was the safety of the marchers as a large number of students opposed the demonstration. The anti-war group reached the safety of the University Center without a serious confrontation and held a candlelight vigil in the building. In the meantime, a group of students gathered near the entrance of the meeting room, apparently considering a confrontation with the antiwar faction; however, the group disbanded after Dykes talked with them and successfully appealed for free expression of ideas.[29]

The faculty observers were Milton Simmons, Jimmy Trentham, Wilbur Washburn, H. J. Smith, Charles Callis, Charles Mangam, J. C. Owens, and Vincent Vaughan. An elderly local woman saw Simmons with the marchers, and she offered some pointed criticism for his supposed participation. When informed that he was not one of the marchers but had been sent by Chancellor Dykes to be an observer, she testily replied, "I know what I saw!" Apparently, she never changed her mind.[30]

On another occasion, an antiwar group threatened to lower the flag, but Dykes met with them and explained the flag was not to be bothered. It wasn't. A rumor also surfaced that a group planned to burn the ROTC Building, but this proved to be an empty threat.[31]

In June 1970, the board of trustees, following more serious demonstrations at Knoxville, adopted three resolutions designed to discourage such future occurrences. The first resolution restricted the use of the university's campuses and buildings to students, faculty, staff, guests, and other individuals invited to the university. The second established a specific policy regarding the cancellation or suspension of classes, and the third prescribed procedures for investigating disruptive incidents. Some students condemned the resolutions as being too repressive, but the overwhelming response from most sources applauded the firm stance taken by the board of trustees.[32]

Ed and Carolyn Boling at UT Martin for the Century Club banquet on January 28, 1977.

On May 28, 1970, a little over two weeks after the peace march, the "dawn patrol"—this group included faculty and staff members—was called to a midnight meeting to launch a campus sweep that night against illegal drugs. The Tennessee Bureau of Investigation instigated the raid, and members of the "dawn patrol" went with TBI agents to the rooms of students suspected of being involved with drugs. Twelve students on and off campus were arrested in the raid, and appropriate action was taken against them. The search was not concluded until nearly dawn, and some bleary-eyed professors who had participated in the raid greeted their classes that morning.[33]

During the mid-1970s, streaking became the number one spectator sport for the campus and community. Many of the local residents, and some from surrounding towns, brought their lawn chairs to advantageous spots around the university center and eagerly awaited the "romp in the rough." Necks craned as the cry, "Here they come!," rang out. A flash of the flesh, and the runners were gone, hopefully avoiding the watchful eye of campus administrators who frowned on this antic. Some of the more daring coeds joined in this show of anatomy. As one observer commented, "Some of the runners weren't completely naked; a few had on socks and shoes." Some of the slower streakers were identified and were subjected to disciplinary action. The *Pacer* reported approximately sixty streaking incidents, some involving as many as eighteen participants, in a two-day period in March 1974. The paper also estimated that as many as 1,300 gathered each night to watch the spectacle.[34] Like most campus fads, streaking soon faded from the scene except for the occasional student who, remembering the glory days of the past, will still make a mad dash, minus clothing, through a dorm.

Robert Neal Glasgow, who served as judge and city manager for Martin for many years, had a unique solution on handling streakers. If caught in town, they would be jailed just as they were apprehended until their parents or some other responsible party could secure their release.

Glasgow demonstrated compassion and wisdom oftentimes when students appeared in his court. "Write a letter to your mother, telling exactly what you've done," Glasgow would order. "If you stay out of trouble for a year, I'll throw the letter away. If not, I'll mail it." Needless to say, few students reappeared in his court.[35]

A member of the Volunteer State Athletic Conference since the early 1950s, UT Martin opted for a new conference affiliation in 1970. The school joined with Troy State University, Jacksonville State University, Livingston University (now the University of West Alabama), Florence State University (now the University of North Alabama), and Delta State College to form the Mid-South Conference. In the following year, two Louisiana institutions, Nicholls State University and Southeastern Louisiana University, joined the league, and it was renamed the Gulf South Conference. Later, Mississippi College and Northwestern State University (Louisiana) became members.[36]

As UT Martin prepared to exit the Volunteer State Athletic Conference and enter the Mid-South Conference in 1970, a determined group of players journeyed to Nashville for the VSAC basketball tournament. Led by seniors and all-tourney performers, Mike Rudolphi and Don McDonald, the team stormed to three successive victories and the conference championship.[37]

Women's athletics at UT Martin gained momentum after tennis was accorded varsity status in 1956. By 1969, basketball, badminton, and volleyball had joined tennis as varsity sports, and UT Martin was recognized as a leader in women's athletics in Tennessee. In the same year, Bettye Giles, who had joined the physical education staff in 1952, was named as the school's first and only women's director of athletics. She would retain this position until her retirement in 1994. The women's athletic department was organized as a separate entity from the men's department, and James C. Henson, who headed both the Physical Education Department and men's athletics, provided five hundred dollars in budgetary support for the new department. In 1974, the school, for the first time, budgetarily provided separate funds for women's athletics. The basketball, volleyball, badminton, and tennis teams received $8,800 for travel, but there were no athletic scholarships. In 1975, this amount was increased to $40,000 for travel, uniforms, equipment, and a basketball coach/trainer. In the fall of 1976, the first scholarships for women finally arrived when Amy Underwood was awarded with a basketball grant-in-aid. Other scholarships followed and today UT Martin sponsors nine women's sports. Two important factors in the rise of women's athletics were the Educational Amendment Act of 1972 (Title IX) and the ardent desire of many young women at UTM for athletic opportunities. Bettye Giles and others also must be praised for their leadership on the arduous road to success.[38]

A student who was very vocal in the quest for starting women's basketball at UT Martin was Lin Dunn. According to Giles, Dunn pestered every one from the chancellor on down about a women's basketball team. She had been a standout player at Dresden High School, and she firmly believed UT Martin should have a team. Ironically, she graduated in the spring of 1969, and women's basketball was started that fall. Following graduation, Dunn became a coach and has headed programs at Purdue University and other colleges. Currently, she is coaching in the Women's National Basketball Association (WNBA) at Seattle.[39]

Lucia Jones, who joined the physical education faculty in 1970, and shortly afterwards became very successful as the volleyball and badminton coach, has fond memories of the camaraderie which existed among the early women athletes. "We played to win, but we also wanted to have fun," she recalled. Snow skiing, floating down a river in inner tubes, and other activities were among the side excursions. She laughingly remembered a volleyball trip to Idaho where "the girls borrowed cafeteria trays and had a great time sliding down the snowy hills."[40]

Earlier, in 1970, UT Martin was at the forefront in forming the Tennessee College Women's Sports Federation (TCWSF). The organization began with eighteen colleges/universities, and in only four years, by 1973, its membership had grown to thirty-four institutions. Tennessee followed Illinois and Texas as the first states to organize women's athletics at a state level.[41]

In the fall of 1970, a tall, slender, and very talented athlete, Pat Head, best known today as coach Pat Head Summitt of the Tennessee Volunteers, arrived on campus. She played volleyball and basketball, but basketball was her primary love. Upon her arrival, she informed Bettye Giles that she had come to play basketball. Giles said, "Fine, but the volleyball season is first, and you have to play it since it is a conditioner for basketball." "I do?" Pat asked. "Yes," Giles replied. This was not exactly true, but Giles knew that Nadine Gearin, who coached volleyball and basketball, needed Pat in both sports. All three parties laugh today about Giles's little deception.[42]

Pat Head with Nadine Gearin, her basketball coach at UT Martin. The occasion is Pat Head Recognition Day at Martin on September 25, 1976.

Head was the leader when UT Martin won the TCWSF state championship in 1971. There was no national championship at the time, but Head's reputation had spread and a legend was being born.

In the meantime, the Association for Intercollegiate Athletics for Women (AIAW) emerged, and in 1972, the first national women's basketball tournament was held at Illinois State in Normal, Illinois. UT Martin was one of sixteen teams from across the nation selected to play in this prestigious event. The team defeated Long Beach City College (California), now Long Beach State, in their first game, but lost the second contest to Mississippi State College for Women. The tournament also exposed Pat Head to national attention, and as a junior she was selected as a member of the United States Women's Basketball Team in the 1973 World University Games in Moscow. The United States team won a silver medal, and the reputations of Head and UT Martin were further enhanced. Head would later win other international/Olympic medals, and to date, she has guided UT Knoxville to six national titles.[43]

UT Martin remained a member of the TCWSF and the AIAW until 1981 when the women opted to join the men as members of the National Collegiate Athletic Association (NCAA). The AIAW disbanded in 1983 after losing an antitrust suit to the NCAA in 1982. The AIAW had contended that the NCAA was trying to take over and control women's athletics. Effective in

1984, both men's and women's teams across the nation were to be members of the same national association. As stated above, the women's teams at UT Martin had satisfied this requirement by moving to NCAA membership in 1981.[44]

Bettye Giles and Chancellor Margaret Perry agreed in advance that when Giles retired in 1994, men's and women's athletics would be placed under one director of athletics.[45] Thus, Benny Hollis, the director of men's athletics, became the chief administrator for all sports at UT Martin in 1994.

Though retired, Giles remains very active in university activities, especially women's athletics. She can view with pride the progress of the women's teams, and she still serves as a very capable spokesperson for the further development of the women's programs.

On Thanksgiving morning in 1970, the most notable landmark on the UT Martin campus, the old administration building, which was abandoned and slated for demolition, was destroyed by a mysterious fire.[46] According to N. B. "Buster" Williams, fire chief for the city of Martin, "Since the fire started in five different places, arson or vandalism was considered as a likely cause for the blaze." Quick work by the fire department prevented damage to other buildings, but all that remained of the administration building were the walls and columns. The cornerstones, which were positioned in 1900, were salvaged and are now on exhibit in the Paul Meek Library, along with some of the contents of the cornerstones. Williams also recalled that from the late 1920s until 1999, the fire department responded to about 176 fires on the UT Martin campus. "The campus has been one of our better customers through the years," Williams remarked.[47]

The sign, "Welcome to Martin, one of nine happy towns in America!" greeted students after *Esquire* magazine in the December 1970 issue selected Martin for this honor. The nine happy towns chosen by Esquire were characterized by their small population (from 2,000 to 19,200), rural or semirural surroundings, and lack of heavy industry. Martin, the only Southern town selected, was noted as one of the places where there is "an absence of noise, bus exhaust, dirt, rudeness, $400 apartments, $4 plastic lunches, insolent taxi drivers, blackouts, riots, crime waves, and people jams." Other favorable points included "uplifted cultural standards" because of the presence of UT Martin, low property taxes, and a low crime rate.[48] Parents checking colleges for their children to attend undoubtedly were impressed by this favorable description of Martin.

In the fall of 1971, to the delight of some students, freshman and sophomore military science became voluntary. Students who wished to enroll in ROTC could satisfy the basic lower division physical education requirements by taking the two years of military science. Non-compulsory ROTC programs became the norm across the nation, partly as a result of student unrest during this period.[49]

Fortunately for UT Martin, several of the military science personnel, following retirement from active duty, elected to remain in Martin, and some were employed on the campus. One of the best known was Col. George

Pictured left to right are James Odell Jones, Baxter Fisher, and Larry Cardwell. Jones joined the UTJC faculty in 1946, and shortly afterwards he became head of engineering, a position he held until his retirement in 1982. Fisher and Cardwell were long-time faculty members in the department.

Freeman, who headed the ROTC program from 1966 until 1969. He and his wife, Lorene, were both highly respected and popular on campus and in the community, and he later served as director of housing at UT Martin during the 1970–78 period. Lt. Col. Bill Duffy is currently in charge of the Office of Extended Campus and Continuing Education, and Lt. Col. Bill Kaler serves as assistant athletic director and academic coordinator for athletics. Col. Al Pendergrass, Col. Jack Myers, and several others also chose to reside in the Martin area following retirement.[50]

An interesting coincidence occurred in 1971 when Mildred Payne, a beloved and very capable English teacher at UT Martin, who served a stint as acting chair of that department, received the outstanding teacher award. At the same time, her son, Dr. James Franklin Payne, received a similar award at Memphis State University. Jim Payne graduated from UT Martin in 1962, the first student to receive a degree in liberal arts from this campus. He is currently semi-retired but still teaching, and has enjoyed an illustrious career at the University of Memphis. His past assignments included associate dean in arts and sciences, acting dean of that school, and chair of biological sciences.[51]

A welcome change occurred in 1971 when the athletic teams at UT Martin received a new nickname. While the school was a junior college the sports teams were called the Junior Volunteers. In 1951, when UTJC was elevated to senior college status, the Volunteer nickname remained, but the athletic teams were often referred to as the Baby Vols or Little Vols. Carey Bates, vice president of the Student Government Association and a 6'5," 240-pound tackle on the football team, understandably explained that "he was tired of being referred to as a 'Baby Vol.'" The new nickname chosen by the student body in a close vote was Pacers. Some thought this was an appropriate selection since UT Martin was a pace-setting university, but others weren't enthused. "What is a Pacer?" and "What will be our mascot?" were questions which plagued the selection.[52] Later, it was decided that the pacer horse would be the mascot, and the Martin Bank purchased a horse and a sulky for the school in 1981. Shortly afterwards, Chuckie made his appearance at football games. Following a touchdown, the original driver, Curtis Sullivan, would enjoy a ride in the sulky as Chuckie paced around the field. Sullivan is also credited with selecting the name Chuckie for the horse. With a little imagination, one can determine the origin of the name in 1980. The mascots, Pacer Pete and Pacer Polly, had arrived on the scene in the meantime. The school colors, orange and white, were retained and a third color, royal blue, was added. Most agreed a new nickname was needed, but Pacers was never enthusiastically endorsed by students and fans.[53] Consequently, it would be replaced in the 1990s by another nickname—Skyhawks.

Archie Dykes, after four years as chancellor at UT Martin, accepted the position of chancellor at UT Knoxville in 1971. During his tenure at Martin, the phenomenal growth of the campus had continued. The enrollment climbed from 3,169 to 4,907, new construction totaling over $17 million had been completed or was underway, and various new programs of study were introduced, including a bachelor's degree in engineering technology, a master's degree in home economics, an associate degree in nursing, a bachelor of science degree in law enforcement, and several new majors in arts and sciences.[54] While the search was being conducted for a replacement for Dykes, Norman Campbell, head of arts and sciences and academic affairs, served as acting chancellor from September 1, 1971 through November 30, 1971.

Campbell, known as "Straight A. Norman" during the 1929–1931 period when he was a UTJC student, joined the faculty in 1943. Hired as a chemistry professor, he, like most of the faculty members, wore many hats. Through the years, he served as the yearbook sponsor and chaired the athletics committee, the research committee, the graduate council, and others. Among his many committee assignments were the instruction committee, the committee on tenure and promotion, and the space and utilization committee. When he retired in 1976, he was the vice chancellor for

Pictured left to right are UTJC alums Ed Jones, Norman Campbell, and George Thomas. Jones served in the United States House of Representatives from 1969 to 1989. Thomas, an attorney in Dresden, served a stint as county judge, and also was a leader in the movement to achieve senior college status for UTJC.

academic affairs and director of graduate studies. Soft spoken and a meticulous planner, Campbell was a highly respected faculty/staff member. While serving as acting chancellor, several of his colleagues showed the high esteem in which he was held when they suggested, "Norman, you would make an excellent chancellor." However, he never sought the position. Following his retirement in 1976, he taught part-time at Bethel College.[55]

Phillip J. Miller, who joined the English faculty in 1969, later reminisced about his employment interview with Campbell, an event that gives insight into Campbell's wisdom and compassion. Miller, who had battled cancer, was very candid when discussing his physical condition with colleges who were interviewing him for a possible faculty position. "Mr. Miller," Campbell explained, "we do not discriminate on the basis of age, race, sex, or physical condition. If you say your health is good enough to do the job, you're hired." Currently Miller, an avid runner, is a highly respected and well-liked faculty member, and serves as chair of the English Department, director of faculty research and faculty development, and NCAA faculty athletics representative.[56] To say Campbell made an excellent decision would be an understatement.

The search committee, after reviewing the credentials of several candidates, recommended Larry T. McGehee as the replacement for Dykes. McGehee and his wife, the former Elizabeth Boden of Louisville, Kentucky, and daughter Elizabeth, arrived in Martin on December 1, 1971. Another daughter, Molly, would be born in Martin.

A native of Paris, Tennessee, McGehee earned his bachelor's degree at Transylvania University, the bachelor of divinity degree at Yale Divinity School, and the master of arts and doctor of philosophy degrees at Yale University. Prior to his appointment at Martin, McGehee was on the staff at the University of Alabama. Among his positions at Alabama were academic vice president, executive vice president, assistant to the president, assistant vice president for university relations, and director of university relations.[57]

McGehee drew national and international attention for a two and one-half minute, 250-word commencement address delivered at the University of Alabama commencement in May 1972. The address covered six vital subjects, and it was lauded for both brevity and content. Undoubtedly, graduating students across the nation hoped other commencement speakers would emulate the brevity of McGehee's speech.[58]

In 1973, at the request of McGehee, Jimmy Trentham moved from chair of biological sciences to provost, a new campus position. A primary responsibility was to deal with the vice chancellors and deans, a dedicated and hardworking group who were not timid in voicing concerns to McGehee about decisions with which they disagreed. Highly respected, Trentham quickly forged rapport with the group, and a cordial working relationship was established. Later, in 1976, when Norman Campbell retired, Trentham assumed the additional title of vice chancellor for academic affairs. The lure of the classroom was too great to resist, however, and he returned to teaching on July 1, 1979. Trentham had

Chancellor Larry McGehee and Dr. William H. Baker, dean of the School of Business Administration, are pictured in this 1977 scene. Baker is credited with the development of a premier business adminis- tration program at Martin. A World War II veteran of the bloody Pacific campaign, he also was noted for going to battle for his staff.

The building in the back- ground was built as a men's dorm. The Wagon Wheel, a recreational area for students, was located in the basement in the 1950s and 1960s.

hoped to return to teaching earlier, but the deans and vice chancellors had prevailed on him to stay longer. Interestingly, he is the only person to occupy the provost position in the school's history. Also, in recognition of his teaching abilities, Trentham on two occasions received Outstanding Teacher of the Year awards from the University of Tennessee National Alumni Association. In addition, the UTNAA granted him a highly coveted Distinguished Professor award, and CASE (Council for the Advancement and Support of Education) cited him in 1988 as an Honored Nominee-Professor of the Year Program. Trentham retired in 1997.[59]

The face of the campus continued to change in the 1970s as new buildings were erected. The University Courts, providing housing for married students and faculty members, the fine and performing arts building, and the chancellor's residence were completed in 1970, along with new buildings for the motor pool and campus maintenance. Other projects of the decade included G-H Residence Hall (now Browning Hall) in 1971, and the domed swimming pool for dorm residents in 1974. Other new major buildings erected were Gooch Hall (1975) and the physical education complex (1976).[60] The P.E. complex would later be named the Kathleen and Tom Elam Center, after the longtime board of trustees member and his wife.

In 1970, a residence for the chancellor was erected on campus. Prior to this date, Claxton and Meek had provided their own homes, but the need for additional entertaining as the school grew necessitated a school residence for the chancellor. The Dykes family, including wife Nancy and children John and Thomas, were the first to occupy the new facility. Some wags referred to the new residence as "Shoney's" because it was the home of "the big boy."[61]

This was the era of protest, and some students demonstrated against the building of the domed pool. Some referred to it as the "huge bird bath," and others objected to the cost ($90,000) and a lack of dressing facilities. Never greatly used by the students, the domed pool would be razed in 1999 by a UT Martin alumnus who planned to use the geodesic dome in his horticulture business.[62]

Gooch Hall was at first referred to as the "H.E.N. House" since home economics, education, and nursing were located in the building. Chancellor Larry McGehee didn't like the H.E.N. designation since many women faculty members were in the building. As a forerunner to being "politically correct," he decreed that the structure be referred to as the EdNuHec[63] Building. In 1972, Mr. and Mrs. Cecil M. Gooch from Memphis donated $802,000 to UT Martin for scholarships. This was the largest gift the school had received up to that date, and the building was named for them in a ceremony in 1976. Lloyd A. King, professor of chemistry and the major fundraiser for the school for a number of years, was primarily responsible for the solicitation of the Gooch gift.[64]

King, in addition to fundraising and other endeavors, was a longtime chairman of the athletics committee; however, he is best remembered as a chemistry professor who wrote on the blackboard with both hands and erased with his elbows. This well known and amicable professor retired in 1977 after serving on the faculty for thirty-one years.[65]

The death of Paul Meek, chancellor emeritus of The University of Tennessee at Martin and vice president emeritus of the University of Tennessee, on November 2, 1972, deeply saddened the multitudes who had come to know this outstanding academician who personified the school at Martin. A familiar campus figure even during retirement, Meek was remembered as an excellent leader, a person with sterling character, and one whose long

Lloyd King, a popular chemistry professor is pictured in a classroom scene.

shadow would remain evident through future years. He and his wife, Martha, and their children, Paul, David, and Anne, were beloved figures in the campus community, and news of his death dampened the spirit of the homecoming activities, which occurred shortly afterwards.

Meek's death marked the end of a life of service and dedication to the youth of the state. During his tenure from 1934 to 1967 as head of the Martin campus, the enrollment increased from 92 to 3,169, the faculty grew from 12 to 165 professors, and campus property value increased from $200,000 to $20 million. He also served in numerous capacities as a community leader.[66] The 1967 *Spirit* was dedicated to Meek, and a quotation from the yearbook aptly

J. E. McMahan, George Horton, Paul Meek, Earl Knepp, Gene Stanford, shown near the time of Paul Meek's retirement in 1967. When the five "old-timers" retired, they had a total of 183 years of service at UT Martin.

summarizes his impact: "A creative mind has left its mark—a mark so meaningful it should not be forgotten."[67]

Martha Meek, perhaps best of all, provided an intimate insight into the life of Paul Meek when she said, "The school was his 'dream' through all the years, and he knew joy in every achievement and in all the staff and students. He knew no sorrow when the problems of the years brought temporary disappointment, for his faith was sure that the dream would become an educational center for our area and the state."[68] Paul Meek's dream lives and continues to grow, a monument to the man who dedicated much of his life to UT Martin.

As a memorial to their parents, the children of Paul and Martha Meek— Paul, David, and Anne—established the Paul and Martha Meek Awards, which are presented at graduation. These two awards are the only ones given during commencement. Other awards are made on Honors Day.

Also in the 1970s, J. E. McMahan, Gene Stanford, George Horton, Earl Knepp, Horace B. Smith, Mary Rachel Armstrong, and Wayne Tansil—names synonymous with the institution—were "old-timers" who retired after years of service to UT Martin. All had joined the faculty/staff during Meek's tenure except for Gene Stanford, who had arrived during Porter Claxton's administration.

McMahan, affectionately known as "Mr. Mac," was the first of the group to retire. He had relinquished his position as head of the Department of Agriculture to Dr. Glen Hall in 1965, but he continued to teach full-time until he retired on September 1, 1971. Mr. and Mrs. McMahan were honored at an appreciation dinner, and two of his former students, State Commissioner of Agriculture Guilford Thornton and Dr. Cavit Cheshier, executive secretary of the Tennessee Education Association, were among the speakers who paid tribute to "Mr. Mac." Another former student, F. G. "Moe" Cavin Jr., served as master of ceremonies.[69]

On September 1, 1972, Gene Stanford and Horace B. Smith, two other "old-timers" retired. Stanford had served as the chief financial officer for the school since 1930, and his astute monetary management had helped the institution weather the depression and other difficult times. Avid campers and travelers, Stanford and his wife, Verletta, would spend much of their time following his retirement visiting sites throughout the United States.[70]

H. B. Smith, who joined the staff in 1946, had earlier worked as a high school principal. Prior to becoming dean of students at UT Martin in 1962, he served as acting chairman of the Department of Liberal Arts, student personnel officer, chairman of the Department of History, chairman of social sciences, and professor of history. Characterized by a calm demeanor and a deep concern for students, Smith is also remembered as an outstanding history teacher. His last official act was to be the commencement speaker at graduation exercises in the summer of 1972.[71]

Wayne Tansil, who was the school's first director of public relations, retired on August 1, 1973, after twenty years of service. At various times, in addition to his other duties, Tansil taught history, journalism, public affairs, and English. He also was the faculty advisor to the student newspaper, as well as being responsible for media releases

H. B. Smith presents an ROTC award to Darrell Smith (no relation). Darrell Smith would serve as a fighter pilot in Vietnam and later was a pilot for several years with Northwest Airlines.

Three other "old-timers" who were important figures in the growth and development of UT Martin were, from left to right: Henry Allison, dean of admissions and records; Wayne Tansil, director of public relations; and Russell Duncan, director of the University Center.

and other duties relating to his office. A high school teacher and merchant in his earlier years, Tansil held a bachelor's degree from Northwestern University and a master's degree from George Peabody College.[72]

George Horton and Mary Rachel Armstrong, both of whom had served the campus well for many years, retired on September 1, 1973. Horton was in the final Hall-Moody class in 1926–27, and he continued his studies at the school the following year when it became the University of Tennessee Junior College. A campus leader and a three-sport letterman, he also was voted the "best necker" by the coeds. He received his bachelor's degree from UT Knoxville and a master's degree from North Carolina State University. He returned to Martin in 1937, and during the ensuing years he headed both the Department of Biological Sciences and the liberal arts curricula. In addition to his academic responsibilities, Horton served on numerous campus committees. He took particular pride in the preprofessional students whom he advised, and many of his former students expressed gratitude for his guidance. Some complained about his exacting demands, but many would later admit that Horton's requirements had them well prepared for medical school and other professional areas. Following retirement, he continued to be a valuable resource on former students and the school's history.[73]

Mary Rachel Armstrong joined the UT Martin home economics faculty in 1952 as professor and head of the department. In 1969, she was elevated to dean when the department became the School of Home Economics. Under her leadership, programs in home economics education, early childhood education, and a master of science degree with a major in home economics were initiated. Deeply concerned about world hunger, Armstrong worked for the United Nations from 1945 to 1947 as a nutritionist, helping to care for displaced persons. Later, she would spend two years (1955–57) in India and would also be a leader in helping to solve nutrition needs in the United States. After her retirement, the Mary R. Armstrong Social-Living Area in Gooch Hall was dedicated in honor of her many contributions.[74]

Earl Knepp, a lovable campus figure for thirty-eight years retired on September 1, 1974 at the age of seventy. A Kansas Jayhawker, he joined the faculty in 1936 to teach agricultural engineering and other agricultural courses. In addition to serving as the sponsor for several student organizations, he was responsible for the farm livestock for many years. Later, he supervised the construction of campus buildings, and he was named as the resident engineer in 1964. He later remarked that his toughest job as resident engineer was bulldozing the peach orchard to build the first "Y" dormitory. "The peaches were just about ripe when a bulldozer mowed them down," he later lamented. Former students, faculty members, friends, and construction firm representatives gathered to honor Knepp at a retirement dinner. The Earl Knepp Scholarship Endowment Fund was established as a tribute to this outstanding educator who was a favorite of both students and faculty/staff members. Robert Smith, who had worked with Knepp, became the resident engineer when Knepp retired.[75]

Knepp, following his retirement, became the victim of an unusual and successful "kidnapping" plot. He was undergoing treatment for a back injury at Volunteer General Hospital in 1981 when two UTM cheerleaders sneaked past the hospital's staff, "seized" Knepp, and transported him to the UTM-Troy State football game. There he was placed in a special seat on the fifty-yard line and presented a jacket proclaiming him to be UTM's "No. 1 Sports Fan." More than six thousand fans roared their approval. To that date, Knepp had only missed one home football game at UTM in forty-four years, and he was a willing victim of the kidnapping escapade. Further investigation of the plot revealed that Chancellor Charles Smith, Nick Dunagan, hospital administrator Tommy Bryant, and Dr. E. C. Thurmond, Knepp's physician, were involved in the "conspiracy."[76]

Members of the home economics staff. Seated left to right are Aaltje VanDenburg and Mary Rachel Armstrong. Standing left to right are Mary Ida Flowers and Doris Latta.

Prominent among the many charitable activities sponsored by the fraternities and sororities was the Push for St. Jude. Alpha Phi Omega, a service fraternity organized in 1970, started this very worthy event in the early 1970s and continued it for thirteen years. Gamma Sigma Sigma, a service sorority, and other organizations assisted with the pushes through the years. It would later be revived and continued by the ATOs. This drive to raise money for St. Jude's Children's Research Hospital located in Memphis occurred during spring

The Alpha Phi Omega's Push for St. Jude, March 18, 1978.

break. The fraternity members pushed wheelbarrows from Martin to Memphis, collecting donations along the way to assist the hospital. Two separate routes were used at times. One went down Highway 45 to Milan and then followed Highway 70 to Memphis. The other route was on Highway 22 to Union City and then down Highway 51 to Memphis. Church, civic, and school organizations and private businesses along the routes furnished meals and lodging for the pushers.

Roger Redding, an Alpha Phi Omega chairman for one of the pushes and now a vice president for the UT hospital in Knoxville, described the arrival of the pushers at their destination. "It was the most emotional moment I've ever had. That moment your aches and pains seemed to go away." Redding calculated that during the first six years the pushes raised over $122,000. Later pushes in this very worthy endeavor were equally successful.[77]

Destined to be one of the most active student organizations on campus, the Undergraduate Alumni Council was established in 1973. Sponsored by the Office of Alumni Affairs, the UAC consists of forty members selected from the undergraduate student body. The group was formed to offer services to the university community and help make students more aware of alumni activities. The largest annual undertaking for this organization is homecoming. Most homecoming activities are the responsibility of the UAC, except for the selection of the royalty which is coordinated by the Student Government Association. Strictly service oriented, the UAC has compiled an admirable record through the years.[78]

The first of several coaching changes in the 1970s occurred in early 1971 when it was announced that Dr. Robert H. Paynter would become the new head basketball coach and director of athletics, replacing head basketball coach Floyd Burdette and James C. Henson. Prior to this appointment, Paynter had been serving as administrative assistant to Chancellor Dykes. A native of Richmond, Kentucky, he received his bachelor's degree from St. Mary's College (Minnesota), the master's degree from Eastern Kentucky University, and a doctorate in education from UT Knoxville. His coaching experience included a fourteen-year stint as head coach at the University High School of East Tennessee State University.

Burdette had served as basketball coach for eighteen seasons, compiling a 200–201 record. His teams claimed three western division VSAC crowns and won the VSAC tournament in 1970. An associate professor in the Department of Physical Education and Health, Burdette remained as a faculty member until his retirement in 1980.

Henson, who had served very ably as a coach, director of athletics, and chairman of the Department of Physical Education and Health, remained as chair of that department and tennis coach. At that time, his tennis teams had won four western division VSAC crowns, the latest in 1970.[79]

Another change occurred in 1974 when, for the first time in the school's history, full-time football coaches were employed. Bob Carroll, who compiled an 84–82–4 record in eighteen years as head coach, relinquished his coaching duties to become assistant director of athletics. During his coaching tenure from 1957 through 1974, Carroll was a member of the history faculty and his four assistants—Vernon Prather had joined the staff in 1969—taught physical education classes.[80]

George MacIntyre was selected as the new head football coach. A graduate of the University of Miami (Florida) where he was a standout quarterback, MacIntyre was the defensive secondary coach at Vanderbilt University when he accepted the position at UT Martin. He started his coaching career in the high school ranks and later coached at Miami, the University of Tampa, and Clemson University. His six assistants were Ron McCrone, Vester Newcomb, Fred Pickard, Bill Ware, David Lee, and Don Wiggins. The personable MacIntyre led the team to 2–8, 8–3, and 8–3 records in three years at the helm. He left Martin to join the staff at the University of Mississippi and later became the head coach at Vanderbilt University. Vester Newcomb moved up as head coach for the 1978 and 1979 seasons, compiling a 7–13 record.[81]

A near tragedy occurred in January, 1974, when the Pacer bus, returning from a men's basketball game at Florence State University, was forced from Highway 22 south of Lexington, Tennessee, by an oncoming car. The bus tumbled about fifty feet down a steep embankment, injuring twenty-seven basketball players, cheerleaders, and staff members. Fortunately, the bus landed on some fresh dirt at the bottom of the embankment or the injuries could have been much worse. Center Jerry Diekmann and cheerleader Cathey Bradford required overnight hospitalization and the other twenty-five persons were treated for minor injuries and released. Coach Bob Paynter had to reschedule two games until his battered and bruised players could recover. The Pacer bus was demolished in this mishap.[82]

In May 1975, two sports, golf and wrestling, were dropped as intercollegiate sports for financial reasons. Both had been very successful, and the fans of these sports expressed dismay over the decision. The golf team, under the tutelage of Grover Page, had been a perennial contender in the Division II national tournaments and had just finished as the runner-up in the Gulf South Conference. Also, UT Martin was slated to host the national Division II and Division III tournaments in June 1975 when the decision was made to discontinue the two sports. The school did host the golf tournaments, which were held at Ft. Campbell, Kentucky, and the golf team, though this would be their final event, finished eighth in the nation. After a six-year hiatus, golf was reinstated in 1981.[83]

The wrestling team, which was started six years earlier, had just finished a 9–4 season. The wrestlers, coached by Richard "Bud" Reiselt, had winning records of 8–2 and 6–5 in the two previous years.[84]

At the conclusion of the 1977 winter quarter, an amazing event occurred— David H. "Gruder" Graham graduated. A student for nearly nine years, "Gruder" gave meaning to the phrase "professional student." Extremely active in extracurricular activities, he is well remembered as the "Pacer Racer." Dressed in an orange jumpsuit and a royal blue fireman's hat, Gruder delighted the fans, especially the children, as he sped around the football field in a white miniature car. Larry Alexander, a UT Martin alumnus and a fraternity brother of Graham, furnished the car. Following a Pacer touchdown, the stadium echoed with the cry, "Go, 'Gruder,' go!" He willingly obliged, oftentimes making a turn with only two wheels on the ground.

All good things must come to a close, and Gruder graduated in 1977 with a degree in Business Management and enough hours for a Ph.D. degree. As his mother commented, "David was at UT Martin for only four terms—those of Johnson, Nixon, Ford, and Carter." Following graduation, Graham has enjoyed a successful career in state government, even though he was somewhat tardy in joining the ranks of the employed.[85]

On November 14, 1979, an anti-Iranian demonstration consisting of about three-hundred students was held in front of the administration building. The American embassy in Tehran, Iran, had been seized by an armed mob on November 4, and the diplomats and military personnel inside were being held as hostages. A few of the hostages were released within days, but fifty-three Americans remained prisoners in the embassy. The Ayatollah Khomeini and his followers had seized power in Iran, and hatred of the United States was rampant in that country. The hostage seizure and the anti-American fervor released a surprising well of anger and emotion by the Americans. Emotional patriotism was displayed across the nation as Americans held anti-Iranian demonstrations. Students at UT Martin were outraged by the actions of the Iranians, but, as in past demonstrations, there were no violent incidents on campus. John Eisterhold, dean of International Programs at UT Martin, urged peace, and he explained that some of the Iranian students at Martin did not necessarily share the view of the Khomeini government. Some had even considered buying space in the *Pacer* and the *Weakley County Press* to condemn the actions of the Iranian government. Eisterhold's statements helped to calm the crowd. Unfortunately, the hostages were not released until they endured a 444-day ordeal. Jimmy Carter, in the last hours of his presidency, released several billion dollars in Iranian assets that he had frozen in American banks. Iran, in turn, released the hostages who were welcomed home by an emotional country.[86]

During the Thanksgiving holidays in 1979 and following the anti-Iranian demonstration, a lone Iranian student stood in the quadrangle protesting. No one knew what he was protesting about on the isolated campus; however, the campus security personnel advised him that if he wished to protest he would be much more visible if he stood on University Street. "No" he replied. "I'm very happy right here," and he continued his lonely vigil, observed mostly by scampering squirrels and chirping birds.[87]

The administration of Larry McGehee at UT Martin came to a close on August 31, 1979, when he transferred to Knoxville to become assistant to the president. His major responsibility in his new position was to secure gifts for arts and humanities. Dr. John W. Prados, vice president for academic affairs, served as acting chancellor at Martin from September 1, 1979, until December 14, 1979.[88] In the meantime, a search committee had interviewed candidates, and Charles E. Smith was selected for the chancellor's position, which he assumed on December 15, 1979.

Smith, a native of White County, Tennessee, started his career in journalism after receiving his bachelor's degree from UT Knoxville. He served one year as managing editor of the *Putnam County Herald* and *Cookeville Citizen* and two years as editor of the the *Sparta Expositor*. He was a staff member of the *Nashville Tennessean* for three years before joining the University of Tennessee staff in 1967 as editor of the UT News Bureau. In 1968, he was named director of public relations for UT Knoxville and then served as executive assistant to the UTK chancellor, Archie Dykes, from 1971 until being appointed executive assistant to President Edward J. Boling in 1973.

On March 1, 1975, he was named acting chancellor at the University of Tennessee at Nashville, with the appointment becoming permanent in 1977. In 1975, Smith was also named vice president for public service in UT's statewide administration. When UTN was merged by court order with Tennessee State University on July 1, 1979, he continued his duties as vice president for public service until leaving UT in August to become editor of the *Nashville Banner*. Prior to assuming this position, Smith had been a candidate for the vacant chancellorship at UT Martin, but he withdrew his name and elected to become editor of the *Banner*. As the search continued for a replacement for McGehee, Smith opted to become a candidate again, and he was selected to become UT Martin's fifth chancellor.[89]

Dr. Jimmy Trentham, who had served as Vice Chancellor for Academic Affairs and Provost until July 1979, received strong support from a campus constituency for the chancellor's position. He had garnered plaudits from deans and faculty members alike for his exceptional handling of campus affairs, and many felt his background and abilities provided excellent credentials for the chancellorship. But Smith's experience as chancellor of UT Nashville and in the UT system were factors undoubtedly in his favor.[90]

In December 1979, Smith and his wife, Shawna Lea, and children, Chip and Tandy, joined the Martin community. He assumed his new duties on December 15, a position he would occupy until September 27, 1985.

Energetic, outgoing, and somewhat demanding, Smith served very capably as chancellor. On one occasion, when a speaker was listing the possible things Smith's middle initial of E. might signify, such as energetic, one of his staff members vocally opined, "I know one thing it doesn't stand for and that's 'easy'!"[91] A fluctuating enrollment, the woes of inflation, and a lack of support for higher education were among the myriad problems facing Smith as he became chancellor at Martin.

The 1980s brought changes not only on campus but also throughout America and world-wide. Ronald Reagan was elected as president (1980 and 1984); the existence of AIDS was reported in the United States (1981); a severe recession hit the United States, and the United States invaded Grenada (1982); 241 United States Marines were killed in a terrorist attack in Beirut (1983); crack cocaine appeared in American cities (1985); United States planes bombed targets in Libya (1986); George Bush was elected President (1988); the Berlin Wall was dismantled; and the United States invaded Panama (1989).

Closer to home, former President Jimmy Carter visited UT Martin to help honor House Speaker Ned Ray McWherter, and the mandatory physical education requirement was eliminated (1982); the state legislature made hazing a misdemeanor and raised the drinking age to twenty-one (1984); the Home Economics Department was accredited, and Alpha Phi Omega, a service fraternity, became coed (1985); Alex Haley, the author of *Roots*, spoke on campus (1986); Marriott Corporation took over the dining services, and a McDonald's was built on University Street (1988); Senator Albert Gore Jr. spoke on campus, and the African-American Greek organizations united under the banner of the National Pan-Hellenic Council (1989).

A rapid growth of student enrollment in the 1980s did not occur. The fall quarter enrollment in 1980 was 5,375. The number reached a high of 5,696 in 1983, but then declined to 5,064 in 1985. The primary factor was a decrease in the number of graduating high school seniors, but, regardless of the reasons, the result was tighter budgets during the years of declining enrollments. Colleges throughout the state faced similar problems with enrollments and budgets.[92]

Former President Jimmy Carter is talking with Speaker of the House Ned R. McWherter in this 1982 scene when McWherter is being honored at UT Martin.

One of Smith's first acts upon becoming chancellor was to launch a study of athletics at UT Martin. He appointed a committee, known as the Intercollegiate Athletic Committee, to examine all facets of the athletics program and to hold public hearings. The committee was composed of area citizens, Don Ridgeway, David Murphy, and Charles Hyde. Faculty members were Tom Noble, Ernie Blythe, and Louise Knifley. Mike Turner, president of the Student Government Association, and Steve Hyers, SGA vice president, completed the panel. Fans, students, coaches, and members of the faculty and staff spoke during the hearings. Some observers would later comment that "some speakers offered help, insight, encouragement, and hope. Others just saw it as an opportunity to bask in the limelight and perhaps to offer criticism."[93]

Following the hearings, Smith hired Ray Mears as director of athletics and Art Tolis became the head basketball coach. Bob Paynter, who previously held both positions, retired. Mears, the first full-time director of athletics in UT Martin's history, was serving as director of promotions for the athletic department at UT Knoxville when he received the appointment at Martin. Prior to this, he had coached the Volunteer basketball team for sixteen years, compiling a record of 278 wins and 112 losses. Ill health forced Mears to retire as head basketball coach, and he then became director of promotions. Dubbed the "Barnum of Basketball," Mears had delighted Big Orange fans with victories

Bill Haney and Coach Fred Pickard share a light moment during an interview. Pickard was the head football coach at UT Martin from 1982 through 1985. Haney and Tom Britt are responsible for the broadcasting of UTM athletic events.

and showmanship. It was hoped that his promotional skills would invigorate athletics at UT Martin.[94]

Art Tolis, a former assistant coach at Louisiana State University for six years, was highly respected as a coach and a recruiter. Smith and Mears both expressed confidence that Tolis could develop a winning program at Martin.[95] Tolis headed the basketball program for two years and was replaced by Tom Hancock upon his resignation in 1982. Tolis compiled records of 12–13 and 21–11, including a 65–41 win over Mississippi State University at Starkville, during his second season. Dennis Bussard, head basketball coach and tennis coach at Babson College in Wellesley, Massachusetts, at the time, was tapped as assistant director of athletics by Mears. He also was assigned to coach the men's tennis team, a position which James C. Henson, who retired in 1980, had filled very successfully for three decades.[96]

"We plan to recruit the best academic students in our service area with the same intensity that many universities seek outstanding athletes," Charles Smith remarked early in his tenure as chancellor.[97] With funds from the estate of the late C. M. Gooch of Memphis, plus other gifts, the University Scholars program was born. Dr. Ernest W. Blythe Jr., who served as director of the program from its inception in 1981 until his retirement in 1997, recalled that Nick Dunagan, the chief development officer, was very innovative in procuring the necessary funds.[98] Currently, thanks to additional gifts from donors like Charles E. "Bub" Cole, Margaret and Randy Perry, Mrs. Sara Dunagan, Lew and Mary Jo Dougherty, Houston Gordon, and Mrs. K. W. Rogers, forty of the sixty scholarships are endowed.

As originally designed, participants in the University Scholars program were chosen based on ACT scores, high school grade point averages, interviews, and recommendations. The program was organized with courses and activities designed to stimulate the talents of the selected students. From fifteen to sixteen scholars were picked annually, and each was rewarded with a lucrative scholarship package. The original format remains in effect at the present, and Dr. Bill Zachry, who worked with Blythe as associate director, assumed leadership of the program when Blythe retired.[99]

Other endeavors, like the honors seminar, which was started in 1985, attract gifted students to UT Martin. The institution, thanks to the generosity of many donors, is able to compete successfully with other colleges for talented and highly motivated students.

Another project which brought about 150 outstanding high school students to the UT Martin campus in the summer was the Governor's School for the Humanities. Milton Simmons, vice chancellor for academic affairs from 1979 to 1983, recalled that the program started on a limited basis in the early 1980s. By 1985, it was fully organized, thanks to assistance from faculty members like Bill Zachry and Ernie Blythe. The program was three weeks in duration at first, but then it was expanded to one month. Simmons, a favorite of the participants and "Uncle Miltie" to many of them, cited David Loebekka and other faculty members for their efforts in making the Governor's School very successful. At first, the program at Martin included the sciences, humanities, and the arts. Other state colleges in Tennessee followed UT Martin's model and

Harold Conner, Assistant to the Vice Chancellor and Director of Minority Activities, hands out a free T-shirt to a lucky freshman during Freshman Studies. Conner was UT Martin's first African-American administrator and a favorite with all students. Freshman Studies was started in the early 1970s and continues today as a week-long orientation program for freshmen.

Chancellor Charles Smith, campaign chairman Don Pennington, and UT president Ed Boling admire the check denoting UT Martin had reached its $2 million goal a year ahead of schedule.

established Governor's Schools which concentrated on designated academic disciplines. John Eisterhold is the current director of the school at Martin, and each summer talented and motivated youngsters arrive for a month of intense study and fun.[100]

In May 1982, a permanent home for West Tennessee history became a reality with the dedication of the West Tennessee Museum/Archives on the UT Martin campus. The museum was housed at first in the Henson House (so-called because it was purchased from Mr. and Mrs. James C. Henson). Later, the museum was moved to the home economics building, where the Holland McCombs papers were located. On March 28, 1987, the building was dedicated as the Holland McCombs Center and Archives. Holland McCombs, on the occasion, was present and reminisced about his boyhood days when most of the campus was farmland belonging to his family. Upon completion of the renovation and expansion of Paul Meek Library in 1993, the historical documents were transferred to the special collections area in that building. The museum in the McCombs Center continues to house historical relics, and Dr. S. K. Airee is the present curator.[101]

The highly successful Tennessee Tomorrow campaign closed during Smith's initial year as chancellor. It was the first system-wide fundraising endeavor in which UT Martin participated, and it was headed by Nick Dunagan, the chief development officer at Martin. Volunteer chairmen were Jim Glasgow, King

Rogers, and Ray Smith. Started in 1977, the three-year campaign netted $2.8 million in gifts for UT Martin and a total of more than $57 million for all UT campuses.[102]

Also, UTM's first independent capital gifts campaign, the Campaign for Quality, was launched during Smith's tenure. Initiated in 1983 with a goal of $2,000,000, the campaign goal was reached in 1985, a full year ahead of schedule. Reese Smith from Nashville, chairman of the UTM Development Committee, and Dyersburg's Don Pennington, chairman of the Campaign for Quality, headed the highly successful drive. Chancellor Smith praised the work of Pennington, Reese Smith, and the other volunteer development committee members who participated in the campaign. He also credited UTM Vice Chancellor for Development Nick Dunagan in the design and execution of the undertaking. "Nick Dunagan conceived a brilliant plan and led its execution to perfection," the chancellor stated. "His leadership has paid rich dividends for this University." These funds were used to fund scholarships, the lecture series, and many other components of the institution's academic programs.[103]

During this era of tight budgets and soaring inflation, students across the state became highly concerned with rising education costs. Forsaking demonstrations for dialogue, students from UT Martin, UT Knoxville, East Tennessee State University, Middle Tennessee State University, and Tennessee Technological University journeyed to Nashville in February 1981, to meet with state political leaders. UTM representatives, Eric Griffin, Brad Hurley, Shari Miles, and Mike Vaughn, along with other Tennessee college students, expressed concern that student costs were rising at a faster rate than state appropriations. The students asked for a long range financial plan for students, stability in state funding, a revamping of the state funding formula, and other measures in lieu of major tuition increases. Speaker of the House Ned Ray McWherter and Lt. Governor John Wilder (a UTJC alumnus) gave the students a sympathetic hearing, but, in turn, pointed out that the slumping economy was the major culprit. State funds at this time were short and taxation opportunities were limited, the leaders explained. Also, Ray Blanton, while governor, had resisted an increase in student fees. Therefore, the political leaders thought a fee increase was probably due.[104]

Shortly afterwards, student representatives met with Governor Lamar Alexander at the executive mansion to express again their concerns about fee increases. Steve Hyers, UTM student representative to the UT board of trustees, and UTM Student Government President Rose Boyd were among the students who met with Alexander. He, like McWherter and Wilder, voiced support for the student concerns, and later proposed that a student expense plan be prepared by the state and universities to span a five-year period. Out of this proposal came a plan whereby the students would pay 30 percent of their basic college expenses, and the state and other sources would cover seventy percent. This was the so-called 70–30 plan. Alexander also stated more funds should be available for student loans.[105]

At the beginning of the 1980–81 academic year, Chancellor Smith made $15,000 available to start the Academic Speakers Program, which was designed to bring scholars from various academic areas to the UTM campus. "The main idea of the Academic Speakers Program is to give students and faculty the opportunity to interact with scholars and prominent people in a variety of academic areas," stated Dr. Milton Simmons, vice chancellor for academic affairs, when the program was inaugurated. Simmons was responsible for administering the funds, and he worked with the deans and department heads to schedule the speakers. The goal was to have one to two speakers per month come to UTM to give a general address, conduct classes and hold seminars for students and faculty. Peter Taylor, noted author of short stories from the University of Virginia; Roger Morris, political scientist who served under three presidential administrations; and the World Hunger Forum were among the initial programs brought to the campus. Through the years, many prominent speakers have participated in the program, which continues today.[106]

Interestingly, international students provided a major source of additional income during the years of stringent budgets at UT Martin. Dr. Milton Simmons, who was dean of Arts and Sciences (formerly Liberal Arts) in 1973, recalls that UTM's International Program was triggered by an outside impetus. Dr. Jose Veciano, a local pathologist and a Cuban refugee, asked Simmons to meet with him and Bill Pearson, a dentist from Memphis. Pearson's wife, Carman, was from Venezuela, and they questioned Simmons about the possibility of having some Venezuelan students enroll at UT Martin for intensive English classes. If the students did well in the English courses, it was requested that they then be integrated into the various curricula at the university.

Simmons accepted the challenge, and in the summer of 1974 ten Venezuelan students arrived at Martin. Aided by Jimmy Trentham, provost at the time, Phil Watkins, head of student affairs, and a capable secretary, June Coleman, a fledgling international program was born. Simmons recalled that the students were exceptional young men who did well in their academic pursuits. Thirty more Venezuelan students arrived on October 1, and the program mushroomed. By 1975, the number had swelled to 75. The Venezuelan government, buoyed by oil prosperity, paid the expenses for the students, and this additional income was welcomed by UT Martin.[107]

The growth of the program, however, placed a tremendous responsibility on Simmons, who was still dean of arts and sciences. It was decided that the international program would be placed under the office of student affairs, and Dr. John Eisterhold, professor of history, was named as head of the program. Eisterhold expanded the program into other areas including Middle East and Far East countries. When Charles Smith became chancellor, he gave strong support to the international program, and it continued to grow.[108]

In December 1980, Smith and Eisterhold, who now had the title of dean of international programs at UT Martin, successfully negotiated a $450,000 educational contract with Nihon University in Japan. This agreement provided

training for two hundred Japanese students on the UTM campus with no use of state funds. The students, along with ten Nihon University professors, arrived at Martin in July 1981, for a ten-week program consisting of concentrated study of the English language and an introductory survey course in American engineering technology. The contract, believed to be one of the largest single international contracts to be awarded to that date by a foreign university to an American institution of higher learning, culminated eighteen months of negotiations.[109] Initiatives, such as this contract, provided sorely needed funds for UT Martin.

Another and more lucrative contract totaling $1.35 million was signed with Nihon University for the following year. The new agreement called for a repeat of the ten-week summer program plus two additional quarters of academic work during which time Japanese professors taught regular Nihon engineering courses to Japanese students in UTM classrooms. Again, about two hundred Nihon students and ten Nihon faculty members participated in the project. Area merchants, as well as the college, benefitted from the influx of the Japanese students and faculty members.[110]

Chancellor Charles Smith is pictured with Japanese students from Nihon University who were studying on the UT Martin campus.

During Eisterhold's tenure of twenty-three years as head of International Programs, the program expanded to have a full time staff of twenty-one, and, at times, as many as four persons were overseas teaching at international universities. Besides Hirosaki University (1975), "other sister university relations" were formed in Japan with Niijima Gakuen Women's Junior College (1983), Taskasaki City University of Economics (1991), Hiroshima Jogakuin University (1994), and Korea's Hangsung University (1996). The peak year for enrollment of international students was probably in 1991 when UTM's international student population reached 402. These students came from approximately forty-five different nations.[111]

Eisterhold, whose recruitment efforts were primarily in Asia and South America, estimated that he traveled about one million air miles during the time he headed the program. Also, he pointed with pride that the International Program had to be self-supporting and that it provided additional funds to both

---

1967

The name of the school is changed to the University of Tennessee at Martin.

Paul Meek retires, and Archie Dykes is named chancellor.

Linda Sue Workman is crowned "Miss Tennessee."

The football team wins the Tangerine Bowl.

1968

The University of Tennessee is converted to a statewide administrative system.

The rodeo team is formed.

1969

The *Tennessee Spirit*, the forerunner of the *Campus Scene*, is first published.

1970

Andy Holt retires as president of the University of Tennessee, and Ed Boling replaces him.

The board of trustees adopts resolutions to discourage student demonstrations.

UT Martin exits the Volunteer State Athletic Conference to join the Mid-South Conference.

The Tennessee College Women's Sports Federation (TCWSF) is formed.

The old administration building burns.

Esquire magazine selects Martin as "one of the nine happy towns in America."

A degree in engineering technology is implemented.

1971

Military science becomes voluntary.

The athletic teams receive a new nickname, "Pacers."

Archie Dykes leaves UT Martin to become chancellor at UT Knoxville; and Norman Campbell serves as acting chancellor.

The Mid-South Conference expands and becomes the Gulf South Conference.

UT Martin and the area. Another important by-product was the cultural diversity provided to the campus and community.[112]

In 1981, the international flavor at Martin was further enhanced when two sophomores, Tommy Hyde from Greenfield and Vicki Peterson from Millington, became UTM's first international exchange students. Both were majoring in business foreign studies, and they were provided with full Japanese Ministry of Education scholarships to attend Hirosaki University for a year of study. At the same time, two Hirosaki University students enrolled at UT Martin under the exchange program. Hirosaki University, located in Hirosaki, Japan, with an enrollment of approximately five thousand students, was considered UT Martin's sister institution and the exchange program continued through the years. Hyde received further international training when he won a scholarship from Taiwan for 1983–84 to study at the Mandarin Training Center.[113]

THE UNIVERSITY OF TENNESSEE AT MARTIN (1967–1983)

Larry T. McGehee is chosen to be chancellor at UT Martin.

1972
The death of Paul Meek is mourned by the campus.

1973
Jimmy Trentham is named as provost.
Undergraduate Alumni Council (UAC) is established.

1974
Ten Venezuelan students enroll at UTM, marking the beginning of the International Programs.

1978
George Bush speaks on campus.

1979
An anti-Iranian demonstration occurs on campus.

Larry McGehee transfers to Knoxville, and John Prados becomes acting chancellor.
Charles E. Smith is named as chancellor.

1980
Academic Speakers Program is started.

1981
The University Scholars program is initiated.
UT Martin becomes the home of WLJT, Channel 11.

1982
Mandatory physical education is eliminated.
The West Tennessee Museum/Archives is dedicated at UT Martin.

1983
UTM's first independent capital gifts campaign, the Campaign for Quality, is launched.

During his tenure as chancellor, Smith put a priority on increasing faculty salaries. Historically, salaries at UT Martin were lower than at comparable universities, and Smith sought to correct this inequity. Whenever funds were available, he and his staff put emphasis on faculty salaries, and in 1985, Smith was able to point with pride that the average salary of UTM faculty was $27,492. This was a 58.5 percent increase over the 1979 average, but Smith noted that there was a dire need for further improvement.[114]

Campus expansion during the 1980s continued, though at a slower pace. In 1980, a concession stand, a press box addition, and two restrooms were added to the football stadium. In 1984, the agricultural pavilion, later to be named in honor of Governor Ned R. McWherter, was built, and in 1988, a new ROTC building was erected at the football stadium. The ROTC building was constructed with a slanted roof to accommodate new stadium seating, which was added with private gifts. The old ROTC building, a World War II army surplus building, was burned in 1988 to provide space for a parking lot. In 1989, a stalling bar next to the ag pavilion completed construction for the decade. During this interval, the administration building received some cooling and duct work improvements, Cooper Hall (now Crisp Hall) was renovated, and the roofs of G-H dorm, the library, and the university center were repaired. In 1989,

---

1985

The initial chair of excellence at UT Martin is approved.

Charles Smith transfers to Knoxville, and Nick Dunagan becomes acting chancellor.

1986

Alex Haley speaks on campus.

Margaret N. Perry is selected to be chancellor.

The University of Tennessee National Alumni Association celebrates its 150th birthday.

1988

Lamar Alexander becomes the eighteenth president of UT.

UT Martin switches from the quarter to the semester system.

The football team wins the Gulf South Conference title and advances to the NCAA Division II playoffs.

Marriott Corporation assumes responsibility for the dining services.

1989

WestStar is started.

Senator Albert Gore Jr. speaks on campus.

1991

Joe Johnson is named president of UT.

Operation Desert Storm occurs.

1992

UT Martin achieves membership in the Ohio Valley Conference.

Ed Neil White, director of facilities planning, correctly observed, "We're not going to be building too many structures in the next ten years; we're going to be updating the ones we have to current standards."[115] His assessment was correct as only limited building occurred in the next decade.

An addition to UT Martin occurred in 1981 when the school became the home of West Tennessee's Public Broadcasting Service–affiliate television station, WLJT, Channel 11, with the opening of studios and offices on campus. Before this, the transmitter was located in Lexington, Tennessee. The station would eventually be headquartered in the old cafeteria, which was remodeled for the new campus addition. Nick Dunagan praised Darrell Rowlett, who was in charge of instructional television for the state Department of Education, for his assistance with the procurement of WLJT. Rowlett, a UT Martin alumnus, advised Charles Smith that the state was going to divest itself of the television station, and he mentioned that a group of citizens could form a public corporation and acquire the station. Rowlett assisted with writing a grant, the West Tennessee Public Broadcasting Council was formed, and the station, though not a part of the University, was located at UT Martin. Funded with private gifts along with state and federal assistance, Channel 11 has provided invaluable services through the years to the campus and West Tennessee.[116]

THE UNIVERSITY OF TENNESSEE AT MARTIN (1985–2000)

1993
UT Martin receives the Professional Grounds Management Society Grand Award.

1994
UT Martin is named the safest college campus and community in Tennessee.

The University of Tennessee celebrates its two hundredth birthday.

1995
The athletic teams receive a new nickname, "Skyhawks."

1996
A four-year engineering program is approved.

1997
A record enrollment of 6,012 is reached.

1998
Margaret Perry retires, and Nick Dunagan serves as interim chancellor until Philip W. Conn is selected as chancellor.

1999
Joe Johnson retires, and J. Wade Gilley is chosen as president of UT.

2000
UT Martin celebrates its one hundredth birthday.

Dr. Nick Dunagan, executive vice chancellor and vice chancellor for development and administration, served as chancellor on two occasions—from September 28, 1985 until June 30, 1986 and from February 1, 1998 until June 30, 1998.

During Smith's tenure the first chair of excellence was established at UT Martin. The other UT campuses also participated in this unique program. The primary goal of this endeavor was to attract the most notable professors to a campus. While serving as governor, Lamar Alexander had managed to get the "better schools" legislation passed, a program designed to improve the public school system in Tennessee. Representative John Bragg from Murfreesboro, aided by the other members of the general assembly, included the chairs of excellence program for Tennessee's publicly-assisted universities in the "better schools" legislation. Under this program, the state would put up $500,000 for each chair and the universities were to match that amount, creating $1 million endowed professorships. The challenge was that the institutions were required to raise the money for the matches from private gifts or other institutional sources, with at least $250,000 from private donations.

The $1 million for a chair, when invested, provided an adequate annual return to attract distinguished professors. Since the endowment was permanent, it was not threatened by economic conditions or other factors. President Ed Boling called the chairs of excellence "probably the single most important development in the history of the University."[117]

The initial chair of excellence on the Martin campus was the Tom Hendrix Chair of Excellence in Free Enterprise. Mr. and Mrs. Tom Hendrix from Selmer, Tennessee, provided $250,000, and the other $250,000 came from other UTM resources. The chair, which received legislative approval on March 7, 1985, was designed to enhance the economic education of UTM students and to allow more research into the free enterprise system. In addition, it provided for outreach work to improve the teaching of economics in elementary and secondary schools. Dr. Gary Young, currently dean of the School of Business Administration at UT Martin, was the chair holder from June 1985 until July 1987. He was succeeded by Dr. Jeff Ray Clark, Dr. Saul Barr, and currently Dr. John Bethune.

Two additional chairs of excellence were created at UT Martin in 1988. These were the Gilbert F. Parker Chair of Excellence in Food and Fiber Industries and the Horace and Sara Dunagan Chair of Excellence in Banking. The Parker chair was created as a legacy to Lake County farmer Gilbert Parker, who left a sizeable gift to the university upon his death in 1976. The Dunagan chair was developed from a $250,000 gift from the family of Horace Dunagan, a UTJC alumnus who later became a very successful banker. Banks in West Tennessee, Western Kentucky, and Southeast Missouri provided the other $250,000. Dr. Norman L. Betz was the initial holder of the Parker chair, a position he filled from January 1, 1990 until

December 31, 1994. He was followed by Dr. David Shoup. The Dunagan Chair was first occupied by Dr. L. Wayne Dobson, followed by Dr. Jim Tripp, and Dr. Thomas Payne.[118]

In September 1985, Smith transferred to Knoxville to become vice president for administration for the UT system. Smith's new position made him the liaison for UT with the state government, legislators, and the federal government. He would also be responsible for facilities planning and building programs. Smith, in his new position, was third in rank in the UT system under President Ed Boling and Joe Johnson, the executive vice president. Johnson, as the university's chief operating officer, had a myriad of responsibilities, and Smith's appointment was designed to alleviate some of the load on Johnson. As Smith departed for Knoxville, he assured the Martin campus that the school would have "a special friend in the office of the Vice President for Administration; someone who understands the strengths and needs of the campus; someone who believes in its unique role in the state's higher education system; and someone who cares deeply about its continued well-being."[119] Interestingly, Smith followed Porter Claxton, Archie Dykes, and Larry McGehee as former UT Martin chancellors who assumed new duties at Knoxville.

Smith later became commissioner of education for the state and then served as head of the board of regents until his retirement from that position in December 1999.

When Charles Smith transferred to Knoxville, Nick Dunagan was named acting chancellor, a position he filled very ably until June 30, 1986. A 1968 graduate of UT Martin, Dunagan received a law degree from the University of Missouri and later, in 1990, he earned a doctorate in higher education administration at Vanderbilt University. Following a one-year stint as a law clerk in the Missouri Supreme Court, he returned to Martin where he practiced law for one year. In 1973, he joined the UT Martin staff as director of development. He served in a variety of positions before being named executive vice chancellor and vice chancellor for development and administration in 1986. Knowledgeable in all facets of the university, he was an excellent choice to serve as interim chancellor during this period. Early on, he declared that he was not a candidate for the chancellorship but he stated he was willing to accept the responsibility until Smith's successor was chosen.[120]

Chancellor Margaret Perry served as chancellor from July 1, 1986 until January 31, 1998. Only Paul Meek had a longer tenure as chancellor.

After reviewing numerous applications, the search committee recommended that Dr. Margaret N. Perry be appointed as chancellor. She assumed her duties on July 1, 1986, becoming the first woman chief administrator of a four-year public college in Tennessee and the first UTM graduate to serve as chancellor. A native of Waynesboro, she received her undergraduate degree from UT Martin in dietetics in 1961. She earned her master's and doctoral degrees from the University of Tennessee, Knoxville, and later became associate dean of the College of Home Economics at UTK. From 1973 to 1979, she served as dean for graduate studies at Knoxville. In 1979, Perry joined the staff at Tennessee Tech where she was associate vice president for academic affairs until her appointment at UT Martin. UT President Edward J. Boling cited her credentials as "an impressive mix of academic and administrative skills."[121]

As a UT Martin graduate, Dr. Perry understood the mission of the school. Possessing common sense, a friendly and outgoing demeanor, a strong work ethic, a willingness to listen, and a solid background in higher education, she served as a very capable leader at UT Martin for nearly twelve years. She served under three presidents—Ed Boling, Lamar Alexander, and Joe Johnson—and only Paul Meek enjoyed a longer tenure as chancellor at UT Martin. A staff member recalls, "It was a pleasure to work for Chancellor Perry. Often times in meetings we looked at solutions for various issues. She would carefully listen, and then would bring up points which we had overlooked or had not even considered. She did not necessarily 'think in the box.'" Others offered similar opinions.[122] Her husband, Dr. Randy Perry, joined the UT Martin staff as dean of engineering technology and engineering. Their two sons, Paul and Sam, also became familiar campus figures.

A primary concern for Chancellor Perry was the enrollment, which had declined in the mid-1980s. Under her leadership, the enrollment rebounded to

Standing before the Alliene and Jimmy Corbitt Room in the Paul Meek Library are left to right: Joel Stowers, director of the library; Col. Jimmy Corbitt; and Dieter Ullrich, special collections librarian/archivist. Corbitt taught at UTJC during the early 1930s, and he has provided the school with a significant endowment to secure genealogical and other historical materials.

a record 6,012 in 1997. During this time, admission standards, ACT scores, and grade point averages for beginning freshmen steadily advanced. In addition, graduation rates moved to the top tier in the state, and available scholarships tripled. The legacy of high rates of acceptance into graduate and professional schools continued, and an academic pinnacle was reached in 1996 when all programs capable of being accredited were accredited.

During Perry's administration, four-year degree programs in nursing, the fine and performing arts, and engineering were added. A degree in engineering technology had been implemented in 1970, but the demand for a degree in engineering continued. In fact, several sources had advocated a four-year program in engineering for years, but to no avail. A two-year engineering program had been formally added in 1944, but many thought a degree in engineering at UT Martin was an area necessity. With a calm demeanor which belied a strong determination, Perry left no stone unturned, and her persistence was rewarded when a four-year engineering program was approved in 1996.

Under Chancellor Perry's leadership, the master of business administration and master of accounting degrees were reactivated and became highly successful. In addition, UT Martin became the first UT campus to offer classes via interactive television.[123]

Another highlight occurred when UT Martin, nationally registered as a botanical garden, received the 1993 Professional Grounds Management Society Grand Award for maintenance of the campus grounds.[124] Guy Robbins, the person in charge of the campus grounds at the time, deserves much of the credit for this prestigious award. Additional accolades followed in 1994 when UT Martin was named the safest college campus and community in Tennessee and the sixth safest in the nation by the book *Crime on Campus: The Personal Guide to Student Safety*.[125]

Other campus highlights included the gutting, expansion, and modernization of the Paul Meek Library and the installation of fiber optic cables to every major building on campus, thus becoming the first public institution in Tennessee to completely connect the entire campus for technology. Crisp Hall, formerly the ag engineering building, was renovated in 1991; all steam lines were replaced; the heating systems were converted from coal to steam; plans were completed to expand Boling University Center; and plans to renovate Brehm Hall were initiated.[126]

The Children's Center, a model child care facility, was completed in 1993, and was later named in honor of Dr. Perry. She and Paul Meek are the only two UT Martin chancellors to have buildings named for them. Another addition, the Equine Center, was opened in 1994, giving the rodeo team an excellent practice facility.

Another notable achievement, and one that was dear to Margaret Perry's heart, was Project Success. This was a program designed to help single parents on welfare earn a degree. Some heartwarming stories can be told about the successes of the participants in this unique endeavor.

The quiet determination of Chancellor Perry was evident when UT Martin sought admission into the Ohio Valley Conference, an NCAA Division I league. UT Martin had competed against schools in the OVC through the years, and those knowledgeable about athletics thought UTM should be a member. For over twenty years efforts had been made to gain admission, but with no success. With an "All for One" slogan, dedicated workers, and a well conceived plan of action, a basketball attendance figure of 22,000 and other requirements were reached. Division I status was achieved, and membership in the OVC followed in 1992.[127]

The athletic teams also had a new nickname, the Skyhawks, when the 1995 fall semester opened. Replacing the nickname the Pacers, the word "Skyhawk" came partly from the historical linkage with Hall-Moody Institute, whose athletic teams were called the Sky Pilots. Also, pilots were trained at UTJC during World War II. The hawk was selected because it is indigenous to West Tennessee.[128]

During this period, a new softball field was constructed. It would later be named in honor of Bettye Giles, the pioneer in women's sports at UT Martin. Also, football, tennis, track, and baseball facilities were improved.[129]

A significant challenge to Chancellor Perry was a threat by the National Council for Accreditation of Teacher Education (NCATE) not to accredit the longstanding education program at UT Martin. NCATE standards had been changed, and UTM had an accreditation visit the year after the standards changed. The visiting team was prepared to recommend a "not accredited" to the education program, and some of Perry's staff recommended that the decision not be challenged. "It's just not right, and we're going to fight it," Perry retorted. A trip to Washington followed in January 1992. Chancellor Perry; Gary Rush, the dean of education; Bob Smith, the dean of arts and sciences; and Homer Fisher, senior vice president from Knoxville appeared before the NCATE board to appeal the decision. Perry presented facts not considered by the visiting committee, and the decision was reversed. Perry's tenacity again was the deciding factor.[130]

Perhaps one of Chancellor Perry's toughest challenges was related to ROTC. Enrollment during a crucial time had declined, and the Army was preparing to dismantle several programs throughout the country in 1996. UT Martin was one of the schools targeted to lose its ROTC program, and Perry decided to battle the decision. Following special efforts from ROTC alumni and congressional representatives, Chancellor Perry, Nick Dunagan, and Ben Kimbrough from Clarksville journeyed to Washington to talk with Sara Lister, assistant secretary of the Army for manpower and reserve affairs. Kimbrough, Tennessee's civilian liaison with the United States Army, was a key figure in arranging the appointment.

"The first fifteen minutes or so consisted of a formal discussion with Chancellor Perry explaining why UT Martin should retain its ROTC program," Dunagan recalled. "Shortly afterwards, Perry and Lister established

excellent rapport when it was discovered that both had been reared on farms. We left the meeting feeling good, but it was not until several days later that we were informed that our ROTC program would remain intact."[131] Once again, Perry's determination yielded favorable results.

Two other campus figures who played vital roles in the battle to save the ROTC program were Lt. Col. Bill Duffy and Dr. Ted Mosch. Duffy, in command of the program at Martin, worked tirelessly to increase the enrollment. Mosch, a highly respected political science professor and a retired colonel in the United States Army Reserve, was chairman of the military science committee on campus. He made numerous calls to politicians, ROTC alumni, and others for support.[132]

During Perry's administration, WestStar, a leadership training program for selected citizens in West Tennessee, was started. The three key figures in the development of the innovative program, started in 1989, were Nick Dunagan, executive vice chancellor; Cathy Holland, a UT Martin graduate who was then employed by the Tennessee Department of Economic and Community Development; and Dr. Bob Smith, UT Martin dean of arts and sciences at the time. The ECD had identified area leadership development as a priority, and Smith agreed to head the new program. During the next decade, mayors, county executives, city/county commissioners, state officials, and volunteer leaders were among the 260 graduates who received leadership training

Directed by Kevin Lambert, the New Pacer Singers are popular ambassadors for the campus, performing at alumni functions and other events throughout the United States.

through WestStar. In 1999, Bob Smith became provost/vice president for Academic Affairs at Slippery Rock University in Slippery Rock, Pennsylvania, and Nick Dunagan accepted primary responsibility for the program, which has been lauded for its success in leadership training.[133]

Early in Perry's administration, several systemwide events occurred. The University of Tennessee National Alumni Association (UTNAA) celebrated its 150th birthday in 1986; Ed Boling retired as president, and Lamar Alexander was selected as UT's eighteenth president in 1988; and Joe Johnson was appointed to the presidency in 1991.

"Run all the way across Tennessee? You've got to be kidding!" was a common reaction when David M. Roberts, associate vice president for alumni affairs and annual giving for the UT system, announced plans for a torch run in the fall of 1986 to transverse the state. The trek was to commemorate the 150th anniversary of the University of Tennessee National Alumni Association, and the torch represented the symbolic torch of learning, a familiar emblem of UT. Ignoring the skeptics, Roberts and his staff, joined by about six hundred alumni, implemented a very successful and fun-filled journey which passed through some eighty towns and cities. Alumni chapter meetings were held in counties along the way to celebrate the 150th anniversary. Volunteer torch bearers joined the caravan at each county line for a run of a mile or more. Facing bitterly cold weather during much of the route, the runners arrived at Martin in time to participate in the homecoming parade on November 1. Appropriately, the theme for UTM's homecoming was "Torch the Gamecocks"—Jacksonville State University was the football opponent. On each UT campus a structure was erected to hold a permanently lighted torch in celebration of the 150th anniversary. The perpetual flame at Martin was originally located in front of Paul Meek Library, but it is temporarily dismantled at the present due to construction.[134]

Dr. Boling was held in high esteem on the Martin campus, and following his retirement, the university center was named the Ed and Carolyn Boling University Center. Boling joined two earlier presidents who had buildings named for them—C. E. Brehm Hall, formerly the agriculture-biology-library building, and the Andy Holt Humanities Building. The engineering and physical sciences building would be named in 1999 in honor of Dr. Joe Johnson.

On July 1, 1988, Lamar Alexander, former governor of Tennessee took office as the eighteenth president of the University of Tennessee. He replaced Ed Boling who retired after eighteen years at the helm of the University. Joe Johnson, executive vice president of UT and a person greatly admired by his colleagues and alumni alike, was the choice of many, but the board of trustees broke with tradition and selected Alexander. Past presidents H. A. Morgan, James D. Hoskins, C. E. Brehm, Andy Holt, and Ed Boling had all been employed by the university prior to being elevated to the top position. One had to go all the way back to 1904, when Brown Ayres was selected, to find an "outsider" who became president. This system of promoting from within had provided excellent presidential leadership, and many were dismayed that it was

discontinued. Fortunately, Johnson remained as executive vice president, and he continued to make invaluable contributions during Alexander's tenure.[135]

Alexander, the first Tennessee governor to serve consecutive four-year terms, had proven to be a strong advocate for education. His parents had been teachers in Maryville, and, as governor, he introduced a master teachers program and a better schools program to improve public education. For higher education, Alexander promoted a system of centers of excellence and chairs of excellence to enhance research and public service at the state's public universities.[136]

The lure of politics captivated Alexander again, and he resigned from the UT presidency in 1991 to become United States secretary of education under President George Bush. After Bush's defeat by Bill Clinton in 1992, Alexander returned to the private sector; however, in 1995 and again in 1999, he unsuccessfully sought the Republican nomination for President.[137]

Following Alexander's resignation from UT in 1991, the board of trustees named Joe Johnson as the nineteenth president. The news of Johnson's appointment brought enthusiastic acclaim from UT alumni and others who had become acquainted with him during this many years of dedicated service to the UT campuses.

Rope pull is a challenging and much anticipated event during the week of Homecoming.

A native of Vernon, Alabama—he jokingly says he is from L. A. (Lower Alabama)—and a Phi Beta Kappa graduate from Birmingham Southern College, Johnson earned a master's degree at UT Knoxville in 1958 and a doctorate in 1968. After a three-year stint in Nashville as deputy commissioner of finance and administration during the administration of Governor Buford Ellington, he joined Andy Holt's staff in 1963 as his executive assistant. He later served as chancellor at UT Memphis, vice president for institutional research, vice president for finance, vice president for development, and executive vice president and vice president for development. During his tenure as president, Johnson and his wife, Pat, were frequent visitors to UT Martin, and the campus proudly remembers that he was at UT Martin on June 30, 1999, his last day in office before retirement.[138]

During this interval of leadership change, in the fall of 1988, UT Martin switched from the quarter system to the semester system.[139] As some students commented, "At least now we only have to register for classes twice instead of three times each year."

Also, excitement rippled across the campus in the fall of 1988. After eleven years without a winning record, the football team posted a 11–2 slate. The Pacers won a share of the school's first ever Gulf South Conference football championship, and then advanced to the NCAA Division II playoffs. In the opening game, Butler University fell to UT Martin, 23–6, on a rainy, chilly day in Martin. The next week, the team journeyed to Kingsville, Texas, to play Texas A & I and were defeated 34–0. A grand season had come to a close, but the players, coaches, and fans could view the 1988 accomplishments with pride. Individual accolades followed. Don McLeary was selected Gulf South Conference coach of the year, quarterback Leon Reed was named offensive player of the year in the Gulf South Conference, and tackle Emanuel McNeil was honored as defensive player of the year. McNeil was also picked as national defensive player of the year by *Football News and Gazette*. Receiver William Mackall and offensive lineman Grady Andrews joined Reed and McNeil for All-America honors.[140] Unfortunately, winning records in future years proved to be elusive. Following the stellar 1988 season, a 6–5 mark in 1993 was the only winning season to be recorded in over a decade.

The 1990s began on a somber note when the United States, as in earlier decades, became involved in a foreign conflict. When Iraq, which had invaded neighboring Kuwait, refused to withdraw, forces from the United States and its allies went to the rescue of the tiny nation. Operation Desert Storm commenced in January 1991, and Iraq was defeated by the end of February. The war was short and decisive, and most Americans viewed much of the action via television. New and more sophisticated weapons were also evident during the broadcasts. During the conflict, a campus poll showed that UTM students supported President George Bush's decision to attack Iraq by almost five to one.[141] Several UTM students were called to active duty during the crisis, and faculty members made every effort to assist them as their studies were temporarily shelved.[142]

At first the coeds participated in tug-of-war contests, but now, like the men, they have a rope pull competition.

In 1994, UT Martin joined the other UT campuses to celebrate the two hundredth birthday of the University of Tennessee which traced its roots back to the founding of Blount College in 1794. Gala events were held on each campus as people across the state participated in the bicentennial celebration.

A political first was achieved in the 1990s when Dr. Richard Chesteen, professor of political science, sought the 1994 Democratic nomination for governor. No other faculty or staff member had vied for the governorship until this time. With the backing of a student group, the Campus Dreamers, Chesteen plunged into the fray with

The Alpha Phi Omegas at All Sing in 1995.

enthusiasm, but victory eluded him.[143] Two UTJC alumni, Ed Jones and Ray Blanton, did achieve the pinnacles of political success. Ed Jones served in the United States House of Representatives from 1969 until 1989, and his papers are housed in the Ed Jones Room in the Paul Meek Library. Blanton served three terms in the United States House of Representatives (1967–1973) and one term as governor of Tennessee (1975–79). Other alumni have achieved notable success in the political arena on the state and local levels.[144]

The 1990s also saw UT Martin alumni for the first time achieve the rank of general while serving on active duty with the United States military forces. Robert C. Hinson, a member of the United States Air Force and a 1970 UT Martin graduate, was elevated to brigadier general in 1995. Dennis Cavin, a 1969 graduate, was also promoted to brigadier general in the United States Army in 1995. Both Hinson and Cavin currently hold the rank of major general. John Gladwyn "Glad" Castellaw, a 1972 graduate, is a brigadier general in the United States Marine Corps.[145]

The 1990s proved to be an especially tragic decade for the campus as a large number of faculty members died while still employed by the university. Among this group of outstanding educators were Norvel Cook, Charles Gillon, Wilson Hall, Ted James, Fereshtel Mahootchi, John Mathesen, Elizabeth Pentecost, Carl Seale, and Robert L. Todd. The 1980s had also witnessed the untimely loss of some key educators who were still on active duty—Jack Beeler, David Briody, Ross Elder, Walter Gorman, Carol McElvain, and Earnest Rezabek.[146]

Tragedy cast its gloomy shadow over the campus once more when Julian Nunamaker, an All-America football player at UT Martin in the late 1960s and later a professional player with the Buffalo Bills, died in February 1995 from injuries suffered in a car accident. Noted for his funloving attitude and warm personality as well as his athletic abilities, Nunamaker was memorialized by his friends and former teammates when an endowed football scholarship bearing his name was established at UT Martin.[147]

In 1996, Rob Harbison became only the second athlete in UT Martin history to compete in the Olympics. A former member of the rifle team and an officer in the United States Army at the time, he shot his way to a sixth place finish in the 1996 games in Atlanta. A 1988 graduate, he joined Pat Head Summitt as the only two UTM Olympians. Earlier, Harbison had served as a tank platoon leader in Operation Desert Storm.[148]

For the first time in the history of the school, a dormitory fire claimed the life of a student. On January 11, 1997, Jong-do Ki, or "Ben" as his friends called him, died from smoke inhalation during a blaze in Ellington Hall. Three other students in the dorm and two UTM police officers were hospitalized following the fire. Jong-do Ki was a twenty-three-year-old Intensive English student from Kwang-ju, South Korea, and the campus mourned the loss of this quiet and very pleasant young man.[149]

Liesel Davis, whose father Phil is a professor of chemistry at UT Martin, became the youngest UT Martin student to earn a master's degree. She received her master's in business administration on May 11, 1996 at the age of nineteen. She had completed her bachelor's degree in accounting a year earlier.[150]

Another first was set when Ola Kizer received a degree in human environmental sciences in December 1999 at the age of eighty-six. She became the oldest person to earn a degree from any UT campus.[151] Until this date, Edith May, who received her degree in 1990 at the age of seventy-three, was the oldest student to graduate from UT Martin.[152]

At the annual fall faculty meeting in August 1997, Margaret Perry announced that she planned to retire on January 31, 1998. She had provided excellent leadership since becoming chancellor in 1986, and she observed, "We've reached every goal we set ten years ago when we had our campuswide planning sessions, and I believe the time is right to bring in new leadership . . . ." She also acknowledged a strong desire to spend more time with her family.[153] The unanimous campus consensus was that she was leaving some gigantic shoes to fill.

Jim Byford, dean of the School of Agriculture and Human Environment at UT Martin, is the author of **Close to the Land,** *a book which shows the importance of reconnecting to the land. He typifies other faculty members who have authored books relating to their disciplines and interests.*

President Joe Johnson, who expressed strong admiration for Perry's leadership, quickly formed a search advisory committee. Nick Dunagan was tapped as interim chancellor, and he, as he had done previously, declared that he did not wish to be a candidate for the vacancy. After interviewing the top candidates, Dr. Philip W. Conn was recommended by the committee to Johnson and the board of trustees, and he assumed his new duties on July 1, 1998.

Prior to accepting the chancellorship at UT Martin, Conn was president and professor of business at Dickinson State University in Dickinson, North Dakota. His previous positions included vice president for university advancement and associate professor of management at Central Missouri State University, 1985–1994; vice president for university and regional services, associate professor of sociology, and vice president for research and development at Morehead (Ky.) State University, 1977–84; and director of alumni affairs, editor of the *Berea Alumnus*, and placement director at Berea College, (1968–70). During the mid-1970s, Conn was executive director of the Kentucky Legislative Research Commission.

Phil and Donna Conn in August 1998 during a meeting of West Tennessee mayors and county executives at the residence of former governor Ned R. McWherter in Dresden.

Conn earned a bachelor's degree in biology from Berea College in 1963;

a diploma in social policy from the Institute of Social Studies, The Hague, Netherlands, as a Rotary International Fellow; a master's degree in sociology from UT Knoxville; and a master's degree and a doctorate in public administration from the University of Southern California. President Johnson cited Conn's training and background as major factors in his selection as chancellor, and he observed, "Following Margaret Perry will be a challenge, but I think Phil and Donna will do it."[154]

Tragedy struck the Conn family in November 1998 when Donna succumbed to cancer after a lengthy battle with the disease. Her warm and engaging personality had endeared her to the campus and community within the few months she had been in Martin. President Johnson expressed the feelings of the university and the community when he said, "She was a grand lady who will be deeply missed. The entire University of Tennessee family shares in this great loss." This remarkable lady, who accomplished a legacy of praiseworthy deeds within her short lifetime, left behind her husband and four children–Chad, Cason, Cyndi, and Christy. Cason, shortly afterwards, went to the Albania-Kosovo area as an

Apache helicopter pilot with the American peacekeeping forces, and the campus shared the anxiety of the Conn family during this interval.[155]

During Chancellor Conn's tenure, he has sought to enhance the natural beauty of the campus with some outdoor sculptures and other accouterments. The area between the university center and the Paul Meek Library has been terraced and flower beds prepared. Also, plans for a bell tower in this area, dubbed the "Centennial Circle" to coincide with UT Martin's one hundredth birthday, have been prepared. In addition, he received a special grant to improve the appearance of the adjacent UT Agricultural Research Facility. A white fence which borders University Street and extends behind the chancellor's residence has been erected.

Conn also has promoted a concept whereby high school students can enroll simultaneously in a course that, for example, satisfies their high school senior English course and their college freshman English course. In the fall of 1999, nearly two hundred honor students enrolled in this program, another innovative example of how UT Martin seeks to meet the needs of West Tennessee students.

In addition, the office of extended campus and continuing education, under the direction of Bill Duffy, has been located in Jackson. Again, this is an effort to serve the West Tennessee area better. Another source of pride is that UT Martin's four-year engineering program, implemented during Margaret Perry's tenure, is now fully accredited.

Chancellor Conn is also very concerned with what he terms "the total collegiate experience." His desire is that students have an enjoyable campus life, and emphasis is being placed on intramural sports, student forums, concerts, and other enriching experiences. It is hoped that students will gain social, organizational, and communication skills from these activities to go along with their academic pursuits.[156]

The athletics program has also been under scrutiny during Conn's tenure. A commission of faculty and staff members, students, alumni, and local citizens completed a study of the total program in 1999, and it is hoped that their recommendations will revitalize athletics at UT Martin. Phil Dane, vice chancellor for business and finance, will become director of athletics in June 2000, when Benny Hollis retires.[157]

A lack of adequate state funding and an enrollment decline are among the challenges which confront Conn. Also, a new era of leadership at the UT system level is bringing additional changes. UT Martin, like colleges across the nation, must constantly evaluate and update its programs to meet the needs of an increasingly complex society.

Another leadership change occurred when Joe Johnson retired on July 30, 1999, and was replaced by Dr. Wade Gilley. Plaudits poured in when Johnson announced his retirement. UT Martin had always considered him to be vitally interested in the school, and he verified this when he stated, "The Martin campus and the Martin area have a special place in my heart. The Martin

Pictured on August 21, 1999, at the ceremony in which the Engineering-Physical Sciences Building was named for Joe Johnson are (left to right) Pat Johnson, Joe Johnson, Phil Conn, Board of Trustees member Jerry Jackson, Margaret Perry, and Board of Trustees member Barbara Castleman.

campus is a unique campus. It does a truly unusually fine job for the young people of Northwest Tennessee and other parts of the state."[158] To show appreciation to Joe and Pat Johnson for their many years of outstanding service, UT Martin honored them on August 21, 1999. The engineering-physical sciences building, as noted earlier, was named in honor of Dr. Johnson; a special sculpture was placed in the Paul Meek Library in honor of Pat Johnson; and an appreciation dinner, with an outpouring of friends, was held that night. Chancellor Conn, who served as master of ceremonies at the dinner, remarked, "The contributions made by Joe Johnson to the University of Tennessee during more than forty years of service are amazing. We at UTM are particularly appreciative of the special interest and commitment he has expressed toward our institution. We know that Joe Johnson admires UTM, and clearly the admiration of him across this campus is strong."[159]

Dr. J. Wade Gilley, with an impressive array of academic credentials and experience, assumed his duties as president of the University of Tennessee on August 1, 1999. He became the twentieth person to occupy the presidential chair in the 205-year storied history of UT. Prior to accepting this position, he had served as president of Marshall University in Huntington, West Virginia, since 1991. Earlier assignments included the presidency of Bluefield State

College in West Virginia; secretary of education in Virginia from 1978 until 1982; and senior vice president at George Mason University in Fairfax, Virginia.

Gilley earned his bachelor's, master's, and Ph.D. degrees from Virginia Tech. He also did postdoctoral work at the University of Florida and the Harvard Graduate School of Business.[160]

During his first few months as president, Gilley has outlined plans for the reorganization of the University of Tennessee campuses. At this date, the proposal is being studied by the board of trustees for final approval. The effect of the plan on UT Martin is not yet evident; however, future changes appear to be likely.

As UT Martin celebrates its one hundredth birthday in 2000, the founding fathers undoubtedly would beam with pride at the growth of the school from a fledgling one-building institution to a bustling primary campus of the University of Tennessee system with over 26,000 living alumni. Today, UT Martin's land, buildings, and equipment have a value of over $154 million. This includes the 250-acre campus, a 680-acre experiment farm, forty-four academic and support buildings, six dormitories, and 256 apartments for married students. A backward glance over one hundred years reveals tremendous change and progress, but the goal to be an exemplary educational institution has remained constant. In 1900, when Hall-Moody was established, the founding fathers had a premier education for the area's young people as the primary objective. Challenges awaited them at every turn, but they continued to press forward. When the school became a part of the UT system, the primary objective remained the same, and challenges—the Great Depression, World War II, the influx of the "baby boomer," etc.—awaited once more. Again, they were met, and this undaunted spirit continues to hover over the campus as UT Martin begins a new century in an ever-changing and fast-moving world.

Notes

PART I: A HISTORY OF HALL-MOODY (1900-1927)

1. Actual count from 1900 census roll. A copy is located in the Tennessee Room, Paul Meek Library, UT Martin.

2. *Tennessee Code Annotated* 13, Tables Volume, 1014–15.

3. "Weakley Education," *Weakley County Press, Centennial Edition* (28 June 1973): 71.

4. "General History," *Last Leaf, 1900–27,* (Martin, 1927) Hall-Moody Junior College: 7, 9.

5. *Minutes* of the Forty-seventh Annual Session of the Beulah Baptist Association held with the Martin Baptist Church on October 2, 1900, 5.

6. *Hall-Moody School Journal* 5 (Martin: Hall-Moody Institute July 1909): 12.

7. Ibid., 14.

8. *Last Leaf*, 7.

9. Neil Graves, *A Picture History of Hall-Moody*, (The University of Tennessee National Alumni Association and The University of Tennessee at Martin, 1975); 5.

10. Ibid., 3. See also Sanborn map, 1907. Sanborn maps are published by Sanborn Fire Insurance Company in Chicago, Ill., and were provided by N. B. Williams, fire chief for the city of Martin.

11. *Call* (Nashville: Benson Printing Company, 1921): 78. See also *Last Leaf,* 32, 34; and *Hall-Moody School Journal* (1909): 34.

12. *Last Leaf*, 14.

13. Ibid., 16.

14. Sanborn map, March 1927.

15. William Hall Preston, "A Description of Hall-Moody Junior College," William Hall Preston Papers, 1927, 1–3.

16. *Last Leaf,* 9.

17. Ibid., 31.

18. "Hall-Moody Institute v. Copass," *Reports of Cases Argued and Determined in the Supreme Court of Tennessee* (The Supreme Court of Tennessee, Nashville, Tenn.: Marshall & Bruce Co., 1903, photocopy); 595. A delightful account of this case, written by Louise Davis, appeared in the *Nashville Tennessean Magazine*, 15 May 1966. Her story primarily focused on Copass, and the author, while admiring the work of Davis, also examines the aftermath of the case.

19. Ibid., 604–5.

20. Ibid., 597–99.

21. Ibid., 599.

22. Ibid., 582–83.

23. Ibid., 608.

24. Ibid.

25. Ibid., 597.

26. Ibid., 603.

27. Ibid., 594.

28. Ibid., 595.

29. Ibid., 592.

30. Ibid., 593.

31. Ibid., 592–93.

32. Ibid., 585–88, 591–92.

33. Ibid., 609.

34. T. H. Farmer, "A History of the First Baptist Church and Hall-Moody Institute, 1912," 3–4.

35. *Last Leaf*, 19.

36. Elmer B. Inman, "A History of the Development of the University of Tennessee, Martin Branch," (Ph.D. diss., The University of Tennessee, 1960); 18–20.

37. *Hall-Moody School Journal (1901–02)* 1 (Martin: 1901) Hall-Moody Institute: 7–9.

38. *Hall-Moody School Journal (1909)*: 19.

39. Inman, "History," 35–36.

40. *Last Leaf*, 34.

41. Ibid.

42. *Call*, 122.

43. *Hall-Moody School Journal (1909)*: 5.

44. *Last Leaf*, 9.

45. Ibid., 12.

46. James Riley Montgomery, *The Volunteer State Forges Its University: The University of Tennessee, 1887–1919* (Knoxville, 1966), 146–64.

47. Inman, "History," 22–23.

48. *Hall-Moody School Journal (1909)*: 30.

49. Inman, "History," 24.

50. *Hall-Moody School Journal (1909)*: 31.

51. Ibid., 30.

52. Ibid., 31

53. Graves, "Picture History," 6.

54. Inman, "History," 24–25.

55. Ibid., 25–26.

56. Graves, "Picture History," 18.

57. *Hall-Moody School Journal (l90l–02)*: 15.

58. Inman, "History," 13.

59. *Hall-Moody School Journal (l90l–02)*: 15.

60. Hollis Kinsey, interviewed by the author, Tupelo, Miss., 12 February 1998. Kinsey attended Hall-Moody in 1926–27 and UTJC in 1927–28. He and H. Kirk Grantham operated a Pepsi-Cola plant in Tupelo for many years. Kinsey died on November 20, 1999, at the age of ninety-three.

61. Inman, "History," 38.

62. *Hall-Moody School Journal (1909)*: 16.

63. Ibid., 8.

64. Ibid., 12.

65. *Hall-Moody School Journal (1909)*: 9–10.

66. *Last Leaf*, 27–28.

67. Van Morgan to Chancellor Margaret N. Perry, 5 July 1995. Morgan, a Hall-Moody alumnus, later served at UTJC as an assistant coach under H. Kirk Grantham. He grew up near the campus, and he has many vivid memories of the school during its early years. He currently resides in Paducah, Kentucky.

68. *Hall-Moody School Journal (1909)*: 14.

69. Virginia Vaughan, *People and Places of Downtown Martin* (Paducah, Ky.: Turner Publishing Co., 1997), 27–29.

70. Clarence Kolwyck to Neil Graves, 20 November 1975. A Hall-Moody alumnus, Kolwyck became a prominent attorney in Chattanooga.

71. *Hall-Moody School Journal (l909)*: 14.

72. Inman, "History," 26.

73. Ibid., 27.

74. Ibid., 27–33.

75. *Last Leaf*, 12.

76. Inman, "History," 29.

77. Ibid., 33–36.

78. *Last Leaf*, 15.

79. Ibid., 14.

80. Ibid., 15.

81. Paul Meek to Dr. Andrew D. Holt, 9 February 1968. This letter followed the designation of the administration building as the Hall-Moody Administration Building by the board of trustees.

82. Inman, "History," 36–37.

83. *Call*, 113.

84. *Last Leaf*, 38.

85. *Call*, 23.

86. *Last Leaf*, 38.

87. *Call*, 103–17.

88. Kolwyck letter.

89. *Last Leaf*, 42.

90. Ibid., 16.

91. Ibid., 42.

92. Ibid., 42, 87–91.

93. Ibid., 16.

94. Ibid., 16–17.

95. Ibid., 94.

96. Ibid., 80.

97. Ibid., 17.

98. Neal O'Steen, *Tennessee Partners* (Knoxville: The University of Tennessee National Alumni Association, 1986), 282.

99. *Last Leaf*, 66–67.

100. Ibid., 2.

101. Ibid., 18.

102. Ibid., 99.

103. Ibid., 96.

PART II: UNIVERSITY OF TENNESSEE JUNIOR COLLEGE (1927-1951)

1. James Riley Montgomery, *Threshold of a New Day: The University of Tennessee, 1919–1946* (Knoxville, 1971), 215.

2. *Public Acts of Tennessee*, 65th General Assembly, 1927, Senate Bill 301, section 9, 28–29.

3. Montgomery, "Threshold," 215.

4. "Transition of the Hall-Moody College to the University of Tennessee Martin Branch," *Volette* (24 May 1955): 2.

5. Mary F. Fuqua (Foster Y. Fuqua's daughter), interview by the author. Also Mary F. Fuqua to author, 30 January 1999.

6. Montgomery, "Threshold," 216.

7. Ibid.

8. *Private Acts of Tennessee,* 65th General Assembly, 1927, Senate Bill 385, section 172, 172.

9. *Private Acts of Tennessee,* 65th General Assembly, 1927, Senate Bill 575, section 247, 247.

10. *Public Acts of Tennessee*, 65th General Assembly, 1927, Senate Bill 301, section 9, 28–29.

11. Inman, "History," 50. In addition, see Montgomery, "Threshold," 229. Also, George Horton in his papers states that he, J. E. McMahan, Myrtle Phillips, and M. P. Bowman were present for this occasion on 17 November 1944. In 1946, M. P. Bowman accepted a position as dean of admissions and registrar at Austin Peay. The Horton papers are on file in the Paul Meek Library.

12. "Honor Roll of American Public Schools," *Look* (1 October 1946): 40.

13. Montgomery, "Threshold," 216.

14. Inman, "History," 48.

15. Holland McCombs talked about Woodley Farm in his presentation during the sixtieth birthday celebration in 1987. Earlier, in 1986, he donated $100,000 to renovate the home economics building.

16. George Horton, "The Transition: The Last Years of Hall-Moody Junior College and the Opening of U. T. Junior College," The *Tennessee Spirit* 1:3 (October 1969): 7. See also: Roy L. Lamb to President H. A. Morgan; Porter Claxton to R. V. Richardson; Morgan to Lamb, Claxton Papers.

17. Montgomery, "Threshold," 221.

18. Inman, "History," 64.

19. Montgomery, "Threshold," 221.

20. Ibid., 218.

21. Ibid.

22. Ibid., 229.

23. Horton papers, Paul Meek Library, University of Tennessee at Martin, 33. Enrollment data furnished by the office of admissions and records. Since faculty members were added during the academic year and one resigned, the exact number for much of the year totaled fifteen, excluding Bob Wilkins, the custodian.

24. Claxton papers, Paul Meek Library, University of Tennessee at Martin.

25. Clayton papers. Correspondence with Willson and A. W. Hobt, head of physical education at Knoxville, clearly demonstrates Claxton's lack of authority in selecting teachers.

26. Montgomery, "Threshold," 218.

27. Claxton to Hobt, 7 May 1932. Claxton papers.

28. Ibid. Hobt sent a letter to Claxton on 21 April 1932 in which he criticized Evelyn Mabry. Claxton, in an impartial manner, defended her work. Though he and Mabry would marry in 1934, Claxton was very objective in his evaluation of her job performance.

29. E. C. Pritchett, Frank Taylor, and other former students, interview by the author, n.d.

30. Keffer to Claxton, 3 August 1929, Claxton papers. See also Claxton to Keffer, 5 August 1929, Claxton papers.

31. Willson to Morgan, 21 October 1931, Claxton papers.

32. UT Junior College budget as revised on August 6, 1927.

33. Montgomery, "Threshold," 219.

34. Gene H. Stanford, *The Stanford Story Regarding Thomas William Stanford of Pennsylvania and His Descendants* (Lexington, Tenn.: Gene Stanford, 1992), 45. Through research, Stanford traces the roots of his ancestors in this delightful work.

35. UT Junior College budget for 1927–28.

36. Claxton to Willson, 31 December 1931, Claxton papers.

37. *Last Leaf*, 95.

38. Dan Kroll, "Beloved Bob Wilkins is Senior on Faculty," *Volette* (11 March 1947): 2.

39. Rowlett to Brehm, n.d. Meek papers. See also Brehm to Meek, 12 September 1947; Meek to Brehm, 17 September 1947; Brehm to Meek, 22 September 1947, Meek papers.

40. Claxton to W. K. Wells, 13 February 1930, Claxton papers.

41. Willson to Dean F. M. Massey, Knoxville, Tenn., 8 November 1930. A clipping from the *Weakley County Press* concerning the incident is attached to the letter. Claxton papers.

42. Unsigned letter, 19 November 1928 from the railroad is in the Claxton papers, along with the names given to the railroad official. The author has talked with some of the "riders," one of whom was E. C. Pritchett, his father-in-law.

43. Claxton to Massey, 11 October 1927, Claxton papers.

44. Duncan to Morgan, 2 April 1932, Claxton papers. See also Willson to Duncan, 13 April 1932, Claxton papers.

45. Willson to Claxton, 13 December 1933, Claxton papers.

46. Harrison interview by the author, July 1994.

47. Hillis interview by the author, February 1999. "Miss Flossie," as she was known, was a favorite of the students, and she and her husband, Russell, later became leaders in the UTJC reunions.

48. Claxton to Willson, 8 February 1934, Claxton papers. See also Willson to Claxton, 9 February 1934; Willson to Claxton, 10 February 1934, Claxton papers.

49. Willson to Claxton, 15 February 1934, Claxton papers.

50. Willson to Morgan, 21 October 1931, Claxton papers.

51. Montgomery, "Threshold," 219.

52. Ibid., 220.

53. Ibid.

54. Some sources cite eighty-five as the enrollment; however, the fall quarter enrollment was ninety-two, and it probably dropped during the academic year.

55. Montgomery, "Threshold," 220.

56. Ibid.

57. *Minutes*, The University of Tennessee Board of Trustees' Committee on the junior college, 21 February 1934.

58. Ibid.

59. Ibid.

60. The Claxton papers.

61. E. C. Pritchett, interview by the author.

62. The Claxton papers.

63. "Paul Meek: Memories," Paul Meek Jr., ed., 1993, 1–4.

64. "Senior Class Officers," *The Volunteer* (1919): 24. *The Volunteer* is the UT Knoxville annual.

65. Claxton to Meek, 15 August 1934, Claxton papers.

66. Meek, "Memories," 4.

67. Paul Meek Jr., *Stories and Practical Jokes*, (1990), 2. In this work Paul Meek Jr. recounts stories which depicted his father's sense of humor.

68. Don Whitehead, "Three Men Remembered from His Childhood," *Knoxville News Sentinel* (23 February 1964): 7.

69. UT Junior College budget for 1934–35.

70. Montgomery, "Threshold," 224.

71. Ibid.

72. See the enrollment chart in the back of the book.

73. Personal knowledge.

74. This story has been retold through the years, and the incident probably occurred just prior to World War II.

75. Another widely circulated story. The supervisor from Knoxville reportedly was Webster Pendergrass, head of the School of Agriculture.

76. Verletta Stanford, interview by the author, 12 February 1997.

77. Frank Taylor and E. C. Pritchett, interviews by the author, 3 April 1977.

78. Horton papers, 45–47.

79. Ibid., 38–39.

80. Personal knowledge. The author was privileged to give an eulogy at Stanford's funeral on 30 November 1994.

81. A pamphlet was printed which emphasized intramural sports for all students, but a lack of intercollegiate athletics helped to curtail the enrollment.

82. Horton papers, 71.

83. Personal knowledge. See also "Derryberry Resigns At Junior College," *Volette* (9 July 1938).

84. Conversations with former players, some of whom were among those who transferred to Memphis State. Ed Parham was one of these athletes, and he shared some articles on the former UTJC students and coaches. Doug Mayo, co-captain of the 1936 UTJC football team, was also very helpful in providing information.

85. The *Volette* and area papers covered this tragic incident. Also Ralph Graves and Ed Parham, teammates of Long, interviews by the author.

86. There was no annual printed in 1936, so the 1937 annual was dedicated in memory of Long. Ralph Graves was the primary force in getting a plaque erected in 1993.

87. Personal knowledge. The author was coached by Phil Dickens at the University of Wyoming.

88. The *Volunteer Junior, 1938* (Paducah, Ky.: Young Printing Co.), 82–83.

89. Personal knowledge.

90. Montgomery, "Threshold," 227.

91. Ibid.

92. Copies of "The Checkerboard" are available in the Paul Meek Library.

93. The *Volunteer Junior* published in 1930 is listed as volume one.

94. Joe Black Hayes, interview by the author, 30 May 1995.

95. *The Volunteer Junior, 1941* (Paducah, Ky.: Young Printing Co.), 69.

96. Personal knowledge.

97. *The Volunteer Junior, 1947* (Martin, Tenn.: UT Junior College), 54–58, 64–65 (author designation, pages not numbered).

98. Author's wife, Kay Pritchett Carroll. Article appeared in the *Memphis Commercial Appeal.*

99. Florence E. Hillis, interview by the author, February 1999. As a staff member, she was greatly involved with Carnicus.

100. Claxton to Massey, 11 October 1927, Claxton papers.

101. Ibid. At first, the women had relaxed rules, but more restrictive regulations were instituted in the immediate future and remained intact for many years.

102. Chancellor Margaret Perry, interview by the author.

103. E. C. Pritchett, interview by the author.

104. "Post Office To Be Established At Spring Quarter," *Volette* (2 March 1936): 1. See also "Post Office is Now Open in Main Building," *Volette* (16 March 1936): 1.

105. Ed Parham, interview by the author, November 1996.

106. N. B. "Buster" Williams Jr., interview by the author, 5 August 1999. Johnny Cash, the popular country and western singer who was a witness to the flood of 1937, would later record a song about the catastrophic disaster. It was entitled "Five Feet High and Rising."

107. Jim Fulbright, *The Aviation History of Tennessee* (A Bicentennial Production of the Department of Transportation, Aeronautics Divisions, 1996), 87.

108. Inman, "History," 61–63.

109. Gene Stanford, interview by the author, July 1994. See also Montgomery, "Threshold," 226.

110. Inman, "History," 61–63.

111. Ibid., 62.

112. Hayes, interview by the author, 30 May 1995.

113. Fulbright, "Aviation," 87.

114. "The University of Tennessee Junior College: Eyes In The Skies," (Paducah, Ky.: Young Printing Company, 1942), 16. Paul Phillips created and designed this colorful pamphlet. N. B. Waller was the photographer.

115. Fulbright, "Aviation," 87.

116. Inman, "History," 66–67.

117. Ibid., 64–66.

118. Ibid., 64.

119. Gene Stanford, interview by the author, July 1994.

120. "Junior College Fire Razes Arts Building," *Commercial Appeal* (21 June 1941). The author did not have access to a page number for this article.

121. Montgomery, "Threshold," 225.

122. Personal knowledge. Meek received the honorary doctorate from Lambuth in 1959.

123. Montgomery, "Threshold," 225.

124. Dieter Ullrich, former special collections librarian-archivist at UT Martin, interview by the author. He presently occupies a similar position at Millersville University in Pennsylvania.

125. Russell Duncan, interview by the author, 18 March 1997.

126. Memorial program provided by Joseph T. Nickell, 15 July 1996. His brother, 1st Lt. Charles Lafayette Nickell, was among the UTJC alumni who lost their lives in World War II.

127. Tom Prewitt, from memorial service, 8 June 1946.

128. N. B. "Buster" Williams Jr. to the editor of the *Weakley County Press* (8 February 1994).

129. Gene Stanford to "Buster" Williams, 15 February 1994.

130. Personal knowledge.

131. George Horton, "The Depression and War Years," *The Tennessee Spirit* (January 1970): 10.

132. Mary Lynn Travis Benson, interview by the author, August 1999.

133. Meek to Brehm, 27 December 1945, Meek papers.

134. Ibid.

135. Earl Knepp, *Recollections: Earl Knepp, 1936–74.* To commemorate UTM's fiftieth anniversary in 1977, Earl Knepp wrote recollections from his tenure.

136. Inman, "History," 77–78.

137. A pamphlet entitled "Make the Junior College a Four-Year School" was widely circulated and provided strong arguments for the elevation of UTJC to four-year status.

138. *Minutes,* Executive Committee of the Board of Trustees, 12 December 1949.

139. Inman, "History," 114.

140. Tomerlin apparently was not timid in making known the wishes of West Tennessee, according to some of his contemporaries who the author interviewed.

141. Smith to Brehm, 6 May 1950, Meek papers.

142. Volz to Brehm, 19 July 1950, Meek papers.

143. The statement "Brehm Cites Views on UT Expansion in West Tennessee" was released by the UT News Bureau, 17 December 1950. Copy in Paul Meek Library.

144. Inman, "History," 114–15.

145. Ibid., 115–16.

146. Ibid., 116.

147. O'Steen, *Partners,* 159–60.

148. Ibid., 160–61.

149. Ibid., 164–65.

150. The front page of the *Weakley County Press,* 16 February 1951, had bold headlines declaring "J. C. Elevation Bill Zips Through Senate, 25–8." A copy of the bill is also printed on the front page.

151. Harold Brundige, James Glasgow, and George Thomas, interviews by the author. Hal Ramer, Ute Halliburton, and Howard Stabaugh from Martin were also cited, along with Ed Jones, a UTJC alumnus and the commissioner of agriculture at the time.

152. Brundige, interview by the author, August 1995.

153. Inman, "History," 118.

154. Ibid., 119.

155. Paul Meek to UTJC faculty, Meek papers, box 69, file 5.

156. A copy of this address is located in Meek's second letter to the faculty, the Meek papers, box 69, file 5.

PART III: THE UNIVERSITY OF TENNESSEE MARTIN BRANCH (1951-1967)

1. The 1977 annual, the *Spirit,* celebrates the fiftieth anniversary of UT Martin (1927–77). There are some excellent articles in the publication (4, 10, 20, 40, 50) on the various time periods.

2. Inman, "History," 120–23.

3. Ibid., 126, 143–44.

4. Phil Watkins, interview by the author, July and August 1999.

5. Inman, "History," 161. Also, the Office of Records, UT Martin, agrees with the 1953 figures, but for 1954 that office lists seven graduates in agriculture and four in home economics, interview by the author, 7 January 1999.

6. "Trustees Convene Here In History-Making Session," *Volette* (15 April 1952): 1.

7. Ibid.

8. Inman, "History," 124–26.

9. Ibid., 138.

10. Ibid., 138–39.

11. Ibid., 142.

12. Personal knowledge.

13. Personal knowledge. Much of the work on a campus is accomplished by those who receive little attention; however, the author wishes to acknowledge the vital roles of the custodians, maintenance people, the secretaries, and others who are extremely important figures.

14. *UTMB Volunteer, 1956* (Martin, Tenn.: UTMB), 2.

15. *The Volunteer Junior, 1954* (Martin, Tenn.: UTMB), 3.

16. Nick Dunagan to the author, 3 March 1995. John Gauldin, interview by the author, April 1995.

17. Personal knowledge.

18. Personal experience.

19. Personal knowledge.

20. Personal conversation with a former student who wishes to remain anonymous.

21. The author was a member of the "dawn patrol."

22. The author was the staff member in the orchard.

23. Personal knowledge.

24. Horton papers, 48.

25. Personal knowledge.

26. Personal knowledge. Also see "Sadie Hawkins Day is Fun for All," *Volette* (22 November 1949): 1. See also "Sadie Hawkins Day Dance Enjoyed by Everyone Present," *Volette* (8 December 1953): 2.

27. Nancy Lawson McDonald, interview by the author. Also see *UTMB Volunteer, 1959*, 134; *Volette* (20 May 1958): 2; *Volette* (9 February 1960): 1; and *Volette* (23 February 1960): 1.

28. Ibid.

29. Personal knowledge.

30. "The Vanguard Theatre," *The UTMB Volunteer, 1956* (Martin, Tenn.: UTMB 1956): 159. See also Harriet Fulton, *Background Material, Fine Arts Building*; two page history on the music department and the quarters used before the fine arts building was completed (np, in author's collection).

31. Fulton, *Fine Arts,* 1.

32. Ibid., 2.

33. "Junior College To Give Athletes Financial Aid," *Volette* (28 March 1950): 1.

34. Guy Wadley, interview by author, April 1999.

35. Personal knowledge.

36. Personal experience.

37. Personal knowledge. See also "Baseball," *The UTMB Volunteer, 1957* (Martin, Tenn.: UTMB, 1957): 204–5.

38. Personal knowledge. There was talk about starting intercollegiate track in the 1930s, but the results were meager. See also "Track," *The UTMB Volunteer, 1959* (Martin, Tenn.: UTMB, 1959): 215.

39. William R. Duffy II, "Policy Paper on Title IX of the Educational Amendments of 1972 and Its Initial Import on Women's Intercollegiate Athletics at UT Martin," (Research for HLIAD84 10, UT Martin: 1996): 4.

40. Personal knowledge. See also Inman, "History," 210–11.

41. Personal knowledge.

42. "Football Highlights," *The UTMB Volunteer, 1957,* 191.

43. Personal knowledge.

44. Personal knowledge.

45. Personal knowledge.

46. Fulton, *Fine Arts,* 1.

47. Horton papers, 111.

48. Ibid., 112.

49. Personal knowledge.

50. "Students Petition Governor Browning," *Volette* (31 May 1949): 1.

51. Paul Meek to J. P. Hess, business manager at Knoxville, 3 May, 8 June, 20 June, 6 October 1950. Meek papers.

52. Inman, "History," 155.

53. Knepp, *Recollections,* 2.

54. Inman, "History," 202.

55. Ibid., 202–3.

56. O'Steen, *Partners,* 103, 157; Horton papers, 146; and Meek to Holt, 9 February 1968.

57. Personal knowledge.

58. Inman, "History," 204.

59. Tomerlin sent an invitation to twenty-eight key leaders concerning the meeting. The invitation was dated May 14, 1956.

60. Inman, "History," 176–82.

61. Ibid., 208.

62. Trentham, interview by the author, 26 October 1999. He laughingly recalled that his bachelor's degree at UT Martin was awarded at the fall faculty meeting. While serving in various capacities at Martin he became one of the most highly respected campus figures.

63. Inman, "History," 190–92.

64. Elmer Counce, interview by the author, September 1999. See also O'Steen, *Partners,* 156.

65. O'Steen, *Partners,* 156.

66. *UTMB Volunteer, 1959* (Martin, Tenn.: UTMB): 2–3. See also *Volette* (30 January 1959): 1.

67. O'Steen, *Partners,* 159.

68. A small number of students and a couple of faculty members sought to emulate the antiestablishment trend, but they were mostly ignored.

69. J. Houston Gordon, interview by the author, December 1999.

70. Personal knowledge. The author coached Davis and has read *Across the Mekong.* A copy of the book is available from Davis, P. O. Box 19031, Alexandria, Va., 22320–0032.

71. Inman, "History," 183–84.

72. See the schedule of buildings in appendices.

73. Personal knowledge.

74. See the schedule of buildings in appendices.

75. Horton papers, 120.

76. Ibid., 108, 130.

77. Dean Harold Conner and the Office of Admissions and Records at UT Martin, interview by the author.

78. Personal knowledge.

79. "Trustee's Action Favorable To Frats-Sororities," *Volette* (9 February 1960): 2.

80. See fraternity and sorority chart in appendices.

81. See appendices.

82. Ruby Long, "Phi Sigs Swipe ATO Cannon Before Game," *Volette* (23 October 1962): 2.

83. Personal knowledge.

84. Larry Alexander and David H. "Gruder" Graham, interviews by the author, December 1999.

85. Ibid.

86. "UTMB Marching Band Debuts At APSC Game," *Volette* (2 October 1962): 1.

87. Grover Page, interview by the author, December 1999.

88. *Volunteer, 1964* (Camden, Ark.: Hurley Yearbook Company), 118.

89. "Dr. Paul Meek Is Elevated To Vice President of UT," *Volette* (2 October 1962): 1.

90. Horton papers, 127.

91. "Three Promoted," *Volette* (2 October 1962): 1.

92. "Memorial Service Conducted On Campus For President," *Volette* (26 November 1963): 1.

93. Ibid.

94. Personal knowledge.

95. Personal knowledge.

96. Personal knowledge. Some sources say the officers left their car to write traffic tickets, and when they returned it was gone. Also, Mack Moody and Ron Lewellen, interviews by the author, December 1999.

97. "Library To Try Sunday Opening," *Volette* (26 November 1963): 1.

98. Horton papers, 128.

99. "Mrs. Myrtle H. Phillips Retires At UTMB; Service As Registrar Spans Generation," *Weakley County Press* (14 August 1964): 4.

100. Personal knowledge.

101. "Agricultural Head Has Laid Foundation For Growth and Development In Future," *Volette* (5 November 1964): 2.

102. Harry Henderson, interview by the author, November 1999.

103. See the list of outstanding teachers in appendices.

PART IV: THE UNIVERSITY OF TENNESSEE AT MARTIN (1967–2000)

1. "Governor Signs Name Change, University Adopts New Title," *Volette* (4 May 1967): 1.

2. Nancy Dunagan, "Dedication Ceremonies Held for Meek Library," *Volette* (8 May 1968): 1.

3. "Chancellor Archie Dykes Assumes Campus Duties," *Volette* (18 September 1967): 1.

4. Personal reflections by the author.

5. Personal knowledge. Also, Travis and Linda Workman Shumate, interviews by the author.

6. *Spirit, 1968* (Martin, Tenn.: UTM), 180. As the number one baton twirler in the nation, Sublette's title was "Queen of Colleges."

7. Personal knowledge. See also O'Steen, *Partners,* 204–5.

8. "Robinson and Rodeo Team Ride Together to Success," *Pacer* (11 May 1978): 4.

9. Personal knowledge. See also "History of the UT Martin Rodeo Team," 1999 rodeo program.

10. Brian Holland, "Freak Accident with Horse Kills UTM Rodeo Member," *Pacer* (22 September 1994): 1.

11. Jerianne Thompson, "On-campus Services Held for Devillers," *Pacer* (29 September 1994): 6.

12. Personal knowledge. See also "History of the UT Martin Rodeo Team."

13. Nick Dunagan, interview by author, 3 December 1999.

14. Mimi Coleman, interview with the author.

15. "Robinson and Rodeo Team," 4.

16. Personal knowledge and conversations with students.

17. Personal knowledge and conversations with students.

18. Personal knowledge. See also O'Steen, *Partners,* 225–26.

19. See enrollment chart in the appendices.

20. Personal knowledge.

21. Personal knowledge.

22. Mike Vaughn, "Presidential Plans Stated During Visit to UT Martin," *Pacer* (30 November 1978): 3.

23. See chart for fraternities and sororities in appendices.

24. *Spirit, 1977* (Martin, Tenn.: UTM), 50.

25. Ibid.

26. Dennis Sellers, "Light 'Disappointing' Crowd Causes Almost $5000 Loss," *Pacer* (21 October 1976): 1.

27. O'Steen, *Partners,* 220–24.

28. Personal knowledge.

29. Robert Neal Glasgow, Jimmy Trentham, and Milton Simmons, interviews by the author.

30. Milton Simmons, interview by the author, 9 November 1999.

31. Personal knowledge.

32. "Trustees Move To Halt 'Confrontation, Disruption, Misuse of Facilities'," *Pacer* (24 June 1970): 1.

33. The author was a member of the "dawn patrol."

34. "From the *Volette* to the *Pacer*: Six-and-a-Half Decades of News," *Pacer* (29 October 1992), 9a.

35. Robert N. Glasgow and Nick Dunagan, interviews by the author.

36. Personal knowledge. The author was involved with the organization of the new conference affiliations.

37. *Spirit, 1970* (Martin, Tenn.: UTM), 103.

38. Duffy, *Policy Paper*, 4.

39. Bettye Giles, interview by the author, 23 November 1999.

40. Lucia Jones, interview by the author, 5 November 1999.

41. Duffy, *Policy Paper*, 6.

42. Giles, interview.

43. Duffy, *Policy Paper*, 6.

44. Giles interview, during which she provided "A Brief Look At The National Growth of Collegiate Opportunities for Women," an outline of the progression of women's athletics. This paper by Giles traces the growth of women's athletics from the TCWSF to AIAW to NCAA.

45. Ibid.

46. "Fire Destroys Building Scheduled for Razing," *Volette* (2 December 1970): 1.

47. N. B. "Buster" Williams, interview by the author, October 1999.

48. Sharon Crowell, "Martin Is A Happy Place; *Esquire* Magazine Says So," *Pacer* (11 October 1979): 2. See also Dave Hill, "*Esquire* Article Spurs Praises, Corrections," *Volette* (11 November 1970): 1.

49. Personal knowledge.

50. Personal knowledge.

51. Jim Payne, interview by the author, 22 October 1999.

52. "'Pacers' Picked Name For Athletic Teams," *Volette* (5 May 1971): 1.

53. Personal knowledge. See also "UTM Gets Pacer Mascot," *Pacer* (1 October 1981): 7.

54. "Dykes Accepts Position at Knoxville Campus," *Pacer* (6 October 1971) 7.

55. Personal knowledge. See also "Dr. Campbell Accepts Duties As Chancellor," *Pacer* (6 October 1971): 1.

56. Phil Miller, interview by the author, 8 December 1999.

57. "Search Ended Last Saturday for Chancellor," *Pacer* (17 November 1971): 1.

58. "Chancellor's Unusual Address Captures International Attention," *Pacer* (1 August 1972): 1.

59. Jimmy Trentham, interview by the author, 26 October 1999.

60. See the building schedule in the appendices.

61. Personal knowledge.

62. Personal knowledge. See also Jim Kemp, "UTM 'Concerned Students' Protest Campus Policies," *Pacer* (8 November 1973): 1.

63. Nick Dunagan, interview by the author, 9 December 1999.

64. Aaron Tatum, "Gooch Donates $802,000 Fund; Largest Gift in School History," *Pacer* (11 October 1972): 1.

65. Personal knowledge.

66. Randy Mashburn, "Meek, Who Helped UTM Become Four-Year School, Dies," *Pacer* (8 November 1972): 1, 8.

67. *Spirit, 1967* (Martin, Tenn.: UTM), 4.

68. *Campus Scene* (fall 1972): 1.

69. An excellent account of the retirement dinner for Mr. Mahan can be found in the Horton papers, 152.

70. "Gene Stanford to Retire After 42 Years of Service," *Pacer* (24 May 1972): 1.

71. "Dean Smith to Retire After 26 Years at UTM," *Pacer* (17 May 1972): 1.

72. "Tansil Retires From PR," *Pacer* (4 April 1973): 1.

73. "Retirement Ends 36 Years Teaching for Horton," *Pacer* (9 May 1973): 2.

74. "Mary Armstrong Feted," *Campus Scene* (fall 1973): 1.

75. "Resident Engineer to End 38-Year Career at UTM," *Pacer* (4 April 1974): 7.

76. Nick Dunagan and Tommy Bryant, interviews by the author. See also "Fan Kidnapped," *Pacer* (16 September 1981): 3.

77. Karen Franklin, "A Phi O Push Collects Record Sum for Hospital," *Pacer* (8 April 1976): 1, 4.

78. Personal knowledge.

79. "Paynter Replaces Henson, Burdette," *Volette* (3 February 1971): 1.

80. Personal knowledge.

81. Personal knowledge. See also "MacIntyre Named Head," *Pacer* (16 January 1975): 1.

82. Danny Lannom, "Twenty-seven Injured as Pacer Bus Overturns," *Pacer* (31 January 1974): 1.

83. Personal knowledge. See also Jerald Ogg, "Golf, Wrestling Dropped; Budget Blamed," *Pacer* (29 May 1975): 1.

84. Ibid.

85. David Graham and Larry Alexander, interviews by the author. See also "Nine Year UTM Era Ends; Gruder Graham Graduates," *Pacer* (17 February 1977): 3.

86. Personal knowledge. See also Pamela Allen, "Eisterhold Urges Peace," *Pacer* (15 November 1979): 1.

87. Ed N. White and Nick Dunagan, interviews by the author.

88. Dean Hitt, "Prados Talks," *Pacer* (10 September 1979): 1

89. Dorothy Bock, "Chancellor Smith 'Meets The Press'," *Pacer* (10 January 1980): 1.

90. Personal knowledge.

91. Personal knowledge.

92. See the enrollment chart in the appendices.

93. Personal knowledge. See also Bock, "Chancellor," 1.

94. Pamela Allen, "Ray Mears Under Consideration," *Pacer* (21 February 1980): 1.

95. "Tolis Named Coach," *Pacer* (2 April 1980): 4.

96. Personal knowledge.

97. "UTM Receives Scholarship Money," *Pacer* (15 October 1982): 4.

98. Ernie Blythe, interview by the author, 19 October 1999.

99. Ibid.

100. Milton Simmons, interview by the author, 9 November 1999.

101. Marvin Downing, interview by the author, 2 November 1999.

102. Nick Dunagan, interview by the author, 26 October 1999.

103. "Campaign Reaches Goal A Year Early," *Pacer* (9 May 1985): 1.

104. "Students Attend Tuition Protest," *Pacer* (19 February 1981): 1.

105. Mike Vaughn, "Alexander Proposes Preparation of 5-Year Student Expense Plan," *Pacer* (26 February 1981): 1.

106. Debbie Coble, "$15,000 Provided for Speakers," *Pacer* (26 February 1981): 1.

107. Simmons, interview by the author, 9 November 1999.

108. Ibid.

109. "UTM Awarded Contract For Japanese Students," *Pacer* (22 January 1981): 1.

110. "UTM, Nihon Sign New Agreement," *Pacer* (5 November 1981): 1.

111. John Eisterhold, interview by the author, 16 November 1999.

112. Ibid.

113. Judy Register, "UTM Students Study in Japan," *Pacer* (22 October 1981): 6.

114. Amy Pearson, "Studies On Salaries Show Room For Improvement," *Pacer* (31 October 1985): 5.

115. Freda Nicholson, "Past Decade Brings Many Changes In UTM Scenery," *Pacer* (30 November 1989): 6.

116. Nick Dunagan, interview by the author, 2 November 1999.

117. Nick Dunagan, interview by the author, 3 November 1999. See also O'Steen, *Partners*, 266–67.

118. Nick Dunagan, interview by the author, 4 November 1999.

119. Amy Pearson, "Smith Leaves UTM," *Pacer* (3 October 1985): 1.

120. Personal knowledge.

121. Amy Pearson, "UTM Graduate Chosen As New Chancellor," *Pacer* (17 April 1986): 1.

122. Personal knowledge and comments from members of Perry's staff.

123. The author had earlier compiled a list of Perry's accomplishments for other publications. See also Erin Finnegan, "Perry To Retire At End of January," *Pacer* (21 August 1997): 3.

124. "UTM Earns National Honor," *Pacer* (30 September 1993): 1, 5.

125. Jerianne Thompson, "Book Rates UTM Sixth Safest Campus In Nation," *Pacer* (25 August 1994): 1.

126. Author's summary of Perry's achievements.

127. Eric J. Martin, "OVC Requirements Met," *Pacer* (30 January 1992): 3, 10.

128. Personal knowledge. See also Brian Holland, "Committee Approves Skyhawks Logo," *Pacer* (30 March 1995): 1.

129. Personal knowledge.

130. Nick Dunagan, George White, Margaret Perry, and Jennifer Hahn, interviews by the author.

131. Nick Dunagan, interview by the author, 17 December 1999.

132. Ted Mosch, interview by the author, 17 December 1999.

133. Nick Dunagan, interview by the author, 10 December 1999.

134. Personal experience. The author was one of the staff members who participated in the run.

135. Personal knowledge.

136. Personal knowledge. See also O'Steen, *Partners*, 266–67.

137. Personal knowledge.

138. Personal knowledge. His accomplishments as president were listed on the program for the Pat and Joe Johnson Appreciation Dinner.

139. Personal knowledge.

140. Lee Wilmot, "Review of 1988 Football Season," *Football Media Guide* (1989): 26–27.

141. Sheila Schoonover, "War Survey Shows Decision Supported," *Pacer* (31 January 1991): 1, 10.

142. Personal knowledge.

143. Dale Wilson and Carol Smith, "Chesteen For Governor?" *Pacer* (31 October 1991): 1, 6.

144. Personal knowledge.

145. Personal knowledge. Also Karen Hinson and Ted Mosch, interviews by the author.

146. See the list of faculty members in the appendices.

147. Personal knowledge. The author was Nunamaker's college coach.

148. "Former UTM Rifle Team Marksman Shoots In Olympics," *Pacer* (20 August 1996): 21.

149. Jack D. Elliott, "Saturday Morning Fire Kills One, Injures Five Others," *Pacer* (16 January 1997): 1, 6, 7.

150. Rosemary Rawlings, "UTM Grad Is Youngest Student To Get Master's," *Pacer* (20 August 1996): 7.

151. Maury Caby, "Ola Kizer, 86-Year-Old Student, To Graduate in December," *Pacer* (30 September 1999): 6.

152. Danny Bundy, "73-Year-Old Graduates," *Pacer* (6 September 1990): 7.

153. Erin Finnegan, "Perrys Leave Endowment to Scholar Program," *Pacer* (29 January 1998): 2.

154. Erin Finnegan, "Conn's The Man," *Pacer* (3 April 1998): 1–2.

155. "Chancellor's Wife Dies Wednesday," *Pacer* (19 November 1998): 1.

156. Philip Conn, interview by the author, 25 January 2000.

157. Personal knowledge.

158. "Former UT System President Joe Johnson To Be Honored At UTM," *Pacer* (16 August 1999): 6.

159. Ibid.

160. Diane Ballard, "New President, New Challenges," *Tennessee Alumnus* (fall 1999): 12–14.

Appendices

ADMINISTRATION

Title	Person	Term of Service
Executive Officer (Reporting to dean of agriculture & home economics, Knoxville)	C. Porter Claxton	September 1, 1927 August 31, 1934
Executive officer, dean, UT vice president and chancellor in charge of the Martin Branch	Paul Meek	September 1, 1934 August 31, 1967
Chancellor	Archie R. Dykes	September 1, 1967 August 31, 1971
Acting chancellor	A. Norman Campbell	September 1, 1971 November 30, 1971
Chancellor	Larry T. McGehee	December 1, 1971 August 31, 1979
Acting chancellor	John W. Prados	September 1, 1979 December 14, 1979
Chancellor	Charles E. Smith	December 15, 1979 September 27, 1985
Acting chancellor	D. Nick Dunagan	September 28, 1985 June 30, 1986
Chancellor	Margaret N. Perry	July 1, 1986 January 31, 1998
Acting chancellor	D. Nick Dunagan	February 1, 1998 June 30, 1998
Chancellor	Philip W. Conn	July 1, 1998 Present

Appendix B

BUILDING RECORDS

Year Constructed Or Purchased (P)	Building Name	Year Renovated	Year Razed
1900	Old Administration Building		1970 (fire)
1919	Reed Hall		1975
1921	Freeman Hall		1973
1929	Sociology Building (Was Old Science Building)	1981	
1929	Old Home Ec. Building	1979	
1930	Pumping Station		
1930	Old Gym		
1930	Old Heating Plant		
1930	Cooper Hall—now Crisp Hall (Old Engineering Building)	1941★★ 1991	
1935	Old Cafeteria-ITV (Now Communications Building)	1979	
1935	Physical Plant Greenhouse		1982
1946	Mt. Pelia Lodge		1977
1947	ROTC Building		1988 (fire)
1947	Lovelace Houses		1982
1947	Westview Terrace Houses		1974–76
1951	Agriculture-Biology-Library Building	1972	
1951	Browning Hall—now Business Administration Building	1975	
1957	Clement Residence Hall	1962	
1959	Home Management House		
1959	Hall-Moody Administration		
1961	Engineering/Physical Science	1971	
1963	Steam Plant	1974	
1963	Fieldhouse		
1964	Stadium		
1964 (P)	Collier House		1979
1964	Athletic Storage		
1964	McCord Residence Hall	1966	
1965	Grove Apartments		
1966	Austin Peay Residence Hall		
1966	University Center	1973 1999	

Year Constructed Or Purchased (P)	Building Name	Year Renovated	Year Razed
1967	Ellington Residence Hall		
1968	Paul Meek Library	1993	
1969 (P)	Smith House		
1969 (P)	Meek House		
1969	Atrium Residence Hall—now Cooper Hall		
1969	Humanities Building		
1970	Motor Pool		
1970	Maintenance Building		
1970	University Courts		
1970	Fine Arts Building		
1970	Biology Greenhouse		
1970	Chancellor's Residence		
1971	G-H Residence Hall—now Browning Hall		
1973 (P)	Duncan House		
1974	Residence Hall Pool		1999
1975	Gooch Hall		
1976	P.E. Complex		
1977	Paint Shop		
1977 (P)	Henson House		
1980	Warehouse		
1980	New Greenhouse		
1984	Agricultural Pavilion		
1987	New ROTC Building		
1993	Margaret N. Perry Day Care Center		

★★Early building records were destroyed in the fire at this building in 1941.

Appendix C

TOTAL FALL HEAD COUNT
ENROLLMENT
(1927–1999)

Year	Total	Year	Total	Year	Total
1927	120	1950	457	1975	5211
1928	130	1951	416	1976	5122
1929	180	1952	481	1977	4982
1930	175	1953	535	1978	5125
1931	156	1954	651	1979	5192
1933	92	1955	758	1980	5375
1934	229	1956	804	1981	5583
1935	286	1957	917	1982	5534
1936	299	1958	972	1983	5696
1937	304	1959	956	1984	5375
1938	313	1960	1123	1985	5064
1939	331	1961	1230	1986	4928
1940	336	1962	1363	1987	4800
1941	254	1963	1469	1988	4670
1942	195	1964	1847	1989	5095
1943	115	1965	2472	1990	5369
	(25 male)	1966	2807	1991	5494
1944	161	1967	3169	1992	5660
1945	196	1968	3755	1993	5546
1946	649	1969	4197	1994	5627
	(532 male)	1970	4622	1995	5812
1947	669	1971	4907	1996	5746
	(557 male)	1972	5013	1997	6012
1948	519	1973	4911	1998	5846
1949	435	1974	5002	1999	5741

UT NATIONAL ALUMNI ASSOCIATION
OUTSTANDING TEACHER AWARDS

1966	Wayne Chester	Geography
1967	Mary Ida Flowers	Nutrition
1968	Letty S. Pryor	Home Economics
1969	Dr. Niels Robinson	Animal Science
1970	Charles Callis	Physics
1971	Mildred Payne	English
1972	Dr. John Eisterhold	History
1972	Landon Unger	History
1972	Dr. Jimmy Trentham	Biology
1973	Dr. Jim Andreas	English
1973	Dr. William Dillon	Biology
1973	Dr. John Fletcher	Business
1974	Dr. Ted Mosch	History
1974	Dr. Ernest Razabek	Elementary & Secondary Education
1974	Richard Shadden	Agriculture
1975	Dr. LeeRoy Kiesling	Occupational Education
1975	Dr. Barbara Jones	Music
1976	Dr. Judith Wakim	Nursing
1976	Dr. Bob Hatchcock	Plant Sciences
1977	J. C. Owens	Elementary & Secondary Education
1977	Dr. Rodney Everhart	Elementary and Secondary Education
1978	Margie Dillon	Nursing
1978	Roger Fisher	Sociology
1979	Dr. Charles Harding	Chemistry
1979	Dr. David Loebbaka	Geology & Physics
1980	Dr. Anne C. Cook	Home Economics
1980	Dr. George C. Thomas III	Sociology & Anthropology
1981	Elmer W. Counce	Agronomy
1981	Bonnie L. Hernon	Music & Art
1982	Elige W. Culvahouse	Agriculture
1982	Bettye Giles	Physical Education
1983	Jimmie R. Alewine	Sociology & Criminal Justice
1983	Dr. F. Louis Maldin	Psychology & Religious Studies
1984	Langdon S. Unger	History
1984	Dr. Lonnie E. Maness	History
1985	Dr. Bob G. Figgins	Economics & Finance

1985	Dr. John F. Fletcher	Finance
1986	Dr. Jimmy Trentham	Biology
1986	Shirley Willhite	Business Administration
1987	Dr. David Cooper	Psychology
1987	Dr. Gene Annaratone	Elementary Education
1988	Dr. Phillip H. Davis	Chemistry
1988	Dr. Patrick R. Taylor	History
1989	Dr. Emery Gathers	Computer Science
1989	Dr. Bob Hathcock	Agronomy
1990	Dr. Ted Mosch	Political Science
1990	Dr. David Pitts	Biology
1991	Dr. Richard D. Chesteen	History & Political Science
1991	Dr. Polly S. Glover	English
1992	Lucia Jones	Physical Education & Health
1992	Dr. G. K. Sharma	Biological Sciences
1993	Dr. Sue Byrd	Home Economics
1993	Dr. Judy Maynard	Sociology
1994	Dr. Nell Gullett	Economics & Finance
1994	Dr. Robbie Kendall	Education
1995	Dr. Carroll Slack	Biology
1995	Dr. Gracie Purvis	Physical Education
1996	Dr. Rodney Thomsen	Agriculture & Natural Resources
1996	Dr. Dan McDonough	History & Political Science
1997	Dr. Jimmy Trentham	Biology
1997	Dr. Margrethe Ahlschwede	English
1998	Dr. E. Jerald Ogg	Communications
1998	Dr. Deborah J. Chapman	Health & Human Performance
1999	Dr. Robert Nanney	Communications
1999	Ingrid T. Padial	Modern Foreign Languages

Appendix E

UT National Alumni Association Distinguished Professorships

Harry Hutson	1972–89
Allison Nelson	1972–89
Jimmy Trentham	1990–97
Bill Snyder	1990–96
Ted Mosch	1996–current holder
Bob Duck	1997–99
Maurice Field	1999–current holder

Appendix F

UT Martin Alumni Who Served as UT National Alumni Association Presidents

Madge M. Harrison	1972–73
Larry Bates	1973–74
Jim Hall	1978–79
C. Thomas Barnes	1984–85
Robert Barger	1992–93
Gary Doble	1997–98
Ron Kirkland	1999–2000

Appendix G ——————————

HOMECOMING AWARD RECIPIENTS

Outstanding Alumni Award

First presented in 1986, this award is given to an alumnus or alumna in recognition of outstanding achievement in his/her chosen profession.

1986—Congressman Ed Jones
1987—Coach Pat Head Summitt
1988—Van H. Cunningham
1989—Ted Welch
1990—D. M. "Pete" Gossett
1991—James R. Nichols
1992—Gary Guthrie
1993—Dianne Vest Duncan
1994—L. H. "Cotton" Ivy
1995—Brig. Gen. Robert C. Hinson
1996—Rebecca Rhodes
1997—J. Houston Gordon
1998—Charles Cox
1999—Major General Dennis Cavin

Outstanding Young Alumni Award

First presented in 1990, this award is given in recognition of outstanding achievement by an alumnus/alumna in his/her chosen profession and the recipient must not be over the age of thirty-nine.

1990—Monice Regina Moore Hagler
1991—Michael W. Jacobs
1992—E. Franklin Childress Jr.
1993—Thomas A. Thomas
1994—Barry Joyce
1995—Jennifer Sheraden Berg
1996—Rob Harbison
1997—Roland McElrath
1998—Stan Bell
1999—Anthony Haynes

Distinguished Service Award

First presented in 1986, this award is based on meritorious contributions by an individual on the local, state or national level. It is not necessary that this person be an alumnus/alumna of UT Martin.

1986—Professor Holland McComb
1987—Governor Ned McWherter
1988—Turner O. "T.O." Lashlee
1989—Hardy Graham
1990—Tom E. Hendrix
1991—George L. Freeman
1992—Milton Hamilton Jr.
1993—J. Robert Barger
1994—G. W.F. "Dutch" Cavender
1995—Allen S. Edmonson
1996—John F. Bradley
1997—Van Swaim
1998—Art Sparks
1999—Peggy Edmiston

Chancellor's Award for University Service

First presented in 1992, this award is given to an individual in recognition of outstanding service to UT Martin.

1992—James S. Corbitt
1993—Raymond L. Pollard
        Elijah V. "Lige" Turman
1994—T. Wayne Fisher
1995—Milton D. Simmons
1996—Harry L. & Rosemary Crisp
1997—Col. Tom & Kathleen Elam
1998—Barbara Higgs
1999—Gail Latimer

Retired Faculty

Dr. Dock Adams	June 30, 1991
Mr. Jimmie Alewine	May 31, 1996
Mr. Henry Allison	November 30, 1978
Mr. Paul Anderson	May 31, 1996
Ms. Mary Rachel Armstrong	September 1, 1973
Dr. William Baker	June 30, 1982
Dr. Saul Barr	January 8, 1996
Ms. Martha Battle	June 30, 1988
Mr. Jack Beeler	June 15, 1981–died in service
Mr. William Bennett	July 18, 1983
Ms. Mary Lynn Benson	June 29, 1981
Dr. Norman Betz	December 31, 1994
Dr. Douglas Blom	December 30, 1998
Dr. Ernest W. Blythe Jr.	May 31, 1997
Mr. Kenneth Bordeau	April 30, 1988
Mr. Glenn Bremer	August 31, 1986
Mr. Robert Brengle	August 31, 1986
Dr. David Briody	July 8, 1988–died in service
Dr. R. L. Brittain	August 1, 1977
Mr. Robert Brunner	May 31, 1993
Mr. Floyd Burdette	July 30, 1980
Mr. John J. Burnett	June 30, 1992
Ms. Vera Burnette	December 31, 1971
Mr. Wesley Byuck	May 31, 1998
Mr. Charles P. Callis	May 31, 1997
Dr. Norman Campbell	September 1, 1976
Mr. Larry Cardwell	December 31, 1990
Mr. Gilbert Carp	May 31, 1992
Mr. Robert Carroll	May 31, 1997
Mr. Ed Chenette	June 30, 1978
Mr. Wayne Chester	June 29, 1995
Ms. Annie Sue Clift	December 31, 1991
Mr. Harold Conner	December 31, 1981
Dr. Anne L. Cook	May 31, 1997
Mr. Norvel Cook	December 7, 1990–died in service
Ms. Rayna Cooper	July 31, 1991
Mr. Elmer Counce	June 29, 1987
Dr. Robert G. Cowser	December 30, 1997
Mr. Clarence C. Cravens	1944–retirement year only
Mr. Elige Culvahouse	January 1, 1986
Ms. Margie Dillon	February 29, 1988
Dr. William Dillon	December 31, 1996

Mr. Glenn L. Dobson Jr.	May 31, 1997
Dr. Wayne Dobson	December 31, 1993
Dr. Sanford Downs Jr.	June 1, 1989
Dr. Robert Drake	May 31, 1999
Dr. George Drew	July 31, 1993
Dr. Bobby N. Duck	June 30, 1999
Dr. Leon Dunning	December 31, 1987
Mr. Ross Elder	October 9, 1986–died in service
Dr. Jean Erwin	December 31, 1984
Dr. Rodney Everhart	July 31, 1992
Mr. Baxter Fisher	June 30, 1986
Dr. John Fletcher	December 31, 1988
Ms. Mary Ida Flowers	August 31, 1979
Mr. Paul Foote	August 31, 1982
Mr. George Freeman	June 30, 1978
Dr. Samuel French	May 31, 1999
Ms. Harriet Fulton	June 30, 1978
Dr. James Gagen	June 30, 1996
Dr. Glenn Gallien	August 31, 1980
Mr. Charlie Gammill	December 31, 1993
Mr. John Gammill	January 31, 1987
Ms. Ethel Ruth Gandy	December 30, 1984
Ms. Nadine Gearin	June 30, 1997
Ms. Bettye Giles	September 1, 1994
Mr. Charles Gillon	October 14, 1994–died in service
Ms. Polly Glover	July 31, 1999
Mr. Richard Gogue	August 31, 1988
Dr. Walter Gorman	February 2, 1981–died in service
Mr. Charles Graham	August 31, 1988
Ms. Dorothy Griggs	June 11, 1982
Mr. James Hadden	December 31, 1992
Ms. Peggy Hadden	December 31, 1992
Ms. Mary Ellis Hall	September 1, 1970
Dr. Paul Hall	May 31, 1977
Mr. Wilson Hall	January 10, 1991–died in service
Dr. Brent Hamner	June 30, 1994
Ms. Ruth Evelyn Harper	June 29, 1983
Dr. J. Wesley Henson	December 31, 1998
Mr. James Henson	June 29, 1980
Mr. Louis Hoffman	June 30, 1987
Ms. Nola Hobbs	August 31, 1998
Mr. Paul Horne	December 31, 1989
Mr. George Horton	July 1, 1973
Ms. Louise Hunt	September 1, 1971
Dr. Harry Hutson	December 31, 1989
Dr. M. K. Jain	June 30, 1994
Dr. Ted James	December 26, 1991–died in service
Ms. Marilyn Jewett	May 31, 1989

Dr. Robert Jolly	June 30, 1998
Mr. Howard Jones	June 30, 1992
Mr. James O. Jones	September 1, 1982
Dr. Kellie Jones	December 30, 1988
Dr. George Kao	June 30, 1992
Dr. B. Wayne Kemp	June 30, 1999
Dr. LeeRoy Kiesling	December 31, 1994
Mr. Lloyd King	August 1, 1977
Dr. Harold Kittilson	January 31, 1980
Mr. Earl Knepp	November 1, 1974
Ms. Louise Knifley	June 29, 1982
Mr. Harry Harrison Kroll	1958–retirement year only
Dr. Wayne Lewis	June 30, 1996
Mr. Hal Lister	October 31, 1987
Dr. Allison Nelson Loebbaka	May 31, 1989
Dr. David Loebbaka	December 31, 1999
Ms. Susan Ludwig	February 1, 1992
Mr. John MacMahan	August 31, 1971
Dr. Fereshteh Mahootchi	December 7, 1993–died in service
Dr. Charles Mangam	September 1, 1972
Mr. John Mathesen	January 25, 1990–died in service
Dr. John E. McCluskey	December 30, 1997
Dr. Kenneth McCracken	May 31, 1999
Ms. Carol McElvain	July 17, 1981–died in service
Mr. Gerald McElvain	December 31, 1994
Ms. Jane Miller	June 30, 1994
Dr. Stephen Mooney	May 11, 1971
Mr. James Moore	June 1, 1977
Dr. Gordon Morris	May 31, 1997
Dr. Robert Muncy	December 31, 1991
Mr. Carol Murphey	December 31, 1990
Dr. William Nelson	May 31, 1993
Dr. Addreen Nichols	December 31, 1979
Dr. Thomas Noble	June 30, 1996
Ms. Barbara Norman	July 1, 1982
Mr. Charles Ogilvie	May 31, 1994
Dr. James Owens	June 1, 1977
Mr. Grover Page	July 31, 1990
Ms. Hortense Parrish	July 31, 1980
Ms. Mildred Payne	September 1, 1974
Ms. Elizabeth Pentecost	March 20, 1992–died in service
Dr. Randy Perry	May 31, 1994
Mr. J. Paul Phillips	1954–retirement year only
Ms. Virginia Anne Pope	August 3, 1986
Ms. Dorothy Powell	December 30, 1985
Ms. Betty Rasberry	July 31, 1990
Dr. Ernest Rezabek	April 4, 1982–died in service
Mr. Edmundo Robaina	May 31, 1989

Dr. Niels Robinson	July 31, 1990
Mr. Carl Savage	June 30, 1992
Dr. Carl Seale	September 10, 1992–died in service
Dr. Goetz Seifert	June 30, 1997
Mr. Jesse E. Sherwood	August 31, 1988
Mr. Burnell Simmons	June 30, 1986
Dr. Milton Simmons	December 31, 1995
Dr. Al Smith	May 31, 1997
Dr. Harold Smith	June 29, 1987
Mr. Horace B. Smith	September 1, 1972
Mr. Joel Stowers	March 31, 1999
Mr. William Snyder	June 30, 1996
Mr. Arthur Sparks	August 31, 1985
Mr. James Spears	July 31, 1994
Mr. Robert Stewart	May 31, 1989
Mr. Robert Sugg	June 30, 1997
Dr. Laurie Grennen-Schasel Swope	June 30, 1980
Ms. Doris Tanner	August 31, 1984
Mrs. Barbara O. Taylor	June 30, 1997
Mr. Grady Taylor	October 31, 1979
Dr. Patrick Taylor	May 31, 1992
Mr. Thel Taylor	May 31, 1992
Ms. Mary R. Tice	July 1, 1982
Mr. Robert L. Todd	October 31, 1991–died in service
Dr. Muriel Tomlinson	August 1, 1976
Dr. James Toomey	December 31, 1991
Dr. Jimmy Trentham	May 31, 1997
Ms. Carline Fuqua Turner	August 31, 1980
Mr. Langdon Unger	July 31, 1989
Ms. Aaltje VanDenberg	July 31, 1985
Mr. Vincent Vaughn	August 1, 1977
Mr. Wilbur Washburn	July 31, 1990
Ms. Margaret Weaver	December 31, 1992
Dr. John Wikstrom	May 31, 1995
Ms. Shirley Willhite	June 30, 1998
Dr. Stanley Williams	October 31, 1983
Dr. Frank Windham	July 31, 1989
Dr. John Wittenberg	July 31, 1991
Dr. David Yang	December 31, 1999

Information supplied by: Dorothy Gillon, Chancellor's Office

SOCIAL FRATERNITIES AND SORORITIES

National Interfraternity Council Men's

★1960	Phi Sigma Kappa
★1961	Pi Kappa Alpha
★1963	Alpha Gamma Rho
★1964	Alpha Tau Omega
★1972	Sigma Alpha Epsilon
★1975	Kappa Alpha Order
1982–95	Sigma Pi
1984–89	Phi Kappa Tau
★1995	Sigma Phi Epsilon

National Pan-Hellenic Council Men's

★1971	Kappa Alpha Psi
1976	Alpha Phi Alpha
★1979	Phi Beta Sigma

National Panhellenic Council Women's

★1961	Alpha Delta Pi
★1961	Chi Omega
★1961	Zeta Tau Alpha
★1966	Alpha Omicron Pi
1974–88	Sigma Kappa
★1989	Alpha Gamma Delta

National Pan-Hellenic Council Women's

★1970	Delta Sigma Theta
★1971	Alpha Kappa Alpha
1986	Sigma Gamma Rho
★1978	Zeta Phi Beta

★Currently active on campus

Appendix J

MEN'S ATHLETICS (1927–2000)

Directors of Athletics

H. Kirk Grantham	1927–37
Nick Denes	1937–39
Paul Hug	1939–41
Joe Black Hayes	1942–44
Paul Hug	1945–47
James C. Henson	1947–71
Bob Paynter	1971–80
Ray Mears	1980–89
Don McLeary	1989–94
Benny Hollis	1994–2000
Phil Dane	2000–

Head Football Coaches

H. Kirk Grantham	1927–32
No Intercollegiate Athletics	1933
Everett Derryberry	1934–36
Nick Denes	1937–38
Paul Hug	1939–41
Joe Black Hayes	1942–43★
Paul Hug	1946
James C. Henson	1947–56
Bob Carroll	1957–74
George MacIntyre	1975–77
Vester Newcomb	1978–79
Lynn Amedee	1980–81
Fred Pickard	1982–85
Don McLeary	1986–96
Jim Marshall	1997–99
Sam McCorkle	2000–

★During World War II, athletics were suspended; however, verbal sources indicate six-man football was played in 1942 and 1943 against Lambuth, Bethel, and perhaps others.

Head Basketball Coaches

H. Kirk Grantham	1927–33, 1934–37
No Intercollegiate Athletics	1933
Nick Denes	1937–39
Paul Hug	1939–42
★War Years	1942–45
Paul Hug	1945–47
James C. Henson	1947–52
Floyd Burdette	1952–71
Bob Paynter	1971–80
Art Tolis	1980–82
Tom Hancock	1982–90
Cal Luther	1990–99
Bret Campbell	1999–

Head Baseball Coaches

H. Kirk Grantham	1927–31
Ed Chenette	1957–67
Jim Swope	1968
Roger Shore	1969–70
Jim Swope	1971–73
David Warmbrod	1974
Dick Windbigler	1975–76
Vernon Prather	1977–98
Bubba Cates	1999–

Head Tennis Coaches

Gene Stanford	Early 1930s

(Records do not indicate specific years, and tennis was probably a club sport.)

Joe Black Hayes	1941–42
James C. Henson	1952–80
Dennis Bussard	1981–87
Dennis Taylor	1988–

Head Golf Coaches

Grover Page	1961–75, 1981–

Head Wrestling Coaches

Richard "Bud" Reiselt	1969–73
Philip McCartney	1973–74
Richard "Bud" Reiselt	1974–75

Head Men's Track Coaches

Ross Elder	1959–64
Ernie Gibson	1968–71
Grover Page	1992–95
	(Cross Country only)
Mike Giesler	1996–

There was talk concerning the formation of a track team in the early 1930s, but evidence suggests the depression derailed those plans.

Head Rifle Coaches

C. E. Gatlin	1937–39

(A colonel in the Army Reserve, Gatlin was called to active duty in 1940.)

Bettye Giles	1955
	(Women's team)
Milton Jackson	1963
Bill Stout	1964–68
Richard Murphy	1969
ROTC Staff	1970–72
Joseph W. Condrey	1973–76
ROTC Staff	1977–81
Bob Beard	1982–

During the 1963–81 period the rifle team was sponsored by the Military Science Department. During the 1981–82 academic year, rifle became an NCAA sport, and it remained coed until 1998. At that time, separate teams for men and women were organized.

Appendix K

Women's Athletics (1927–2000)

Directors of Athletics

Bettye Giles   1972–94
(In 1994, all athletics were placed under one
administrator.)

Head Basketball Coaches

Nadine Gearin	1969–78
Judy Southard	1978–81
Anne Strusz	1981–83
Karen Lawler	1983–89
Sharman Coley	1989–96
Kim and Gary Van Atta	1996–

Head Volleyball Coaches

Nadine Gearin	1969–73
Lucia Jones	1973–84
Milly MacDonell	1984–98
Chris Rushing	1998–

Head Tennis Coaches

Bettye Giles	1953–73
Carolyn Byrum	1973–74
Gracie Purvis	1974–77
Darcy Holland/	
Helen Carroll	1977–78
Darcy Holland	1978–79
Laurie Lynn	1979–83
Cathy Strange	1983–87
Dennis Taylor	1987–

Head Softball Coaches

Milly MacDonell	1985–92
Mellanie Surratt	1992–99
Amy Cole Fuller	1999–

Head Track and Cross Country Coaches

Brian Schmit	1992–93
Brenda Webb	1993–96
Mike Giesler	1996–

Head Coed Badminton Coaches

Nadine Gearin	1969–70
Lucia Jones	1970–77
Linda Ramsey	1977–78
Bettye Giles	1978–79
Linda Ramsey	1979–84

Head Soccer Coaches

Ruth Holden	1997–99
Nathan Pifer	2000–

Information compiled by Bettye Giles

ATHLETICS HALL OF FAME

1983
Charter Members
Floyd Burdette
Robert Carroll
Bobby Fowler
H. Kirk Grantham
Leonard Hamilton
Julian Nunamaker
Pat Head Summitt
Frank Taylor

1984
James Henson
Hugh Lashlee
Joe "Nip" McKnight
Marvin McKnight
Clifton Pritchett
Paul Redick
Virgil Yates

1985
Lionel Barrett
Bettye Giles
Ed Jones
Gordon Lambert
Ralph Rutland
Ray Scott
Gerald Tabor

1986
George Horton
Marvin Long
Mark Luttrell
James Pritchett
Mike Rudolphi
Darrell Smith
Elmer Vaughn

1987
Thomas Ellis
Bobby Hayes
Don Jackson
Dolph Larimer
Vernon Prather
Chip Rockholt
Larry Shanks

1988
Ronnie Armstrong
Wilbur Edmiston
Nadine Gearin
Nathaniel "Nate" Holmes
Jim Love
Roland McMackin
Roger Shore

1989
Mary Ann Archie Childers
Gary Doble
Charles Graham Gordon
Ron Lewellen
Don McDonald
Halliday T. Short
Joe Taffoni

1990
Allan Cox
Col. Tom Elam
Terry Giltner
Errol Hook
Don Hubbard
Ray Mears

1991
Michael B. Beeler
Walter Glass
Jim Hart
Amy U. Poteete
Ron Schomaker
Richard Whitfield

1992
W. Ralph Graves
Dan Merritt
Pat Nanney Jr.
Alvin Smalls
Jim Swope
Dr. Ed Welles

1993
Chris Brady
Dan Bunn
Marcus Glass
Lucia Jones
Bill Rhodes
George Zarecor

1994
Mike Coffron
Eddy Eckert
Howard Finley
Rob Harbison
Mitch Stentiford
Johnny Williams

1995
Mary Kate Long Arend
Bobby Brannon
Emmanuel McNeil
Mike Meschede
Jerry Reese

1996
Larry Carter
William Mackall
Vesa Ponka
Joella Ross Presson
Jim Willis

1997
David Clarke
Richard Craven
Roger Cypriano
Mark Florence
Leon Reed

1998
John Burch
Ray Frame
Margaret N. Perry
Paul Randolph

Appendix M

ALL STUDENTS CLUB, ALL STUDENTS ASSOCIATION, AND STUDENT GOVERNMENT ASSOCIATION PRESIDENTS

All Students Club

1927–28	Lionel Barrett
1928–29	Emma Lee Cotham
1929–30	Clifton Pritchett
1930–31	Paula M. Fitts Jr.
1931–32	Glenard Riley
1932–33	N/A
1933–34	William Roberts
1934–35	Elwood Hurt
1935–36	Markey Luttrell
1936–37	Bernard Watson McLean
1937–38	Woody Ryan
1938–39	Charles King
1939–40	Ralph Hudson
1940–41	Herbert Dycus
1941–42	Mark Wilkinson
1942–43	T. C. "Stormy" Clark
1943–44	Sherrill Parks
1944–45	Margaret Burton
1945–46	Ruth Edenton
1946–47	William Yandell
1947–48	Sanford Smith
1948–49	Donald March
1949–50	Joe Hiram Sanford
1950–51	Fred Welch
1951–52	Cavit Cheshier
1952–53	Cavit Cheshier
1953–54	Pete Gossett
1954–55	Pete Gossett
1955–56	Phillip Watkins
1956–57	Dan Arnold
1957–58	Jere E. Freeman
1958–59	Kenneth Houston

All Students Association

1959–60	James Graves
1960–61	Bob Duck
1961–62	Tommy Duncan
1962–63	David Stroud
1963–64	David Stroud
1964–65	Larry Bates

Student Government Association

1965–66	Larry Bates
1966–67	Bill Milliken
1967–68	Paul Blaylock
1968–69	Steve Davis
1969–70	Billy Cunningham
1970–71	Steve Becker
1971–72	William Mallard
1972–73	Ron Simmons
1973–74	Roy Herron
1974–75	Mike Faulk
1975–76	Steve Cox
1976–77	Russ Stoddard
1978–79	Richard Williams
1979–80	Mike Turner
1980–81	Rose Boyd
1981–82	William Kyle Sanders
1982–83	Brad Hurley
1983–84	Reginald Williams
1984–85	Reginald Williams
1985–86	James Kevin Ross
1986–87	James Kevin Ross
1987–88	Phillip B. Barham
1988–89	John Barker
1989–90	Susie High
1990–91	Nick Arnold
1991–92	Richie Hockins
1992–93	Steve Mort
1993–94	Cade Cowan
1994–95	Cherie Gillespie
1995–96	Cherie Gillespie
1996–97	Eric Maupin
1997–98	Ben Hays
1998–99	Jessica Peccolo
1999–2000	Ruth Nutter

Researched by Mimi Coleman

About the Author

Robert L. "Bob" Carroll, who retired in 1997, was a member of the faculty/staff at UT Martin for more than forty years. During his tenure, he was the head football coach from 1957 through 1974, taught history, and was Assistant Vice Chancellor for Alumni Affairs when he retired. He served during the administrations of five chancellors and three acting chancellors, and he saw the enrollment climb from 457 in 1950 when he was a freshman to more than six thousand in 1997. Chancellor Margaret Perry aptly observed, "It is appropriate that Bob Carroll write a history of UT Martin since he has lived most of it."

A native of Milan, Tennessee, he graduated in 1950 from Milan High School. He received a two-year diploma from UT Martin in 1954 and a bachelor of arts degree with honors from the University of Wyoming in 1956. He was the recipient of the Outstanding History Student Award in both his junior and senior years at Wyoming. He earned a master's degree in history and political science at the University of Mississippi in 1962.

While a student at UT Martin, he was selected as the most valuable football player during his freshman and sophomore years and captained the team in his second year. A starting defensive back at the University of Wyoming, he was named as an Academic All-American. He is a charter member of the UT Martin Athletic Hall of Fame, and he was inducted into the Tennessee Sports Hall of Fame in 1993.

A veteran of the United States Marine Corps (1951–1952), he is a former president of the Martin Rotary Club and a former post commander of American Legion Post No. 69. He has taught a Sunday school class at the First United Methodist Church in Martin for the past thirty-two years. He is married to the former Kay Pritchett from Munford, and they have three children: Steve, Cliff, and Kayla.